# KNOCKING
# AT OUR
# OWN DOOR

The Columbia History of Urban Life
*Kenneth T. Jackson, General Editor*

*The Columbia History of Urban Life*

*Kenneth T. Jackson, General Editor*

# KNOCKING
# AT OUR
# OWN DOOR

Milton A. Galamison
and the Struggle to Integrate
New York City Schools

## Clarence Taylor

Columbia University Press  New York

Columbia University Press
*Publishers Since 1893*
New York    Chichester, West Sussex
Copyright © 1997 Columbia University Press

Library of Congress Cataloging-in-Publication Data
Taylor, Clarence
Knocking at our own door : Milton A. Galamison and the
struggle to integrate New York City schools / Clarence Taylor.
p. cm. — (Columbia history of urban life)
Includes bibliographical references and index.
ISBN 0-231-10950-4
1. School integration—New York (State)—New York—History.
2. Galamison, Milton A. (Milton Arthur), 1923-1988. 3. Afro-
American clergy—Biography. I. Title. II. Series.
LC214.23.N7T39   1997
379.2'63'097471—dc21                                        97-7573
                                                              CIP

For Marsha

# contents

# acknowledgments

This book has its origins in a 1987 interview I conducted with Milton A. Galamison. My objective was only to focus on the Downstate Medical Center campaign of 1963 for my dissertation on the black churches of Brooklyn. But during this long and fascinating interview, I learned, not only about his role in the Downstate campaign, but also about the long and intense battle for school integration in New York. The interview with Galamison inspired me to write this book.

A book is seldom the effort of one individual. Thus it is the case with this work. Many people have contributed to the publication of this book and I appreciate their labor. I would like to thank Jonathan Birnbaum for his careful reading of the work and his suggestions. Our long conversations over the phone about Milton Galamison and the New York City school integration struggle not only resulted in extraordinarily high phone bills but were also exceptionally helpful in conceptualizing the book. Likewise, Carol Berkin's reading of the manuscript and comments were thought-provoking and assisted me in shaping this work.

I owe a debt to the members of the 1994 Research and Development Committee at Le Moyne College for their grant. It enabled me to travel and interview Dr. Rhody McCoy and it helped pay for loads of photocopying. I would also like to thank Sharyn Knight, whose painstaking work and suggestions made this book possible. Ellie Lahn's editing was extremely beneficial and I am grateful. I owe a special debt of gratitude to Kate Wittenberg, editor in chief of Columbia University Press, for reading the manuscript and recognizing its significance. I also would like to thank Leslie Bialler for his copyediting and his patience throughout this project. This book would not have been published if it were not for the numerous people who shared their experiences with me about those turbulent decades known as the civil rights years. I would especially like to thank the Reverend Sylvester Shannon for his openness and willingness to discuss his predecessor.

On a personal note, I owe many thanks to Doug and Linda Egerton, John Langdon, Ed Judge, Sarah Ramsey, Bob Kelly, Joe Kelly, Richard Merriman, Margot Gelman, Ben Merriman, Carl Thomas, and Tony Fictchue for their friendship and for creating a supportive environment while I labored on this project.

Last but not least, I would like to give special thanks to Marsha for her continuous help and support throughout this project. Her countless hours of reading chapters, making suggestions, and listening to my ideas and thoughts about Galamison, the school integration struggle, civil rights, and history were invaluable. Without a doubt, her greatest contribution has been her patience and love through the years, which makes everything worthwhile.

## Archival Collections

Norma Becker Papers, State Historical Society of Wisconsin, Madison

Bedford-Stuyvesant Congress, Newsletter (Spring 1953), Brooklyn Society, New York

Bernard Donovan Files, Special Collections, Milbank Memorial Library, Teachers College, Columbia University

David Feingold Papers, State Historical Society of Wisconsin, Madison

Files on Discrimination, Special Collections, Milbank Memorial Library, Teachers College, Columbia University

Milton Galamison Papers, Schomberg Center for the Study of Black Culture, New York City Public Library

Milton Galamison Papers, State Historical Society of Wisconsin, Madison

Milton Galamison, Transcript of Oral History Interview, Moorland-Spingarn Research Center, Howard University, Washington, D.C.

Mayoral Papers of John V. Lindsay, New York Archives, New York City

NAACP Papers, Manuscript Division, Library of Congress

Diane Ravitch Papers, Special Collections, Milbank Memorial Library, Teachers College

Bayard Rustin, microfilm edition

Schools Council of Bedford-Stuyvesant-Williamsburg, Annual Yearbook, 1946, Teachers Union Collection, Cornell Labor Archives, Cornell University, School of Industrial and Labor Relations, Ithaca, New York

Minutes of Session, Siloam Presbyterian Church, Brooklyn, New York

Annie Stein Papers, The Public Education Association, New York City

Mary Church Terrell Papers, microfilm edition, Library of Congress

United Federation of Teachers Collection, Robert F. Wagner Labor Archives of the Tamiment Institute Library, Elmer Holmes Bobst Library, New York University

United Parents Association, Special Collections, Milbank Memorial Libary, Teachers College

Mayoral Papers of Robert F. Wagner, New York Archives, New York City

## Interviews

William Claxton

Anne Filardo

Mildred Flacks

Maurice Fredricks

Winifred Fredricks

Gladys Galamison

Milton Galamison

Arnold Goldwag

Lois Hampton

Marjorie Leeds

Oliver Leeds

Elana Levy

Hermenia Logan

Rev. Thomas Logan

Rhody McCoy

Leon Modeste

Wendi Modeste

Rev. C. Herbert Oliver

Rev. John Powis

Rev. Sylvester Shannon

Eleanor Stein

Rev. Gardner C. Taylor

Gwendolyn Timmons

Evelyn Weiner

Charles Wilson

In an integrated school your child will receive the benefits of a democratic education that will enable him to live, play and work with children of all backgrounds. Your child will develop a better appreciation of himself as a human being—born free and equal in dignity and rights with other children. . . . When all children have the opportunity to know children of other backgrounds as equals, they lose any feelings they may have of inferiority or superiority.

*Milton A. Galamison*
*January 1961*

# KNOCKING
# AT OUR
# OWN DOOR

Milton Arthur Galamison died in March 1988 of pancreatic cancer. The day of his funeral, Siloam Presbyterian Church was packed with loyal parishioners, family members, friends, and the curious. The Reverend Thomas Logan, former pastor of Saint Michael's and All Angels Episcopal Church, the church Galamison attended as a boy, sat among the mourners. Betty Shabazz, the widow of Malcolm X, was also there. She must have recalled the days when her husband was an outcast with few friends and how Galamison befriended the outspoken black nationalist leader. There were participants in the early school boycotts, such as Jetu Weusi (formerly known as Les Campbell). By the late 1960s, Weusi had become an advocate for community control of public schools in the black communities of New York and a critic of Galamison's integrationist approach.

There were also the less famous sitting in the church, people who had heard about the civil rights leader who had led the famous boycotts of 1964 and was a champion for racial and economic justice. A young woman asserted that she admired the Presbyterian pastor because she recalled her childhood and how Galamison struggled to force the Board of Education to provide her an adequate education. Gwendolyn Timmons, a school supervisor and member of Siloam was at the funeral. She vividly remembers her days as a member of the church's choir in the summer of 1963, when her pastor convinced her and her mother to join the struggle to break the walls of racial discrimination in the construction industry at the Downstate Medical Center. She became a "jailbird for freedom," an experience she treasures because she was given the opportunity to strike a blow at racial injustice.[1]

The late pastor of Siloam drew praise from many circles. The controversial mayor of New York, Ed Koch, who had been accused of fanning the flames of racial tension in the city, said "While on occasion he caused a great deal of controversy, it was always for a good cause." Koch contended that Galamison would be missed. Brooklyn Borough President Howard Golden called Galamison a "crusader to the end." An obituary in the *New York Times* referred to him as a person who fought for jobs for his "fellow blacks and who led school boycotts to urge better education for minority-group children. . . ."[2]

The Reverend Gardner C. Taylor, pastor of Concord Baptist Church and considered the dean of Baptist preachers, delivered a moving eulogy at the service. After noting that he and Galamison had come to Brooklyn in the late 1940s, he described Galamison as a great fighter who struggled on behalf of children. Taylor recalled that, on the eve of the first boycott on February 3, 1964, he went to give Galamison a check in support of the demonstration and found the Presbyterian pastor sitting with children. The scene moved Taylor because it demonstrated that, despite all the city-wide attention Galamison was receiving, he remained a humble man, never forgetting the children.[3]

To be sure, there were many New Yorkers who were not saddened by Galamison's death. To some he was domineering, incapable of working with people, unwilling to compromise or listen to another point of view. He was accused of creating disruptions in the school system and increasing racial tension throughout New York City by organizing several demonstrations designed to force the Board of Education and city officials to integrate the school system.

The Presbyterian minister was not a nationally prominent figure. He never led a national civil rights organization. In fact, Galamison never trav-

eled south to join any of the southern civil rights campaigns. The pastor of
Siloam Presbyterian Church in Brooklyn from 1948 to his death in 1988, he
headed the Brooklyn branch of the NAACP for only a brief time in the
1950s. Although he helped establish a civil rights organization, the Parents'
Workshop for Equality in New York City Schools, it remained a grassroots
organization, consisting mostly of working-class parents. No prominent figures belonged to the Parents' Workshop, only ordinary people interested in
integrating New York City public schools.

Despite his lack of national notoriety, by the early 1960s, Galamison had
emerged as one of the most prominent civil rights leaders in New York City.
Beginning in the 1950s, Galamison became actively involved in the struggle
for school integration. The militant Presbyterian pastor helped forge a
broad coalition of parents, teachers, ministers, and civil rights and community organizations and on February 3, 1964, led one of the nation's largest
civil rights demonstrations for school integration.

However, just when victory seemed imminent, the New York City civil
rights movement suddenly and shockingly came apart, failing to win any
substantial gains from the Board of Education. It is one of the most puz-
zling episodes in the history of civil rights. Why did the movement self-
destruct? The story of Galamison, New York City's leading civil rights
activist in the 1950s and 1960s, is a story of heroism and tragedy.

Little has been written about Milton Galamison. Although he was the
leading school integrationist in New York City, he usually receives only a
brief mention in topical works. In her book, *The School Fix, NYC, USA,*
Miriam Wasserman only briefly mentions Galamison, contending that he
was a man who "probably had some political ambitions, [and] called for a
citywide boycott against the schools to support the demands for integration." While Diane Ravitch has written more extensively on Galamison, she
presents the Presbyterian pastor as an irresponsible militant whose demands for city-wide integration were not realistic.[4]

The best works to date on Galamison are David Rogers's *110 Livingston
Street* and Daniel Perlstein's chapter in his dissertation, "Milton Galamison
and the Integrationist Ideal." Rogers details Galamison's involvement in the
citywide boycott, the Parents' Workshop for Equality in New York City
Schools, and the City-Wide Committee for Integrated Schools. He also gives
insight into the political battles within the civil rights movement. Relying
on Galamison's unpublished autobiography, sermons, and letters, as well as

other sources, Perlstein presents a portrait of the "preeminent integration-ist" in New York. Perlstein correctly places him within the camp of militant integrationists who did not seek the goal of integration for assimilationist purposes or a proletariat alliance. Instead, he attempted to balance integra-tion with a sense of community. Perlstein also provides a good description of Galamison's relationship with the leftist activist Annie Stein. Both Rogers and Perlstein discuss the political relationship Galamison had with Stein and her role in building the school integration movement in New York.[5]

The problem with the accounts of both Rogers and Perlstein is their brevity. Perlstein briefly mentions Galamison's childhood, his leadership in the Brooklyn NAACP, and his militant ministry. Rogers does not touch on Galamison outside of the school struggle. We learn little about what moti-vated Galamison and the connection between his religion and his radical politics. Although Galamison's own unpublished biography sheds some light on his childhood and boycotts of the 1960s, it is full of holes when fo-cusing on his early life and the numerous political activities of one of New York's most dynamic activists. The work provides little information about his education or the people who influenced his political outlook. Moreover, his autobiography contains almost nothing about his family, his early min-istry, and his tenure as president of the Brooklyn NAACP. There is scant information on the grassroots organizations that he led and the people who helped him build the school integration movement.

To be sure, Milton Galamison is an important political figure because of his long struggle to desegregate the largest school system in the United States. Because of his activities for more than a decade that touched the lives of countless people in New York and elsewhere, and the impact he had on New York City's politics, school system, and civil rights community, his life deserves a close examination. As the central figure in the school integration struggle, Galamison is crucial to the history of the civil rights struggle. The early chapters of my work examine not only Galamison and his family his-tory but also the political context that shaped his thoughts and brought him into the militant protest wing of the civil rights movement. Galamison be-came part of a movement that included a progressive religious component as well as the secular left that emerged during the Cold War, a radical civil rights fringe that attempted to direct the movement. It demanded and struggled for the elimination of all racial barriers that hindered black and Puerto Rican children, thus coming into conflict with not only anti-civil rights forces but also the more moderate wing of the movement. The militant wing of the New York City civil rights movement and its personalities, passions, objectives, thoughts, activities, tactics, successes, and failures are important features of this book.

The first two chapters examine Galamison's early life and his emergence as a radical Presbyterian pastor. Chapter 3's major focus is on Galamison's activities and difficulties in the Brooklyn branch of the NAACP. He was able to become president of the local branch and, along with Annie Stein, build a grassroots parents' organization within the Brooklyn branch of the NAACP. This community-based organization helped nourish a subculture of political activity, cultivated leadership, and diligently struggled for desegregation as a means to create a just society. But Galamison alone did not create the New York City integration movement. The movement had its origins in an organizing tradition rooted in parent-teacher associations. Chapter 3 explores these origins and pays attention to the activities of the Brooklyn NAACP School Workshop. As civil rights scholar Charles Payne contends, focusing on the mundane is important because it "puts value on network building and movement building."[6] Local and national civil rights organizations and leaders did not always complement each other. At times they were at odds. Another important theme of the chapter is the tension not only between Board of Education officials and grassroots organizations, but also between national and local civil rights groups, among leaders, and within the Brooklyn NAACP. This tension developed over ideology and approach to struggle.

The backlash from members of the local and national leadership as well as Galamison's difficulty with administrative work made him leave the Brooklyn NAACP and establish the independent Parents' Workshop for Equality in New York City Schools. Chapter 4 provides detail on the origins of the militant grassroots parent organization and its struggle with the Board of Education over desegregation. The Parents' Workshop, which had its roots in the parent-teacher association and the School Workshop, consisted of working parents who joined forces to become the chief organization struggling for school integration. Like the NAACP Workshop, members of the Parents' Workshop developed a social world view that held firm to the belief that an interracial, loving community was possible.

The belief of the militant wing of the school integration movement that community organizing, with its reliance on collective militant action to force the Board of Education to come up with a plan and timetable to desegregate the school system, and the support it gained from the older civil rights organizations would lead to a showdown between the civil rights community and the largest school system in the nation. Chapter 5 highlights the building of a broad but fragile coalition that carried out the first city-wide boycott of the school system, demanding an integration plan and timetable. The February 3, 1964, school boycott in New York City was one of the largest civil rights demonstrations in the nation. Close to half a million children stayed out of school to protest the lack of a policy on school integration. The protest brought together a wide variety of groups and individuals in a broad coalition. With the exception of Bayard Rustin, there were no national civil rights notables leading the protest, unlike the 1963 March on Washington. Instead, grassroots people were responsible for the huge demonstration. Despite the apparent success of the February 3 boycott, the coalition that managed to carry out the demonstration fell apart. Chapter 6 focuses on the reasons for the breakup of the City-Wide Committee for Integrated Schools and the death of the school integration movement in New York.

By 1966, the community control movement had gained momentum in New York, and by 1967 experimental local governing boards had been established by the Board of Education. However, by the spring of 1968, the Ocean Hill-Brownsville governing board was locked in a confrontation with the United Federation of Teachers and the Board of Education over the issue of community control and due process for teachers. Chapter 7 is an examination of Galamison's role in the community control struggle and the dilemmas he faced as an integrationist, grassroots leader, and member of the Board of Education. The book concludes with a look at Galamison's troubles at Siloam in his later years and an assessment of his life and contribution.

An important objective of this work is to depict how Galamison linked religion and leftist politics. His radicalism was rooted in his life experiences, education, and understanding of the Bible. He interpreted Christianity as an ideology that summoned people to eradicate social sin and help create a just society. Another goal is to portray Galamison's relationship to the movement he led. This work also examines the relationship between race and class in America's largest city. Similar to the civil rights movement in the South, New York's battle over school integration demonstrated that race and class were linked. When it came to explaining the reason for inequality among social and racial groups in New York, class and race were both significant factors.

*Knocking at Our Own Door* relies heavily on accounts left by the participants, speeches, on newsletters published by the grassroots organizations, interviews, and letters. The work attempts to place the story of Milton Galamison and the school integration struggle in the context of the modern civil rights movement. In the 1950s and 1960s, the struggle for school integration became the most important civil rights issue in New York. Civil rights, civic, and grassroots organizations as well as ordinary people joined in the crusade to eradicate discrimination and to provide all children with a decent education. The publication of Adam Fairclough's *Race and Democracy: The Civil Rights Struggle in Louisiana: 1915–1972*, John Egerton's *Speak Now Against the Day*, Robin D. G. Kelly's *Hammer and Hoe*, James Goodman's *Scottsboro Stories*, John Dittmer's *Local People*, and Charles Payne's *I've Got the Light of Freedom* have enriched our understanding of the battle for civil rights in the South before and during the 1960s. These works do not just examine the activities of national figures but also give critical attention to the less well known who struggled to eliminate racial oppression. *Knocking at Our Own Door* builds on that historiography.[7] However, for the most part, civil rights historiography has focused on southern civil rights campaigns, especially before the 1960s, leaving the impression that the only region worth studying during the modern civil rights period is the South. Most of the books, articles, and films on the topic have done little to challenge the southern paradigm. By focusing on the struggle to integrate New York City schools, this book suggests a more comprehensive approach to studying the civil rights movement. It offers an alternative to the nearly exclusive southern paradigm. To be sure, the New York experience was different from the South's. Absent in New York were the numerous racist attacks that led to the maiming and killing of civil rights workers and the economic terror launched by the White Citizen Councils and the Ku Klux Klan. However, Galamison and others argued that a segregated New York public school system psychologically crippled countless black and Latino children and helped place them on a road to economic and social disaster. Without a doubt, the New York City school integration struggle was part of the national struggle for civil rights.

# chapter one

# THE SHAPING
# OF MILTON
# GALAMISON

Milton A. Galamison grew up in a racially divided Philadelphia, where, like so many African Americans, he experienced poverty, suffered racial discrimination, and was the victim of a family breakup. However, thanks to a caring grandmother, a nurturing black church, a determination to succeed, and some serendipitous opportunities, young Galamison managed to overcome these obstacles and embark upon a successful career in the ministry.

## African Americans in Philadelphia

The black population of Philadelphia increased from 62,600, or 4.8 percent, of the population in 1900 to 134,200, or 7.4 percent, by 1920. The increase was due to black migration, as thousands of African American men, women, and children moved from the South to northern urban centers.[1]

As factory jobs became plentiful, blacks were locked out because of racism. Historian Roger Lane notes that in 1900, there were "no African American boilermakers, locomotive engineers, streetcar conductors or sheet metal workers."[2]

In contrast, new European immigrants moved rapidly into the industrial sector. Nearly half the immigrants worked in industry, five times as many as blacks. In 1900, the vast majority of black workers were classified as unskilled and worked in domestic and personal service. As a result European immigrants moved up the economic and social ladder while blacks moved down. Although blacks possessed skills that could be used in industry and were far more literate in English than the European immigrants, racial hatred determined black occupations.[3]

Labor institutions were no help. Unions discriminated against blacks. With the exception of a few labor unions such as the cigar makers, typographers, and longshoremen's Association, blacks were excluded. In 1894, the AFL's affiliates' constitutions contained clauses that excluded blacks.[4]

There were few black business owners in Philadelphia at the dawn of the twentieth century. In his classic work, *The Philadelphia Negro*, W. E. B. Du Bois points out that some blacks were prominent caterers and barbers. However, as the twentieth century matured, the number of black entrepreneurs actually declined. Lane notes that in 1885, there were 300 barbers; by 1912 their numbers had dwindled to 166. Blacks were virtually barred from apprenticeships by the first decade of the twentieth century. There was only a handful of black lawyers and doctors in Philadelphia.[5]

The one area in which blacks were able to gain employment after 1870 was civil service. When the Republicans gained control of Philadelphia's government in 1871, blacks gained jobs. Civil service reform also opened the door for blacks because reform meant doing away with patronage. Jobs could no longer be awarded on the basis of loyalty. Instead, people applying for government employment would have to take civil service examinations, an objective way of measuring candidates that offered greater opportunities for blacks. Thanks to civil service reform, blacks gained jobs as messengers, watchmen, schoolteachers, police officers, firemen, clerks, and postal workers. These jobs paid well and provided steady incomes and security. By 1913 there were 200 black postal workers in Philadelphia.[6]

Although World War I provided job opportunities for African Americans in manufacturing, those jobs were lost right after the war because of racial discrimination. But the growth of government led to more blacks being

hired by the public sector. By 1920 there were 274 black police officers, 276
schoolteachers, and 145 black mail carriers in Philadelphia.

By 1930, Philadelphia had 1,951,000 citizens, one of ten cities in the United
States with a population of one million or better. The African American population of 250,880 made up 13 percent of the total population. Although
many suffered during the Depression, Philadelphia's blacks were devastated
by the economic crisis. Half of the black working population of the city was
unemployed. Thirty-six thousand, or 85 percent of the employed black women in Philadelphia in 1930, worked as domestics. Their weekly wages ranged
from $5.00 to $8.00. By way of contrast, the largest group of white workers of
that era was earning between $25 and $29 on average. The 39th ward extended from Broad and Mifflin streets on the Delaware River to the Navy Yard. It
was not uncommon to see 150 to 200 men and women waiting on the streets
for an employer to hire them for the day in that ward. It was reported that
some of the workers exchanged their labor for as little as ten cents an hour.
One woman reported that she received seventy-five cents a day from a white
merchant as a house cleaner. She scrubbed four large rooms and one bath-
room and washed ten windows, along with a general cleaning of the house.
Besides the seventy-five cents, she was given a light lunch of two slices of
bread, cheese, and "as much water as she wants." Except for a barber shop,
there were no businesses operated by blacks in the 39th ward. Moreover, there
were no black professionals in the area. Few blacks owned their own homes.[7]

Blacks had the highest percentage of unemployment. A survey conducted by the University of Pennsylvania's Department of Industrial Research
in the spring of 1930 revealed that 15 percent of persons surveyed were
unemployed. In 1938, 32.5 percent of employable African Americans did
not have work.[8]

Floyd Logan, president of the Educational Equality League, designed to
obtain and safeguard the educational rights of citizens throughout Pennsylvania, noted that out of 207 elementary schools, fourteen were set aside
for blacks. Although black children attended the other elementary schools,
the schools did not employ any black teachers. "In other words, our teachers are entirely restricted to teaching children in these exclusive (the 14
black) schools, while, their white fellow teachers are allowed to teach the
children of all races." Logan contended that this was in clear violation of
the school code of the state, which prohibited racial discrimination. Historian Vincent P. Franklin has noted that during the Depression many

black teachers lost their jobs and none were allowed to teach in racially mixed secondary schools.[9]

By the mid 1930s, there were 41,753 black children in public schools of Philadelphia, about 18 percent of the total enrollment for the city's elementary and high schools. However, out of 7,753 teachers, only 303 were black. The racial makeup of the staff of the public schools was no better. Of the 559 clerks and stenographers, only thirteen were African American. Although there were 1,123 janitors, carpenters, custodians, skilled and unskilled laborers, a mere 87 were black. Although there were 1,400 high school teachers, none were black. This was also true for other divisions. Of the 1,315 junior high school teachers and 151 vocational school teachers, not one was black. Just as all the public schools had black students but few black teachers, the same record was found in the trade and special schools. Because of the struggle launched by the Educational Equality League, the practice of assigning teachers to schools based on race was officially ended in March 1937.[10]

Very few blacks attended high school in Philadelphia. In 1930, the 2,422 black junior high school students made up only 6.4 percent of the 37,809 students. Only 2,006 African Americans made up a mere 5.7 percent of the 39,929 high school students. Vincent Franklin notes that after 1930, when the number of blacks in Philadelphia increased, the number of public schools became more segregated. Forty percent of the elementary schools were predominantly black. By 1935, 50 percent of black high school students attended only three high schools. In 1941 two of these schools had 40 percent of the black student body of Philadelphia.[11]

In 1936, blacks in Philadelphia also lived in the worst housing. In North Philadelphia, the average age for housing blacks lived in was 54.6 years, compared to 40 years for the district as a whole. Blacks were more likely than whites to live in overcrowded housing. The general conditions were bad. Black families made up about 20 percent of the 59,463 families that resided in North Philadelphia. A large number lived in structures with poor heating, 525 places had no bathrooms, 668 had no indoor lavatories. Only 153 accommodations used "mechanical refrigeration," while 2,632 contained some property nuisance, such as bad plumbing, flooded cellars, imperfect drainage, and garbage in the yards.[12]

According to the *Philadelphia Afro-American*, black Philadelphians during the Depression also suffered from the worst health problems. The health department noted that death rate from tuberculosis was four times as great

among blacks as among whites. Blacks accounted for 34 percent of the total
deaths from pulmonary tuberculosis, although whites outnumbered blacks
8 to 1 in the city. William N. Jones, managing editor of the black weekly,
blamed the state of black Philadelphia's health on racism: "there is only one
way to lower the colored tuberculosis rate to that of citizens of other races,
and that is to equalize their economic and social status." Jones, whose weekly column was titled "Talking It Over," noted that inequality of health problems would continue to exist as long as blacks were denied their fair share
of jobs in the public and private arenas.[13]

Galamison, like so many African Americans, grew up in a Philadelphia that
denied African Americans the same opportunities that it offered to whites. As
a child he experienced racism and poverty, and family dislocation.

## The Galamison Family

Joseph Galamison, Milton's paternal grandfather, was born in March 1863,
the year Abraham Lincoln issued the Emancipation Proclamation. Because
of a dearth of information, it is impossible to determine whether his parents
had been slaves or were part of a free black population. Judging from his
occupations and the fact that he resided in a house, he may have become
part of a black middle class.

Joseph Galamison was listed as black in the 1900 census and as mulatto
in the 1920 census. There could be various reasons for this discrepancy.
First, the census workers may not have bothered to ask. Galamison himself
could have told the worker in 1900 that he was black and in 1920 said he was
mulatto. In any case, it seems likely that Joseph had a light complexion.

The 1900 census reveals that Sarah Madden was born in May 1868 in
Maryland, and she was married to Joseph Galamison by 1900. The Galami-
sons had four children and were living with Sarah's mother, Agnes Madden.[14]
Joseph and Sarah's oldest child, Alma, was born in March 1889; followed by
Gladstone, born in February 1893; Agnes, born in February 1898; and Cath-
erine, born in January 1900.

The first time Joseph A. Galamison is listed in *Boyd's Philadelphia City
Directory* is in 1909. While this would seem to indicate that Galamison
arrived in the city at some point in 1908 or 1909, it is quite possible that the
directory had not bothered to list him before that date, because city direc-

tories were notorious for ignoring blacks.[15] Regardless, the directories reveal little information about the Galamisons. Joseph is listed in 1909 as Joseph A. Galamison, a collector living in a house at 1926 Montrose. The following year he is listed as an "agt" (agent) residing at the same address.[16]

The 1915 directory listed Joseph as a salesman, living at the same address. In 1919, the directory gave Galamison's address as 245 N 58th, still listing him as a salesman. The years 1921, 1922, and 1923 gave similar information on Galamison.[17]

The 1920 Census provides more information on the Galamison family. Joseph, 57, was listed as a mulatto born in Maryland. The names of his relatives were also given. Sarah, his wife, 49, was also born in Maryland. Gladstone, 24, was the oldest child still residing in the household. Oliver, 16, born around 1904, was the next oldest boy. Joseph, the youngest of the three boys, was 14. Agnes, 19, was the oldest daughter still residing there, and Kathryn (spelled Catherine by the census taker), 16, was the youngest girl. All the children were listed as having been born in Maryland.[18] This census information suggests that Kathryn and Oliver were either twins or less than a year apart in age. It also reveals that the Galamison family must have resided in Maryland as late as 1906 (the year that the youngest child of Joseph and Sarah was born). The family either moved and resided for a short period in another state before moving to Philadelphia or moved directly from Maryland to the City of Brotherly Love.

In the 1926 directory Joseph was still listed as a salesman. However, he had moved to a house at 5605 Haverford. Kathy A. and Oliver W. Galamison resided at the same address. Oliver's occupation was listed as postal clerk. Kathy's occupation was not listed. The 1926 directory also listed a Gladstone W. Galamison, an actor, residing in the house at 5605 Haverford Ave.[19] All three sons at some time in their lives worked for the postal service, a prestigious profession for African Americans.

Although Milton Galamison contends that his father, Gladstone, was a postal worker, the directory lists him as an actor who lived in his parents' house at 5605 Haverford Ave.[20] He may have been sharing expenses with his parents and his siblings or he may have been supported by his family. He could have been working at the post office part time or full time while pursuing an acting career. Gladstone may have stopped his acting career and joined his brothers in the post office on a full-time basis. In his unpublished autobiography, Milton Galamison does not mention his parents' names,

and he very seldom refers to them. His two mentions of his father are far
from complimentary. He describes Gladstone as a postal worker who deserted the family and refused to support his children, portraying him as a
criminal who left his family to starve.

Gladstone had a family of his own by the early 1920s. Gladstone and Dorothy's first child, Joseph, was born in 1922; Milton was born on March 25, 1923. Gladstone, Dorothy, and the two boys must have lived with Gladstone's parents because the directories do not list a separate address, suggesting that they had to rely on the assistance of Gladstone's family.

Less information is available on Milton's maternal grandparents. Galamison mentions his mother only a few times in his autobiography, informing his reader that she was forced to work to raise him and his brother. Dorothy Woods, Milton's mother, was probably born in Pennsylvania. Her father, Theodore H. Woods, was listed in the 1920 census as a mulatto, 49, and born in Pennsylvania. His wife, Nellie Woods, was twenty years his junior and born in Florida. Dorothy was not listed in the census.

The 1935 directory lists Theodore Woods's occupation as truck driver; he resided with Nellie in a house at 52 North 59th. In 1935 a D. Galamison (most likely Dorothy) also resided at 52 N. 59th, suggesting that by 1935, Dorothy had separated from Gladstone and was living with her parents. The only explanation that Milton Galamison gives for the separation is that his father had completely abandoned the family. However, a cousin of Milton's, William Claxton, recalls seeing Gladstone visit the family on occasion.[21]

By the 1930s, Dorothy Woods and her children were living with her mother, Nellie. Mary Woods, another of Nellie's daughters, also resided in the household. According to those who knew the Woodses, Milton's maternal grandparents separated, creating financial hardship for Nellie, who became responsible for raising her grandchildren. Although Galamison reveals little about his early childhood, he describes the poverty he faced. The family moved constantly in order to avoid paying rent.[22] Dorothy worked in the Strawbridge Clothier retail store as a maid. Mary and Nellie did domestic work, like most working-class black women. The grandmother would use other people's credit in order to purchase clothes for her grandchildren.

Although he grew up poor during the Depression, Galamison did not blame his poverty on the national economic crisis. His blame was much more provincial; he attributed his destitution to his father's abandonment of his family.

My mother worked in a department store and contributed her mea-g[er] earnings to our support. My father was a postal clerk, making a good income throughout the depression. He contributed nothing and it always amazed me that, over a period of seventeen years, the same sheriff's office that so efficiently put us out of the house for non-payment of rent could never find my father to arrest him for non-support.

Poverty and hunger were terrible aspects of Galamison's life that he never forgot. Although he joked about it in his autobiography, his bitterness toward the person who clearly was responsible for his impoverishment is quite evident.

When I read Dick Gregory's discussion of his home life in his book, Nigger, I could not help but draw my own amusing comparisons. Dick writes about rats in his home. No self-respecting enterprising rat would have allowed himself to starve or freeze to death in our home. The New York Urban Coalition slogan says, "Starve a Rat Today." I guess that is what we were doing back in the thirties because I never saw a rat in our house. The presence of rats is a sign of some affluence. Dick writes about hiding the telephone when the welfare investigator revisited. We never qualified for welfare because our absentee, [reprehensible] father always had a good job. And we never had a telephone because it was a luxury we couldn't think of affording. Dick laments the fact that his father only came home at Christmas time. Mine never came home at anytime. I don't think he even knew where we lived. I used to go to my bedroom sometimes and cry when I should have stood on the street corner and shouted for help.[23]

While Galamison blamed his father for the family's poverty, nowhere in his autobiography does he express anger toward his mother. Yet those close to the Galamisons were aware of an estrangement between Milton and Dorothy. He only mentions her a few times, and never acknowledges her contribution in raising him and his brother, which strongly suggests the distance between mother and son. Galamison did not display or communicate deep affection for Dorothy Woods.

The lack of closeness to his mother may be explained by the fact that she worked and was away from home. It may also have been due to Dorothy's

attitude. She may not have been a warm and affectionate person. Reverend
Thomas Logan, pastor of St. Michael's and All Angels, the church Milton attended in Philadelphia, was always puzzled by the lack of closeness between
Milton and Dorothy. William Claxton contends that Dorothy had to work
constantly and had little time to spend with her children. Sometime during
the Depression Dorothy moved out of her mother's house to live with the
Claxton family, probably for economic reasons. Although she was only a
short distance from her children, the separation must have been traumatic
for Milton and Joseph. Probably not understanding the reasons for his mother's absence, Galamison may have resented her for not being there.[24]

Milton was closer to his aunt Mary and grandmother, Nellie Woods, than
his own mother. In 1966, when Mary died suddenly, Galamison's wife,
Gladys, had to break the news to him. She recalled that it was the first time
in their marriage that she had seen her husband cry. Mary never had any
children. She had been married, but the marriage did not work out. Although Mary is not mentioned in the book, those who knew the family say
that Milton was close to his aunt. Mary may have treated the boys as though
they were her own children.[25]

The one person Galamison mentions with affection in his autobiography
is his grandmother, Nellie. He describes her as a kind woman who took care
of her two grandchildren and made sure that they were fed and clothed. It
was not Dorothy, but Nellie, who saw to it that Joseph and Milton received
a proper education. When the family moved, Nellie enrolled the boys in the
new school and conferred with school officials. Moreover, Nellie may have
had a tremendous influence on her grandchild's reading ability. A voracious
reader, she may have been a member of the Book of the Month Club. Although she was poor, books were everywhere in her house, and Gladys cannot remember a time when Nellie did not have a book in her hand. This
passion for reading rubbed off on Milton, who read history, biographies, literature, philosophy, and other serious works all the time.[26]

## Life in Philadelphia

The young Milton Galamison experienced racial bigotry as well as poverty
in Philadelphia. One of the most appalling incidents occurred when he was
in elementary school. His class was on line to go to the auditorium when he

suddenly needed to go to the lavatory. Without notifying the teacher, Mrs. Bradley, he left the line and went to the facilities. Galamison was a bed-wetter, and his grandmother had informed school officials that her grandson had a "weak bladder," something the future Presbyterian pastor would later deny. After he returned to the line, his teacher insulted him by announcing to the entire class that "A white child wouldn't do a thing like that!"[27]

Comments such as these hurt the student emotionally. But beyond heartlessly insulting or embarrassing young black children, these remarks tended to inculcate racial bias and support the established racial hierarchal structure. Inappropriate behavior was linked to a racial characteristic, demeaning black children by promoting white superiority and destroying black self-esteem.

Although he was upset by the episode, Galamison's ego remained intact. A few weeks after the lavatory incident, a white child struck Mrs. Bradley. Long after the commotion had abated in the classroom, Galamison continued to laugh uncontrollably. When the teacher demanded to know what was so funny, the defiant student yelled out "A white child wouldn't do a thing like that." Galamison believes that Mrs. Bradley got the last word when he was struck by a cafeteria worker without provocation a few weeks later. The worker, Galamison claims, was a good friend of Mrs. Bradley.[28] The incident demonstrates that at a young age, Galamison developed a sense of justice and was willing to take action against racial bigotry.

As a child Galamison experienced a number of other racial incidents intended to reinforce black inferiority. He recalls attending a Jim Crow movie theater on Market Street where black children were confined to the balcony. Although as a child he paid little attention to the segregated seating arrangements, the blatant exclusion of black children from the door prize every Saturday morning raised his consciousness about the impact of racial discrimination. Galamison asserts:

Apparently, only the tickets of white children on the orchestra floor were included in the drawing because nobody in the balcony ever won. This particular Saturday there must have been an error. The prize was a set of electric trains and the number called was the number of a balcony ticket. Do you know that the theater management conjured up some explanation to negate the drawing and all three prizes ultimately went to white children on the orchestra floor? I won-

dered then what kind of people those could possibly be who would so
mistreat children. What manner of depravity does a man suffer that
he could deal unfairly with a child?[29]

Galamison remembers an incident when he received a cigarette burn from a
white man for no reason except that he was black. When he crossed into the
Italian section of town, boys would throw rocks at him, chase him, and call
him nigger. He was fully aware that there were Jim Crow restaurants and other
eating facilities that refused to serve blacks, and that there were few black
police officers, firefighters, and teachers in the City of Brotherly Love.[30]
Although Galamison's autobiography does not mention his experience with
racial bigotry in high school, it clearly had an impact and may have been a
motivating factor in his career.

In spite of his interest in reading, racial discrimination limited Milton's
success in high school. Like his brother before him, he was slated for a vocational program—unlike white students, who were programmed for an academic education. Because classes were large, however, he was put untypi-
cally into some college preparatory classes where he excelled, and he did
not, in fact, do well in the vocational classes. Despite his success with academic subjects, however, and his mediocre performance in vocational classes, the school never corrected the error. Galamison's school experience
probably left him bitter. He knew first hand how a racist school system
could handicap children of color. He understood from his personal experience how black children could fail in school because of discrimination.[31]

In spite of the appalling racial episodes in Galamison's life, he recalls an
organic, viable black community that sheltered its members. Besides a caring aunt and grandmother, there were friends and kind neighbors. His cousin William Claxton affirms that he, along with Milton and Joseph, played
with the neighborhood boys, developing strong bonds. The most important institution in the community to young Milton and his family was the
black church.

As in other black communities, the black churches of Philadelphia were
quite active. The black press reported the activities of the numerous main-
line churches, including the African Methodist, Baptist, Presbyterian, and
Episcopalian bodies. They sponsored many activities including musicals,
plays, lectures, as well as offering supplication. The dedicatory organ service
at First African Baptist Church featured classical anthems sung by the choir

and an organ recital. A musicale was given by the senior choir, and a "plantation drama" was performed by the Junior League of Pemel Methodist Episcopal Church. The members of Saint Thomas Methodist Episcopal presented a pageant, and a fashion show was held by the church's usher board. On Wednesday evening the Mount Carmel Baptist Church's usher board sponsored a program that featured the Quaker City Female Band. A lecture on the pyramids of Egypt was given at the Mount Olivet Baptist Church. The "Romance of Rush" was performed by the Romance Club of the church to raise money to purchase chairs for the Sunday School. The Union African Methodist Episcopal's choruses, with the assistance of other church choruses, raised more than one thousand dollars. The Reeve Presbyterian Sunday School performed a cantata for its Christmas celebration.[32]

The clubs in the black churches hosted events for the church and the black community, usually on weekday evenings. Saint Thomas Methodist Episcopal Church's Ladies Aid Society sponsored a "Sauerkraut Supper" one Friday. One Thursday evening, Mrs. Sue McDonald and her singers gave a recital under the sponsorship of the Sunday School. The "Queen of Sheba," a pageant, was given on a Thursday evening at the Holy Trinity Church, while an epiphany pageant, "The Feast of the Lights," was given at the Philips Brooks Memorial Chapel one weekday evening at eight.[33] The black churches of Philadelphia offered African Americans a wide variety of social and cultural activities and access to the recreation and entertainment otherwise denied them by the larger society.

Like millions of blacks in the United States, the Galamisons went to church for social, educational, and religious support. For Galamison and his family, Saint Michael's and All Angels, a small Episcopal church, located on Forty-third and Wallace Streets in Philadelphia, served these functions.

The Episcopal and other high churches in the black community attracted the black elite through emphasis on middle-class culture. Such religious institutions emphasized that one reaches God through reason rather than experience, by learning the catechism and reading the Bible. Priests trained in seminaries delivered scholarly sermons that had an ethical message. The notion of whipping a person into a frenzy was alien to the advocates of the black high church. Ecstatic behavior was associated with the religious institutions of the working class, people who were considered less sophisticated. Members of the high church considered themselves more refined, reserved, educated; in short, quite middle class. But working-class people were also attracted to the high black churches. Many working-class African Americans who aspired to move into the middle class adopted middle-class values. Like their more affluent neighbors, some black working-class members rejected what they saw as unsophisticated behavior among the Pentecostals and some Baptists. They turned to the Episcopalian, Presbyterian, Congregational, high Baptist, and African Methodist churches. This may tell us something about the role of class in the black community. Economics may not be the only determining factor; culture plays a major role.

Despite their poverty, Nellie Woods, her daughter, and her grandchildren associated with the high church. Dorothy joined in 1916, when she was a young girl. Her family were stalwart members. Nellie took her children, Mary, Ted, and Dorothy, to Saint Michael's every Sunday. Dorothy was active in the church choir. Like her mother, Dorothy made sure her children attended the church regularly. Milton became an active member of the church's youth organizations.[34]

In January of 1940, Saint Michael's received a new rector, the Reverend Thomas Logan. Logan, born in Philadelphia, had followed both his father and older brother by becoming an Episcopal priest. Ordained in 1938 at age 26, he first went to Saint Phillip's Protestant Episcopal Church in New York City and served as the first curate. He later became rector of St. Augustine Mission in Yonkers, New York. Saint Michael's was his first real church.[35]

Logan was not quite 28 when he took the reins at Saint Michael's. On several occasions Logan's sermons dealt with racial uplift and stressed social issues, attacking racism and injustice. The Episcopal priest referred to himself as a "race man." He was a young, handsome, and vibrant man who was attractive to many young people, including Milton Galamison. Logan presented the young Galamison for confirmation and appointed him an acolyte. Milton's duties included assisting the priest and distributing the Eucharist at Mass. Milton's position at the altar, wearing a robe every Sunday, visible to all members, meant that he was looked upon as someone special. Moreover, young Milton became very active in the church, drawing attention from the weekly *Afro-American*. In the spring of 1940, the paper noted that Milton Galamison gave an address at the church at the evening service. The paper also noted that the acolytes attended special services at various churches in the city.[36]

In a short time Milton Galamison became close to Thomas Logan. He became the rector's ghost writer, putting together articles for the *Philadel-*

*phia Tribune.* Galamison often visited the rector at his house, did chores for him, and accompanied him on trips and visits to other churches. Although there was only a ten-year difference between the two, the priest became Galamison's mentor. The two spoke often about Galamison's concerns and aspirations, including the teen's desire to go into the ministry.[37]

It is not clear exactly when young Galamison decided that he wanted to go into the ministry; he left no clues in his autobiography. According to Reverend Logan, Milton enjoyed being at the altar; it was a sign of power and prestige. He may have also been attracted to the church teachings. In his grandmother's house he read the Bible. A relative of Milton recalls that, as a teenager, Galamison was self-confident and extremely smart. He realized that he was articulate, a skill that could move him up the social and economic ladder. Those who knew him assert that he was ambitious, determined to succeed. Thus the ministry was a route to success. The attention he received from the congregation and the black press probably influenced his decision to pursue the ministry.[38]

Eventually, it became apparent to the entire church body that the young Galamison wanted to become a rector. Logan recalled a Sunday morning when he had an emergency and had to leave the church; he asked Milton to take charge. It is unknown what Logan expected from the acolyte, but the young Galamison acted as though he were the priest in charge that day. He conducted the service and even delivered the sermon.[39]

In order to reach his goal, Galamison had to go to college. There were, however, two obstacles: a lack of money and a lackluster high school record. Milton had done poorly in his vocational courses because he was unable or unwilling to work with his hands, but he had excelled in academic courses. Overbrooke High School officials, however, had never changed his program. In June of 1940, therefore, Galamison graduated from Overbrooke with a nonacademic diploma.[40]

Excited that a member of his church wanted to go into the ministry and realizing that Galamison had no money for college, Reverend Logan urged him to apply to Saint Augustine in Raleigh, North Carolina. Unlike predominantly white institutions of higher education and some of the more prestigious black colleges, Saint Augustine was willing to accept students with lesser academic credentials. Founded in 1867 by the Episcopal church, the historically black college was devoted to making its students knowledgeable agents of change and positive contributors to society by providing them with opportunities for "personal, social, and cultural growth." In December 1930, the North Carolina Department of Public Education awarded Saint Augustine an "A" rating. In May 1931, the school awarded its first accredited bachelor's degrees at its Sixty-Fourth Commencement.[41] A degree from Saint Augustine would therefore open the doors to a seminary.

Galamison was accepted to Saint Augustine and moved to Raleigh in the summer of 1940. However, despite his enthusiasm, the youthful Philadelphian soon ran into trouble. The school's strict code of behavior collided with Galamison's urban world view and sense of justice. Saint Augustine limited the hours that students could be off campus, students had to sign in and out, and meals were served at specific times. Galamison was not used to these restrictions. It is likely that he did not take to the required code of behavior and Southern etiquette, and may also have been unhappy at being separated from his family.

During his freshman year Galamison became involved in a event that would change the course of his life. Details are sketchy. Galamison, dissatisfied with the food and/or the service, led a student strike. Almost a quarter of a century after the event, the Presbyterian pastor told the *Amsterdam News* that the strike had been successful, but did not give any details. He did assert that, although the strikers had won, the church leaders made life for him unbearable. Even though the church was paying for his education and a decision to withdraw would jeopardize his college career, he decided to leave Saint Augustine after one year.[42] The episode once again demonstrated that at a young age, Galamison was willing to take action against what he determined was injustice. He had developed a sense of righteous indignation and the willingness to challenge authority.

After leaving Saint Augustine, the undaunted Galamison decided that he wanted to continue his college education. He applied and was accepted to Lincoln University, a fine institution located in Pennsylvania, near his family. Founded in 1854 as Ashmun Institute and renamed Lincoln University in 1866 in honor of the slain president, it was the first institution in the United States to offer African Americans higher education. Founder John Miller Dickey received permission from the Presbytery of New Castle to establish Ashmun Institute "for the scientific, Classical and theological education of colored youth of the male sex." The all-male school (it would not admit women until 1952), located in Chester County, Pennsylvania, counts among its graduates Supreme Court Justice Thurgood Marshall, the world-renowned author Langston Hughes, and Kwame Nkrumah, first prime minister of Ghana. During its first hundred years, 20 percent of the country's black doctors and 10 percent of its black lawyers graduated from Lincoln. A large percentage of black federal, state, and municipal judges; college presidents; and ministers were also graduates of Lincoln University.[43]

There was no scholarship program at Lincoln. To help pay his way, Galamison worked at a dry cleaner. Gladys Galamison recalls that "Milton went to school on a nerve." Determined to succeed, he became an exceptional student. During his Lincoln years, Galamison came into contact with a number of students from what would become known as third world nations. In particular, he became friendly with a group of African students who spoke of European colonialism on the African continent. They often spoke of how the West stole precious resources from the Africans, causing poverty. Galamison's conversations with the African students had a profound impact. It made him understand better the impact of European domination and colonialism on the African continent and elsewhere, explaining why many parts of black Africa were underdeveloped. His experience and early understanding of the impact of colonialism would stay with him for the rest of his life.[44]

While Galamison was at Lincoln, the United States entered World War II. After one or two years at Lincoln, he may have decided to contribute to the war effort and applied for a job at the Baldwin Locomotive Works, close to Philadelphia. He was assigned to the boiler gang, which consisted of a person who heats the locomotive boiler with a torch, another who holds a flat iron against it, and a third who hits the flat iron with a ten-pound sledge hammer. Although Galamison was relatively small, weighing only 120 pounds, he received the sledge hammer job. While aware that larger men, including a cousin who worked for Baldwin, had "softer jobs," he did not complain but attempted to succeed. Eventually becoming extremely frustrated because he was unable to perform the strenuous task and did not receive assistance or relief from the two white "bastards" in his crew, he quit and went back to college. But the experience left him bitter. "And I cried. Not because there weren't a dozen other jobs. Not because I wanted to stay on the job. I cried to learn that there are people like that in this world. White people whose bigotry and prejudice renders them inhuman." Once again, the lesson of how racism dehumanizes African Americans and denies them complete citizenship was instilled in the young Philadelphian.[45]

While a student at Lincoln, Milton met Gladys Hunt, born and raised in
Chester, Pennsylvania, in an affluent home. Her parents had been born in
Georgia. Her father, an undertaker who owned a business, became the city's
coroner and a member of the school board. Her mother helped operate the
undertaking business. Although Gladys's mother was a Baptist and her father was a Methodist, her father insisted that she be raised a Presbyterian
because of his positive experience attending a Presbyterian high school,
more associated with the middle class.[46]

Gladys's junior high school teacher was Hermenia Logan, the wife of Reverend Logan. Mrs. Logan recalls Gladys as quaint and proper with long pig-
tails. Gladys attended and graduated from Chancy University with a degree
in education and joined the Chancy Alumni Association. Mrs. Logan, also a
graduate of Chancy and a member of the Alumni Association, recalls Reverend Logan coming to an association meeting with Milton. Mrs. Logan introduced Milton to Gladys and they began to date.[47]

Galamison graduated from Lincoln in 1945 with honors. After graduation, while Galamison remained committed to his goal to become a minister, he made a crucial decision to become a Presbyterian. Some years later
Galamison claimed that he had switched to Presbyterianism because the
Episcopalians were attacking him at Lincoln for his activities at Saint Augustine. This is highly unlikely. His change probably had more to do with his
trouble with the Episcopal bishop. Milton wanted to attend Philadelphia
Divinity school on Spruce and 42nd Streets, an Episcopalian institution, but
the school had a Jim Crow policy. The alternative was to study in New York
City. The bishop insisted that he attend a school at 179 Ninth Avenue in
Manhattan. Demonstrating his defiance he insisted that he wanted to stay
in Pennsylvania, no doubt to be near Gladys and his family.[48]

Because of Milton's success as an undergraduate, Dr. Jesse B. Barber,
dean of studies at Lincoln, and Dr. Larry Foster, a professor of Religion at
the university, recognized that he was academically gifted and tried to persuade him to attend the divinity school at Lincoln. The major problem for
Galamison was that Lincoln was not an Episcopal but a Presbyterian institution. Not only would they have to persuade him to stay at Lincoln, they
would have to persuade him to change to Presbyterianism. This was not an
easy decision. Galamison was raised an Episcopalian and had matured in
the church. His decision would have an impact on others, perhaps disap-
pointing his family, Reverend Logan, and friends at Saint Michael's.[49]

Galamison, however, decided to accept Barber's offer. Gladys, who was raised a Presbyterian, may have influenced his decision. Just as important, Galamison's defiance and his intolerance for racial injustice would not allow him to give in to racial discrimination. Giving in to the bishop would have been capitulating to racism. In addition to the principle involved, this switch offered him an opportunity. Barber and Foster courted the potential recruit by offering him free tuition at Lincoln. He was familiar with the institution and its faculty, and on the completion of his course work he would be assigned a church.[50]

After spending four years at the Presbyterian institution, Galamison had become quite familiar with the faith. He had gained independence from the Episcopal church when he went off to college; that sense of independence grew when he went to Lincoln and paid his own way. Moreover, he had been away from Saint Michael's a number of years and may have grown distant from the congregation. When he married Gladys in 1945, he did not invite the Logans to his wedding ceremony.[51]

Milton Galamison's life was a narrative of ascent. A poor boy managed to rise out of poverty and climb aboard the train for success. Unlike many young African Americans who faced similar hardships, Galamison would make a prominent career, becoming one of the few black Presbyterian ministers in the country. But the young Philadelphian's vision was not limited to self-aggrandizement. By the time he started leading a church, he had a vision of a bright future that encompassed all of humanity.

# chapter two

# FROM WITHERSPOON TO SILOAM: THE MAKING OF A MILITANT PASTOR

By the start of the Cold War, Galamison was a pastor with a promising career. His seminary training, speaking ability, and writings made him well known in religious circles. However, careerism and social standing were only one aspect of the young pastor's life. In 1947, he emerged from the seminary at Lincoln University as a political radical. Adopting a race and class analysis developed from life experience, sharpened by his years at the university and the political climate of the time, the young Presbyterian minister became part of an African-American left political movement that included W. E. B. Du Bois, Paul Robeson, Shirley Graham, and Communist Party officials Claudia Jones and Ben Davis. This group presented an international critique of imperialism, racism, and class exploitation on a global scale, identifying with China, the Soviet Union, and national liberation movements in Asia, Africa, and Latin America. They were critical of a nationalist approach advocating that blacks turn inward. The young pastor also identified with a rich religious tradition, rejecting the strict communist view that religion was part of the superstructure manipulated by capitalists; Galamison realized that the African-American tradition of struggle and Christian devotion could serve to alleviate oppression. His emphasis was on the development of a harmonious multiracial society devoid of racial and class inequality.

In 1947, the 24-year-old seminarian was ordained by the Presbytery Church in Princeton, New Jersey, and assigned to the Witherspoon Presbyterian Church there. It was a middle-class black church with no more than two hundred members. Gladys recalls that Princeton was a lovely area; the people of Witherspoon were warm and made her feel welcome. Galamison's preaching style—elegant and thoughtful with flawless enunciation—was suited to the black high church. His tenor voice was forceful, and he spoke loudly with a great deal of confidence.[1]

Galamison wasted no time in revealing his religious and political views to the small middle-class congregation. His sermons were typed single spaced and ran from two to six pages long. He usually began with an exegesis of a biblical passage and then applied the text to the modern world. In his early sermons Galamison attacked racism and class exploitation. "Think of all the race and class prejudice we have in the world," Galamison told Sunday morning worshippers at Witherspoon:

> It's all so unreasonable, isn't it? It's hate that's stupid and blind and without reason—like the way we suffer from the hate of some white people, who simply hate us without bothering to know us. And this hatred results in war and domestic strife and unrest and suffering, hate because as John says, they are blind. They have no power to see that hate and prejudice are getting us no place but into more and more trouble, wars and social unrest.[2]

Galamison argued that Christians must condemn all forms of prejudice, attacking not only racial bigotry but also anti-Semitism:

> We boast that we worship the true God who came down from heaven in the form of man, and we are loud in our condemnation of the Jewish people who, through centuries have rejected Christ and refused to believe in him as Lord. We would say that for the Jewish people God has never become a Christian. But one needs only to hear a

Rabbi preach today to know that the Jewish people under the name of
Judaism have discovered that beautiful way of life that we like to call
Christian and which is Christian in everything but name.[3]

After condemning those who profess Christianity but carry out horrendous acts, the young pastor contended that Christians have practiced anti-Semitism. Christians in Colonial America barred Jews from New York and "denied them the right to hold property. On Manhattan Island Jews were forbidden to trade. In 1737 Jews were denied the right to vote by the New York Assembly. In Pennsylvania and New Jersey Jews were not allowed to hold political office. In 1868, Jews could not practice certain professions in Maryland unless they subscribed to the Christian faith. Many states adopted constitutions which extended civil liberties only to Christians so that all Jews were automatically excluded."[4]

However, Galamison noted, not until the twentieth century were there organized campaigns of bigotry: "deliberate anti-Jewish and anti-Catholic and anti-Negro movements were begun in America by men and women who boasted being white, Gentile Protestants, one-hundred percent American Christians."[5]

Besides racism and class exploitation, Galamison criticized militarism. In one sermon he noted that war leads only to misfortunes. Although World War I was to have been the war to end all wars, Galamison contended, it only led to the rise of the Soviet Union, Attaturk in Turkey, and Mussolini, Franco, and Hitler. Only peace and humility will end war.[6] The solution was "to resist the forces of wrong and darkness. . . . And to persist in the direction of healthy-mindedness in Christ so that we may live without prejudice and hate." The absence of God meant the presence of strife, war, and racism. Therefore, the best solution to these problems was to put God in their lives.[7]

For Galamison, Christianity was a revolutionary ideology; Jesus, Paul, and other figures of the Bible were social radicals who stood up for the poor and oppressed. They were the examples that Christians should follow. In his sermons at Witherspoon, Galamison criticized capitalism and racism, but he did not directly advocate socialism. Instead, he argued that the best way to gain social and economic justice was by adopting Christian practices. The social obligation of Christians was based on Scripture, and the Bible was a blueprint of how they should conduct their lives, focusing on the spiritual and physical plight of people.

In one of his best socio-religious sermons, given on February 29, 1948, and entitled "The Political Significance of the Crucifixion," Galamison argued that Jesus had opposed the corruption and decadence of the Roman Empire. Jesus, the revolutionary, came to destroy the corrupt state. Galamison, comparing the Roman Empire and the contemporary United States, noted that the state "has guarded not the highest, but the lowest, aspects of human life." He claimed that Jesus had little respect for property rights and the office-holding classes of his day. Office holders only manipulate people for their own selfish needs, and Jesus saw them as parasites. Jesus wanted a society "in which no military forces drained the substance and life of the people." Galamison declared that it was militarism that had crucified Christ. He advised his congregation to give allegiance not to governments and armies but to God.[8]

Despite the atmosphere of the Cold War and the anti-communism hysteria in America, Galamison was quick to condemn the foreign policy of the United States and its allies, colonial masters who subjugated people of color. While he argued that their attempt to end communism would fail and lead only to greater conflict in the world, he was careful to advance not a political solution but one based on Christian principles. Put God and family first. Militarism and imperialism were "asinine" and directly linked to capitalist greed. "Men shall know peace when and only when we are all reconciled in one body to God through the cross."[9] Noting that the great national resources of the world were controlled by "no more than five percent of the population," and that there was great disparity between rich and poor in the United States, he again carefully couched his solution in religious and ethical terms, warning that the seeking of wealth is idolatry: people must turn to God.[10]

The stress on moral and religious resolution demonstrated that he wanted to appeal to people's sense of fair play and social justice. The Bible offered the best means. However, the young pastor also urged his congregation to heed those who offered political solutions to militarism, racism, and class exploitation. In a sermon titled "Speaking Your Mind," Galamison declared that Henry Wallace was "the greatest prophet on the international scene today" because he stood up to the "international thugs in an effort to achieve peace." Wallace, unlike other politicians, had the fortitude to criticize his country because it was using its power and wealth for strategic military purposes. The pastor compared Wallace, who had been Vice President in Franklin Roosevelt's third term and had run as a left-wing third-party candidate

for President in 1948, to the prophet Micaiah because both condemned war.
Portraying Wallace as a hero, Galamison placed him in a left perspective, but
in the context of Christianity.[11]

Despite the pastor's outspoken leftist views, Gladys Galamison did not
recall him having a difficult time. She recalled that people accepted him, and
he was happy at Witherspoon. A strong indication that Galamison liked
Witherspoon and Princeton and planned to stay was his enrolling at Princeton Theological Seminary seeking a Masters in theology.[12]

Despite their fondness for Princeton, their stay in the quaint town was to
be a brief one. The next year, following the death of Rev. George Stark of
Siloam Presbyterian Church in Brooklyn, Galamison was offered the pastorship of the distinguished congregation.[13]

## Siloam

Siloam Presbyterian Church, founded as a Presbyterian mission in 1849 by
James Gloucester (son of John Gloucester, the founder of black Presbyterianism in Philadelphia), had developed into one of the most exclusive black
institutions in New York. (Among its parishioners were many of Brooklyn's
black elite, including Dr. Susan McKinney-Steward, one of the first black
women physicians in the country.) Indeed, Historian Willard B. Gatewood
has suggested that Siloam continued the practice of renting pews to exclude
working-class blacks.[14]

Stark, one of Brooklyn's most prestigious pastors, had been an active Republican, and his activities were often cited in the black weekly *Amsterdam
News*. More importantly, Stark is given credit for having built Siloam into
an institutional church. He moved the church to its present location on Jefferson and Marcy Avenues. The building contains a gymnasium that offered
recreation to children and adults. The church became a cultural center in
Bedford-Stuyvesant, offering numerous concerts, dances, and other activities for the members and community. Stark acquired a manse near the
church. Numerous clubs were established under Stark's pastorship.[15]

Galamison was one of the few black Presbyterian ministers in the country,
and his reputation as a pastor may have attracted Siloam officials. Although
he was content at Witherspoon, Siloam was a much more prestigious position, offering more exposure and greater professional opportunities.

On October 23, 1948, more than 700 members of Siloam attended the installation of Galamison. Dr. Jesse B. Barber, dean of Lincoln University School of Theology, was the guest speaker. He was no doubt proud of the 25-year-old pastor picked to head one of the most prestigious black Presbyterian churches in the nation. Other guests included Dr. Frank Niles of the First Presbyterian Church of Princeton, Dr. Herbert H. Fields of the Presbytery of Brooklyn-Nassau, and the Rev. John Coleman, Rector of Saint Phillip's Protestant Episcopal Church.[16]

Like his predecessor, Galamison would become a celebrity in New York City. One important accomplishment enhancing his reputation was the master's degree he earned from Princeton Theological Seminary in 1949, the same year Gladys gave birth to Milton Jr. Entitled "The Theme of Salvation in the World's Great Religions," the 102-page thesis, well written and well organized, sheds no light on Galamison's political views. Absent from the work is any discussion of social, political, and economic injustice, the themes of many of his sermons. Instead, it is a conventional work examining salvation themes in Hinduism, Buddhism, Confucianism, Islam, and Christianity. Galamison attempted to answer five questions: from what must I be saved; to what will I be saved; who can be saved; when will I be saved; and how can I be saved. Although he contended that all these religions address the questions, he concluded that the first four had great limitations. Buddhism only saves some people from suffering and rebirth; Confucianism saves people from a chaotic social order but does not offer them everlasting life; Hinduism saves some people and not all, and Islam saves people from external sin but not internal transgressions.

"Christianity," according to the author, "is interested in saving man from himself. . . . The Christian has gotten at the root of the problem. Hindu and Buddhist salvation result in the loss of personality, Confucist salvation ends in the attainment of a perfected order created by imperfected man, Mohammedan salvation ends in a heaven where many sensuous earthly practices may be carried on with impunity. Christian Salvation ends in the fulfillment of personality." The Christian must grow to become like Christ. According to Galamison, every soul "becomes a son of God."

When the thesis turns to a discussion of Confucianism, major flaws appear in the analysis. It mistakenly classifies Confucianism, which is actually a philosophical doctrine, as a religion. Moreover, to contend that Islam's major objective is a paradise of "sensuous" pleasure is misleading. Like Christians,

Muslims seek fellowship with God. Galamison also ignores the fact that Christians describe Heaven as Paradise. Perhaps the absence of social, political, or economic themes was deliberate. It may be that Galamison was shrewd enough not to include political or religious views that might jeopardize his graduation.

Galamison's Masters degree, from a prestigious seminary, heightened his status in the church and Presbyterian community. To add to his growing reputation, the young pastor became involved in the *Dumont Morning Chapel* on a pioneering local New York City television station, and made several appearances on the program.[17] In the late 1940s numerous religious bodies, businesses, and media launched the campaign "Religion in American Life." Selecting Charles E. Wilson, President of General Motors, as its chairperson, the organizers of the campaign declared that "we must support the spiritual values of our civilization or we may have no civilization left." In an attempt to get Americans to reaffirm their faith, they carried out a persistent effort to reach households through radio, television, and volunteers who went door to door informing citizens about the activities of churches in their communities.

*The Dumont Morning Chapel* was structured like a regular church service. The program opened with a prayer, followed by a hymn, a scripture reading, another hymn, and a sermon. Galamison's sermons were evangelical, conventional religious messages imploring people to turn to God. In one such sermon Galamison spoke about the moral decline of the family, telling his listeners that the answer to family breakup is to bring God into the home: "I wonder if it's just a coincidence that families that pray together stay together. The Religion-in-American Life committee reports that the percentages of families broken by divorce, separation or desertion run as much as four times as high in families that profess no religious faith as among families in which both parties are church members." He contended that "A lot of bad situations are corrected when God is in the home."[18]

By the early 1950s Galamison was also appearing on the *Radio Chapel*, a Sunday morning program from 9:30 to 10:00 A.M., sponsored by the National Council of the Churches of Christ in the USA. Like the *Dumont Morning* sermons, Galamison's Sunday radio messages were evangelical, urging people to God first: "Our security is determined by our nearness to God and relationship to fellowmen." The cause of war, corruption, labor strife, and the moral decline of the family is not having God in "our lives."[19] On at least one occasion, however, in August 1952, Galamison infused a political message in his radio chapel sermon, "Temporary Triumphs and Final Failures." The Siloam pastor contended that the Founding Fathers

> wrote noble words about life, liberty, and the pursuit of happiness, about human rights and equality. And then we proceeded to apply these great thoughts to ourselves and the people we love. . . . The tragedy is that we have never loved widely enough and this ecstatic speaking has never applied to all the people. It has never applied to Indians, Mexicans, Negroes, Women, nor has it applied to other people in other parts of the world. . . . either every human being is included in our concept of liberty or liberty will be doomed.[20]

Although this moderate critique of America is a far cry from his sermons, it is nevertheless a daring effort on Galamison's part to raise the consciousness of Americans and express the concerns of those considered to be on the margins. Most likely, he did not raise his political concerns on television or radio because he knew it would have been self-destructive during a period of Cold War hysteria. Galamison would have risked his career by criticizing the United States.

Galamison's career had taken off. Besides making radio and television appearances, he contributed to the religious sermon column in the *Amsterdam News*.[21] He had become one of the best-known pastors of Brooklyn. Membership at Siloam had increased from 778 in 1948 to 1,020 in 1952, while Sunday school attendance rose from 209 to 250.[22]

Despite his growing reputation and fame, Galamison was not willing to sacrifice his political beliefs. The young minister wasted little time in revealing his ideological and theological convictions to his prominent middle-class congregation, continuing to hammer away at the evils of racism, militarism, class exploitation, American injustice, and Christian responsibility in his sermons. In one sermon, he contended that sin was both an individual and a collective transgression. While an individual could and does transgress against God, a "few sinful individuals can create an evil social order." This collective sin leads to a corrupt society and stops people from "hearing God."[23]

He declared to Siloam members that the greatest social evils people faced were racial discrimination, class inequality, and war—evils that stemmed from the greed of the rich and powerful. He asserted that class exploitation was a major culprit in the development of inequality. According to the minister, there have always been people willing to destroy liberty and social justice to further their own privileges, people willing to "prostitute public decency for private gain." Using Karl Marx's notion of superstructure, i.e., political, religious, and cultural institutions support the capitalist economic order, Galamison argued that individuals, the dominant culture, the state and its leaders, including the Protestant church in America, had all perpetuated class and race inequality and war.[24]

Galamison emphasized Christian social obligation, telling his congregation that the dire situation created by class exploitation, racism, and war had created a special need for Christians. Followers of Christ must fight all forms of inequality. If one professes to be a Christian, one cannot sit idly by and allow innocent human beings to suffer from poverty, racism, and war. True Christians should be vehicles for change and social redemption.[25]

Although he called Christians to battle, Galamison noted that they could not do it alone. He argued that Christians should ally themselves with anyone, including secular groups working for economic and social justice. Associating with communists and other radical groups was morally legitimate because they had the common goal of eradicating the social evils of poverty and inequality. Secular groups that also adopted the obligation of eradicating injustice were simply embracing Christian principles; consequently, Christians should join forces with them.[26]

In one early sermon titled "If Wishes were Horses," he examined the eighteenth chapter of Luke, the story of the rich man who wanted to follow Jesus but was unwilling to give up his riches. Galamison compared the Allies during the Conference at Versailles following the defeat of Germany in World War I to the rich young man in Luke. They wanted world peace but were unable to give up their colonies, tariff barriers, and economic inequality. The young pastor said it was easy to talk about the ideal condition for peace but difficult to pay the price for it. Although the Christian church speaks of brotherhood, it must heal itself and separate itself from the decaying social order before receiving true brotherhood.[27]

Criticizing the church for its lack of commitment to racial justice, Galamison told his congregation that the Protestant church in America had contributed to the segregation of blacks. Most Protestants worship in segregated congregations. True Christians should reject segregation, resist fleeing to the suburbs, and open their doors to people who are different from themselves. He called on his congregation to take action against the social sins of poverty and racism.[28] In one sermon he argued: "We grumble about high prices; but make no effort to combat the forces of greed. We grumble about race discrimination; but when the anti-intolerance organizations meet, we are conspicuously absent; and we complain about housing conditions, but we have no time for meetings where citizens are waging war on thieves and thugs who make home life impossible for millions."[29]

Galamison did not hide his admiration for the activist political left from his black middle-class congregation. In fact, he contended that true Christian doctrine required Christians to address the evils facing people. On one occasion, after speaking to ministers who defended the Ku Klux Klan, he noted that six young people who were members of Henry Wallace's Progressive Party had been arrested for handing out literature. Galamison admired their conviction and their willingness to risk the scorn of their community and society to make a better world.

For Galamison, the activists had behaved in a manner that was more Christian than that of many professed Christians. If social redemption was a major goal of the gospel, then the church was "bankrupt" in social programs. He contended that Christianity should not stress otherworldliness and ignore social justice and political freedom, because Jesus and other heroes of the Bible addressed social issues.[30]

According to Galamison, Christians who did not become socially and politically active because they feared a backlash should look to the heroes of the Bible, whose suffering was far greater than people in the modern world would endure. Despite their tremendous ordeal, they did not give up the good fight. The Apostle Paul said, in spite of his suffering for Christ, "Thank God He makes my life a constant pageant of triumph." In contrast, Galamison said: "We complain, we immerse ourselves in comfort. We ignore life challenges. We do not join the forces that attempt to eradicate anti-intolerance nor do we give up comfort to deal with so-called Christians who do not want to sacrifice their comfort." The young pastor asked how many of today's churchgoers would be Christians if they had to make the sacrifices that the early Christians made.[31]

Ideologically, Galamison felt connected to progressives and radicals; they worked for the same goals and criticized the same targets: the state and

church. He spoke of the Christian conference he had attended during which
the six Progressive Party activists had been arrested for handing out literature. On occasions he even praised Marxism. According to the Presbyterian
minister, socialism has been an important "historic force." It has been a "def-
inite attempt to define the nature of man. The ideas of human dignity and
justice are the basis of Marx's writings and these ideas created modern
socialism and Russian Communism." Galamison argued that the power that
defined the Russian Revolution was a "concept of man: Faith in oneself,
faith in the common man, in his ideas, his power, in his rights. It is this idea
of man which has dominated Russia and made her one of the great nations
of the world today."[32]

Galamison defended communists from red-baiting, noting enemies of
change often scapegoated communism. "Communism, as the story goes,
is responsible for all the world's woes." Galamison claimed that using
communists as scapegoats was a diversion that takes people's minds off
the real issues:

> This thing came to me in a very real sense during the recent campaign
> to establish a hospital in the Bedford-Stuyvesant area. A number of
> people advised me: "You can't work with that Bedford Health Con-
> gress group, there are some communists in it." But, in any case, would
> the fact that communists were working for the building of a hospital
> in this area lessen the need for one?[33]

Praising communism and the Soviet Union, Galamison argued that God had
a hand in creating the ideology. In a sermon titled "Unexpected Help from
Unknown Sources," he contended that communism "started a fire in Christian camps," challenging Christians to "make the gospel real." He claimed
that the doctrine had won a following because it attacked poverty.[34]

Galamison's sermons acknowledged his internationalism. Besides defending communism and advocating building alliances across racial lines,
the young Presbyterian minister often attacked the theory of nationalism as
"stupid." It created artificial barriers that kept people of different racial and
cultural groups from seeing their common interest. Moreover, it led to irra-
tional feelings of patriotism. "Nationalism is an immaturity. There is absolutely no difference between the man who insists that his country is the best

and the college sophomore who argues that his fraternity is the best. Both haven't quite grown up yet." The real danger in nationalism is that it promotes a feeling of superiority, destroys true brotherhood and creates racial animosity. Nationalism led to the colonization of Africa, India, China, and other third world countries.[35]

Galamison, whose Christian outlook would be classified today as Liberation Theology, was raising the consciousness of his parishioners by giving them a race and class analysis of social problems and turning to the Bible for solutions. Envisioning a world where the collective evils of racism, class exploitation, and militarism could be eradicated, he dedicated his ministry to achieving such a goal. Although the young Presbyterian pastor talked about Marxism, he was no Marxist. For Galamison, class did not supersede race. Although he spoke about class exploitation, he did not advocate a working-class alliance across racial lines to fight for a socialist society. The greatest emphasis in his sermons was on the elimination of racial inequality. Although he had moved into the middle class and clearly was on the road to a successful career, he still faced racial harassment. The key for a true mellifluous community, where all people could enjoy the resources that assured a successful existence, was to obliterate racism.

## Origins of Galamison's Radicalism

What accounts for Galamison's leftist views and his interpretation of Christian doctrine? Sociologist Gary T. Marx found that black members of predominantly white denominations are more politically active: "It is perhaps ironic that those individuals in largely white denominations (Episcopalian, Presbyterian, and Catholic) appear somewhat higher in militancy that those in Negro denominations, in spite of the greater civil rights activism of the latter."[36] While this may, in part, explain Galamison's radical views, there were other factors. As a child he had a sense of fair play and had already displayed his willingness to fight against what he felt was unjust. Reverend Thomas Logan recalls that as a teenager, Galamison stood up to what he thought was wrong. Logan noted that Galamison complained bitterly to him and his wife and refused to attend his high school graduation because he was not allowed to wear his zoot-suit. Although he was conventional in many ways, a member of the Episcopal church, and an acolyte, growing up on the streets of Philadelphia he was exposed to a youthful hip culture. As his cousin and playmate, William Claxton, noted, "We were in the streets playing and hanging out."[37]

Historian Robin D. G. Kelly contends that this period of the zoot suit, hip language, "conk" hair, and hop was a "culture of opposition among black, mostly male youth." The zoot symbolized rebellion against societal norms advocated by Galamison's family, the educational system, Reverend Logan, and the church. Although Galamison was more than willing to follow the path to success, by playing and hanging out on the streets the young Philadelphian was exposed to and adopted this culture of rebellion. He forged an identity in which he coopted values from both a conventional culture and a hip culture. He was a rebel while aspiring to rise in a conventional culture. By graduating from high school in Philadelphia, he demonstrated his success in a society where few blacks graduated. At the same time, his insistence that he wear the zoot suit to his high school graduation illustrated defiance at a high level.[38]

Galamison was fully aware of the furor against the zoot; it symbolized criminality, subversive subculture, hostility to the norms of society. As Robin Kelly notes, the zoot became a symbol of a decadent leisure culture, something that church going folks shunned because it was taboo. But Galamison was willing to confront his society's expectation of appropriate wear. It was a challenge to his mother, to the school, and to the larger society's cultural norms and expectations. Galamison's desire to wear the suit also illustrated his desire to identify with working-class people. While he was moving up the social ladder, he did not forget his working-class roots.[39]

Galamison emerged from high school as a person climbing the ladder of success but at the same time identifying with working-class people. He developed a reputation as a person willing to challenge those in authority. Moreover, the numerous racial incidents, the racist tracking of the school system, poverty, the struggle for survival by his mother and his grandmother, abandonment by his father—all fueled his passion for social and economic justice. His sense of justice and willingness to challenge authority was in part rooted in his experience of racism and economic injustice.

Racial experiences during World War II would have a tremendous impact on Galamison. During World War II, when for the first time blacks were allowed to drive trolley cars for the city of Philadelphia, white transit workers, in defiance of the Transport Workers Union, struck in protest. The episode made him wonder who America saw as its enemy, the "Nazis or the Black people?"[40] Galamison also asserted that he worked as a reporter for the *Baltimore Afro-American* during the war and covered a story about a lynching in the South and a story about two black men who unjustly spent twenty years in prison after being caught with burglar tools. They did not commit any robbery. Their only crime was that they had the tools to commit a crime. For Galamison, these stories augmented the detrimental impact of racism on African Americans.[41]

Galamison's experience in higher education and his reading of history and current events also helped fuel his radicalism. He became attracted to individuals who challenged the status quo and society. While in college he studied philosophy and religion, including the writings of Karl Marx, the works of Bertrand Russell, and Martin Luther. He read a great deal of history and became an admirer of Abraham Lincoln, the abolitionist John Brown, William Lloyd Garrison, and Frederick Douglass. In his early sermons he talked about Galileo, Wendell Wilkie and "his dream of one world," and expressed his admiration for Gandhi because of his struggle against British imperialism, and for Henry Wallace because of his progressive views. He also praised the populist and progressive movements.[42] Clearly, Galamison was attracted to the left for its moral commitment and activity for social justice. As noted, his contact at Lincoln with students from developing nations also gave him a deeper understanding of the impact of colonialism.

Moreover, his experience at Princeton would further convince him of how detrimental racism was in education. Although he was a pastor and graduate student working for a master's degree at Princeton Theological Seminary, he experienced racial bigotry at the prestigious institution. He noted that he studied with a professor who contended that every race except blacks had contributed to civilization. He told the young seminarian that blacks would eventually make their contribution and in anticipation Princeton had opened its doors to African Americans. Galamison felt insulted that despite his own standing as a pastor and a graduate student at Princeton, this man would publicly make such a charge. Galamison most likely felt that this was a personal attack. Moreover, he classified his professor as a racist because he argued that blacks were immature and would eventually grow up as other races had and make their mark. Galamison thought that this professor was either ignoring or belittling the contributions that Africans had already made to world civilization and African Americans had made to America. This experience demonstrated for the young pastor that racism was pervasive, even reaching America's best institutions of higher learning, and in spite of his own social and economic standing in life, he could not escape racial bigotry.[43]

Although he was willing to ally himself with the left, he did not have roots in the labor movement. In fact, throughout his life he witnessed and sometimes challenged the racism of white workers. Scholar Daniel Perlstein points out that the "structure of the labor market mitigated against interracial labor organizing." Blacks were relegated to the lowest-paying jobs and when they attempted to oppose racial barriers in the labor market, they were challenged on occasion by members of the white working class, as in the case of the white transit workers' strike in Philadelphia during the war, and years later in the Downstate Medical Center dispute. Moreover, a racist labor market was not the only arena of discrimination in the North. Housing, health care, and education were other areas where the distribution of services was based on race. Racial discrimination, Galamison contended, did not only deny blacks resources, it took away the "dignity of a person which is the heritage of all God's children." Racism is the refusal to recognize "people as full fledged human beings."[44]

Galamison went so far as to argue that the economic status of black workers was quite different from their white counterparts. Racism increased the misery of black workers. During the 1950s, the Presbyterian pastor declared that what was considered a mild recession for white workers was a "major crisis of unemployment for the Negro wage earner. The income gap between the two has increased since 1952." Although he attributed post–World War II jobs lost to structural economic changes, he noted blacks were also denied access to jobs by racist craft unions. Citing Gunnar Myrdal's *American Dilemma*, Galamison pointed out that blacks were virtually excluded from the construction industry and the printing trades, while black youth was excluded from apprenticeship programs. For Galamison, neither the abolition of class oppression nor the increase of wages led to benefits for blacks.[45]

Galamison's avenue for eliminating racial inequality, especially in education, was integration through grassroots activism. The Presbyterian pastor once warned:

Those of us who think that democracy is inevitable and that integration is inevitable are making a serious mistake. Those of us who suppose that equality will just gradually come and that the world will inevitably become a better place for our children are in error. These things will not be achieved through our keeping quiet nor through our seeking to keep others quiet. We can't ride to democracy on a toboggan. Democracy and equality and freedom will demand all the intelligence and devotion we can muster. . . . And we may be passing laws 100 years from now to enforce the Supreme Court decision of 1954 if we don't busy ourselves on the behalf of our children."[46]

Despite his leftist views, there is no evidence linking Galamison to the Communist Party or other left-leaning organizations. During the 1950s, Galamison did work with the New York Committee for a SANE Nuclear Policy. He allowed the group to use Siloam for a meeting and publicly supported the group's position for peace and nuclear disarmament. However, the Siloam pastor may have also been motivated by the generous financial contributions the group made to the church. In a letter to a member of a peace group thanking her for "sums of money contributed" for the use of Siloam, Galamison pointed out that "Being a non-profit organization ourselves, we try to sympathize and work with other non-profit organizations, particularly when they represent such worthwhile causes. We do, however, have many expenses as you know, and are always grateful for the kind of thoughtfulness that you exhibited." Thus his involvement in the group was not simply ideological or based on simple altruism.[47]

In 1953, he was listed as a communist sympathizer in *Counter Attack*, a weekly publication "devoted to discussing subversive and communist groups." In response to the magazine's accusation, the Siloam pastor accused the publishers of having launched a smear campaign: "Anyone who indulges in such is not living up to the best in American ideology."[48]

To be sure, Galamison differed from most black pastors of Brooklyn. Several had strong connections with the major political parties, were influential in those parties, and received political patronage; most did not associate with left and grassroots organizations. For example, the Reverend Sandy F. Ray of Cornerstone Baptist Church was known as a "stalwart" of the Republican Party, with close ties to Republican top brass including Governors Thomas Dewey and Nelson Rockefeller of New York. At one time,

party officials considered running him for a congressional seat. Reverend
Gardner C. Taylor, one of the few Democrats among the prominent black
clergy of Brooklyn, was named by Mayor Robert Wagner to the Board of
Education; he was one of three men named to replace Joseph T. Sharkey as
Democratic leader of Brooklyn.[49]

The prominent black ministers kept their distance from the left. Most
Brooklyn black clergy stayed clear of the Bedford Health Congress, a grass-
roots organization that diligently campaigned for a hospital in Bedford-
Stuyvesant, because it was labeled a communist front.[50] Ray joined the Cold
War crusade, claiming that blacks were loyal to the United States and would
not submit to "subversive ideology."[51]

Galamison's sermons were not just empty words. Soon after he arrived at
Siloam, Galamison revealed that he was not only going to talk about social
justice, he was also going to actively work for it. In January of 1950, after less
than two years as pastor of Siloam, Galamison made a bold move. He jeopardized his career, standing up to his church and Presbyterian hierarchical
structure, by refusing to pay a tax to the Brooklyn-Nassau Presbytery because the money was being used to build a Presbyterian church in Levittown, on Long Island. Levittown homes, developed by Arthur Levitt during
World War II, allowed many for the first time to purchase homes at a low
cost. However, Levittown's homes excluded blacks. Galamison asserted that
there was no other recourse for Siloam. Noting that blacks could not buy the
new homes, Galamison told the *Amsterdam News*: "We want to see the extension of the Presbyterian Church . . . but we cannot support movements
into areas where we are not certain Negroes would be welcome."[52]

The young Presbyterian pastor's decision was presented at a monthly
meeting of the Brooklyn-Nassau Presbytery. The Presbytery argued that
Levittown's refusal to sell a home to a member of Siloam was no grounds
for that body to condemn the developer. In the end, however, the body
voted to study the situation.[53]

Through these acts, Galamison jeopardized his career with the Presbyterian order, alienated some more moderate members of his church, and
painted himself a radical during the McCarthy period. Despite the risks, he
won admiration and respect for his bold move. The *Amsterdam News* laud-
ed Galamison, claiming that this was one of the first times a black church
had "spoken against segregation within the body of its organizations."[54] The
paper carried a photograph of Galamison with the caption "A Voice Against

Bigotry." Galamison also fought racism within his own religious organization. He informed his church that he, along with other members of the Afro-Presbyterian Council, a group of African-American Presbyterians, threatened to set up a picket line if they were not allowed to present their case on racial discrimination to the General Assembly.[55]

By the early 1950s, Milton Galamison was recognized as one of the most vocal activist pastors in New York City, willing both to speak out and to actively challenge racism and class oppression, despite the paranoia of the Cold War. Although the left was being decimated and prominent progressive leaders became pariahs, Galamison was more than willing to identify with and defend them. He shrewdly combined leftist ideology with Christian doctrine, winning the support of his congregation. To be sure, the support he received from his church gave him the independence to speak out and take action. While other militant voices for social and racial justice were being silenced in the 1950s, Galamison's was just beginning to flourish.

It should be noted that Galamison's travels abroad and in the United States verified for him the detrimental impact of racism on people of African origins. In 1956, he embarked on a four-month visit to Cameroon. He saw the effects of colonialism on Africans:

> In the Cameroon [sic] I saw clearly what the days of slavery must have been like in the United States. I saw extremely limited white people dominating black lives and citizens from different western nations apologizing for their perfidy on a comparative basis. The French excused their corruption on the premise that the Americans were the worst colonizers in civilized history. They pointed to the plight of the American Indian and who could disagree? The Americans excused their behavior on the premise that the French couldn't even hold their own nation together. . . . I saw red-baiting, as if Communists could possibly worsen the plight of the populace.

Displaying a keen awareness of the colonial situation in Africa, he argued that the use of "Communist hysteria" was an attempt by the French to crush the black nationalist movement in the colony.[56]

However, Galamison claims that his most traumatic experience was not overseas but in the United States. In the summer of 1957, Galamison, accompanied by Gladys and their seven year old son, traveled by car to Han-

over, Indiana; Waupaca, Wisconsin; and Kansas City, Missouri to address
various Presbyterian youth conferences about his trip to the Cameroon.
He noted that he drove through West Virginia fearing for his life, because
he thought he might be stopped by police who might have mistaken
Gladys for a white woman because of her fair skin. However, it was near
Columbus, Ohio that he experienced virulent racism. No motel owner
would provide a room for the pastor and his family. They had to travel
into the city to find accommodations. Moreover, once they arrived at
Hanover College in Indiana, a student invited them to his house. But
when the student's parents learned that the Galamisons were black, the
offer was withdrawn. The Galamisons left Hanover for Wisconsin. They
stopped in Chicago only to be denied motel accommodations. "No motel
owner would take us in. No one would provide respite for a tired woman
and a seven-year-old child."[57]

Throughout their travel that summer, the Galamisons were the victims
of racial bigotry.

Through southern Wisconsin the prejudice was equally as adamant.
My wife consoled that we might fare better when we got a little far-
ther north. But then we would be in Canada. A kind restaurant
owner in Southern Wisconsin found us a boarding house where we
spent the night. But returning from Waupaca we ran into the same
problem again. We drove nearly seven-hundred miles from Waupaca
to Cleveland, Ohio and spent the night with some friends because no
one would afford us a place to sleep. I wired the conference in Kansas
of my predicament and suggested that, if they had any spare time,
they ought to spend it praying for this heathen country. My boy said
to me, "Daddy, I know why we can't get a place to stay—because
you're colored."[58]

The experience embittered the Presbyterian pastor. He declared, "No man
wants to be degraded in the eyes of his children, to have his family denied
normal human comforts." Galamison contended that the experience convinced him to challenge racism at all costs. "And I decided in the course of
that trip that if I had to burn this stinking, bigoted country to the ground,
my son and his family would never have to suffer the indignities heaped on
the Black people of my generation."[59]

Galamison became a voice for an activist Christian ideology, arguing that it was the job of Christians to eradicate racism, poverty, and militarism, which were the collective sins of humanity. An integrated society was the means of assuring equality of resources and dignity to all people. Moreover, at a time when communists and other members of the militant left were portrayed as evil, he attempted to broaden the meaning of Christianity not only by stressing a social gospel but also by arguing that leftist forces were moral because they had adopted the similar goals of the Christian social activists. In his sermons he urged community organizing and collective action to forge a just society. Galamison's Christian doctrine of social commitment would be an important aspect of the New York City civil rights movement.

# chapter three

# THE NAACP YEARS

In the 1950s Milton Galamison took center stage in the struggle for school integration in New York City, organizing and leading a grassroots organization that challenged the Board of Education. Under the leadership of Galamison, the Brooklyn branch of the NAACP emerged, between the years 1956 and 1959, as a militant civil rights association organizing working-class parents who grappled with school officials to provide decent education for black and Puerto Rican children. With the Brooklyn NAACP, parents gained another vehicle for expressing in a militant tone to board officials their disfavor over educational policy. The NAACP Parents' Workshop helped convert ordinary black, Latino, and white parents from marginal players in the education of their children to a significant force. While Galamison was helping transform the Brooklyn NAACP into a militant civil rights organization, he and his allies were meeting stiff opposition from more conservative forces among national NAACP leaders and members of the Brooklyn branch who feared communist domination. Hence, the 1950s was a period of intense ideological struggle within the Brooklyn NAACP.

## Leading the Struggle for School Integration

The Brooklyn branch of the NAACP was the borough's most prominent civil rights organization. Its leadership included Brooklyn's black elite. In 1942, the branch's list of ministers consisted of James Adams of Concord, W. O. Carrington of Fleet Street A.M.E., John Coleman of Saint Philip's Episcopal, S. T. Eldridge of Berean Baptist, Albert Scott of Nazarene Congregational, Kimball Warren of Bethany Baptist, and George Thomas of Brown Memorial Baptist Church. By the 1950s its membership included clergy from outstanding black churches including the Reverends Gardner C. Taylor of Concord Baptist Church, C. L. Franklin of Mount Lebanon Baptist Church, and Sandy F. Ray of Cornerstone Baptist Church. In 1952, Concord reported that it had 10,000 members, the largest in Brooklyn. Reverend Franklin reported a congregation of 6,000, and Reverend Ray, 5,000 members. The Reverends Hilton L. James of Berean Missionary Baptist Church and John Coleman of Saint Phillip's Protestant Episcopal Church, also members of the Brooklyn NAACP, reported memberships of more than 1,200. Besides prominent clergy, several attorneys and politicians were active in the Brooklyn organization, including Municipal Court Judge Lewis S. Flagg and Justice Myles Page.[1]

The Brooklyn branch of the NAACP lobbied in Albany and Washington for anti-discrimination legislation. It also participated in voter registration drives. The civil rights organization's major focus was on police brutality. It publicly denounced alleged cases of police physical abuse of African-American citizens, printed and distributed leaflets on police brutality, and sponsored some rallies. In 1949, the Brooklyn NAACP organized a conference on police brutality. That same year, the association also urged Governor Thomas Dewey to appoint a special prosecutor to investigate cases of alleged police ruthlessness in New York. The Brooklyn NAACP also provided lawyers for victims of police brutality cases. Details of alleged police brutality cases appeared in the branch's monthly newspaper, the *Brooklyn NAACP Spotlight*.[2]

However, despite its work in the area of police physical abuse against citizens, voter registration, and the struggle for anti-discrimination legislation,

the Brooklyn NAACP had done little political grassroots work. The civil
rights group made no connection between organization building and militant protest. The leadership of the civil rights group had little interest in the
issues that confronted working people. Kenneth Neilson, described by Roy
Wilkins as an active member of the Brooklyn chapter, complained that the
local branch, as well as other locals, did "not function very well on local
issues which touch the welfare of the masses of people. . . ." He noted that a
mass meeting to push for black operators and conductors on city buses and
subways had been held but the Brooklyn NAACP's participation in the
event had not been mentioned in a report on the gathering. Instead, the National Negro Congress and the Harlem Coordinating Committee for Employment had taken the lead on this issue. "He said that most people knew
about the Association, but did not know that it was doing anything that
intimately concerned their welfare."[3]

The Brooklyn NAACP was very vocal in police brutality cases, but it had
a poor record in winning justice for victims. Despite the attention that the
Brooklyn NAACP gave to police brutality, it seldom won a case. Between
May and July of 1945, nine cases of police attacks on black residents of the
borough had been reported to the organization. None had, for various reasons, "reached a stage where some satisfactory conclusion would result."
Part of its failure had to do with the lack of leadership given to these cases.
Although the Brooklyn NAACP was representing Ruth Hemming in a
police brutality case in 1945, its president, Fred Turner, called an executive
board meeting in order to hear the side of a police officer accused of striking the victim. Although the board did not allow the police officer to speak
at the meeting, after it had been adjourned the officer and members of his
family pleaded with board members to drop the case. Turner later lobbied
members of the board in order to persuade them to settle on a compromise.
After it was learned that Turner had reached a settlement with the officer
without informing board members, some NAACP members called on the
national office to dismiss the Brooklyn branch President.[4] Turner was also
accused of using his influence to assure the election to the executive board
of members who were completely loyal to him. According to some disgruntled members, such a practice made the executive board "nonfunctioning."

By the late 1940s, under the leadership of James Powers, the Brooklyn
civil rights organization became more vocal in police brutality cases. Its
monthly newsletter, *Spotlight*, focused on several alleged police attacks on

black Brooklyn residents. The Brooklyn NAACP seldom organized people for demonstrations, however. It was not immune to the Cold War leanings of the national organization, and it forcefully opposed the militant left. Although Henry Wallace's civil rights program was more far reaching than Truman's, Walter White, National Executive Secretary of the NAACP, campaigned for the President instead of Wallace, who ran on the Progressive Party ticket in 1948. Not only did the NAACP support Truman's civil rights platform, it also joined in the crusade to stamp out radicals. The national office ousted W. E. B. Du Bois from his executive position as director of special research because he supported Henry Wallace and he publicly criticized Walter White for accepting a consulship to the United Nations delegation from the Truman administration. According to Du Bois, when Walter White accepted this consulship the board of the NAACP aligned itself with the reactionary war mongering colonial imperialism of the present administration."[5] Du Bois was arrested, handcuffed, and indicted for serving as an "agent of a foreign principal" because of his anti-war work with the Peace Information Center, and the NAACP did not come to his defense.

In 1950, the national NAACP attempted to purge its ranks of communists and assure that the left played no role in civil rights. The National Emergency Civil Rights Mobilization meeting held in Washington became a battle ground. More than 1,500 NAACP members, mostly from the New York (Manhattan), Brooklyn, and Jamaica (Queens) chapters, were barred from the three-day conference, accused of being "reds" and communist sympathizers.[6]

By joining the government's effort to crush leftist groups and individuals, the NAACP helped isolate themselves from the civil rights movement. It helped separate black radicals from civil rights. Leftist leaders such as W. E. B. Du Bois and Paul Robeson, who connected racial with class oppression, came under attack. More importantly, by joining the Cold War effort, the NAACP narrowed the civil rights movement's focus on race and marginalized class as an integral part of race relations in the United States. Absent from the NAACP's discourse on civil rights were the economic factors that caused and maintained segregation and racial discrimination. There was no serious attempt to broaden the civil rights agenda to include methods of uniting people to battle against poverty, unemployment, and other issues affecting the poor.

When it came to the anti-communist crusade, the Brooklyn branch was

not to be outdone by its national organization. Attorney Jesse P. Griggs, an
"ex officio" of the legal staff of the local branch, charged that communism
had invaded the chapter, paralyzing it. No one was willing to tag anyone a
communist, the attorney claimed, because of the fear of slander. But many
in leadership, Griggs asserted, "know that the deadly germ has entered the
organization." The communists, according to the attorney, had gained control of various committees, spreading propaganda and grooming leaders to
take over the Brooklyn branch. Although Griggs, who offered no evidence,
would later recant his charge, this event revealed how Cold War hysteria
made life difficult for the left.[7]

The Brooklyn branch was so bent on not working with the left that it
proudly announced, in a police murder case in Brownsville, Brooklyn, in
1951, that it had wrestled the case away from the communists "in an effort
to proceed with whatever legal acts necessary without engaging in hysteria
and meaningless agitation."[8] Moreover, one of the slogans the organization
adopted for fund raising was "Segregated We Fight Communism with a Dull
Sword." The Brooklyn branch was a militantly anti-communist organization, suspicious of its leftist members. In 1947, the National organization attempted to assure a disgruntled member of the Brooklyn branch who had
accused the local branch of working with communists by contending, "We
have striven and are striving to make clear to all branches and officers that
members of the Communist party will not be permitted to use our organization as a sounding-board for their political beliefs, nor will the Socialists,
Democrats, or the Republicans."[9]

This was extremely frustrating for the leftists, who wanted the NAACP to
become more active in the fight for school integration. They realized that
the school system was divided by race and class. As more working poor
blacks and Hispanics entered New York they were restricted to predominantly poor minority communities, including Central Harlem, East Harlem, the Lower East Side of Manhattan, Bedford-Stuyvesant, Brownsville,
and Jamaica, Queens. These geographical restrictions were a result of the racial practices in the real estate industry and resistance to integration by the
white communities of New York. Because of the Board of Education's racial
practices, de facto segregation became a common feature of New York City's
schools. While the children of working- and middle-class whites were able
to send their children to underutilized schools where more experienced
teachers were assigned and the best educational services were offered, black

and Hispanic children were confined to the worst schools, receiving an inferior education. As early as 1940, when Bedford-Stuyvesant's black population was increasing, community and civic leaders complained about overcrowding and segregation in many public schools that serviced the community. The Schools Council of Bedford-Stuyvesant and Williamsburg, a
community group consisting of parents and teachers, claimed that their
children were receiving an inadequate education. Twenty of the fifty-six
classes at P.S. 3 on Hancock Street and Bedford Avenue received the normal
six hours of daily instruction, while all other classes received only four
hours because of a teacher shortage. Considered the worst in the city, the
school was called a fire trap, with only one hallway for 1,700 children.
Classes were overcrowded, with forty children assigned to a room; shop
classes were located near the school's boiler, creating a hazard to children.[10]
Public School 3 was not unique; other schools in Bedford-Stuyvesant limited daily instruction for children to four hours and classes were overcrowded. In addition, children were denied hot lunches because of improper
kitchen facilities.[11]

To make matters worse, few blacks were hired as teachers. In 1949,
blacks accounted for only 2.5 percent of the teaching staff of the City of
New York, and only 1.5 percent were regularly appointed. By 1955, the situation had not improved. Well over 50,000 people were employed as
teachers in the system, but only 544 were black, 232 with regular appoint-
ments and 312 as substitutes.[12]

Kenneth Clark asserted that the school system was segregated and that
black children received an inferior education. At an Urban League symposium, the professor of psychology charged that segregated schools left black
children with a sense of inferiority and hindered their educational progress.
Segregation, the psychologist contended, leads to personal humiliation, a
"defeatist attitude and a lowering of personal ambitions."[13]

Clark argued that there was strong suggestive evidence that educational
standards of black children were declining. Blacks recently from the South
and the West Indies "tend to be superior in academic achievement to the
native born New York Negro Child in the 4th through the 6th grades in New
York City schools." A study of the factors influencing the educational
achievement of black children in Harlem schools revealed that the average
reading and math levels were two years behind grade level for those schools
studied. In some classes there was no improvement in scores from the begin-

ning to the end of the school year. The psychologist also pointed out that most teachers in the schools were inexperienced and poorly supervised.[14]

According to Clark, the "best available estimates" showed that in thirty-five schools in districts 10 through 14, there were 103 classes with retarded mental ability (CRMD); students who scored a 75 on an I.Q. test could be placed in these classes. The social psychologist contended that many students were assigned to these classes based on group test results. On the other hand, only three schools in Harlem had programs for intellectually gifted children (IGC), with no more than six classes. Clark noted a "small preliminary study of a number of schools in New York City" revealed that teachers in schools located in black and Puerto Rican neighborhoods had lower expectations for their students and believed that the curriculum had to be adjusted to accommodate their lower ability. The high school drop-out rate was higher for black and Puerto Rican children than for white. Black and Puerto Rican children were given fewer opportunities to participate in school and work in the cooperative system, because employers were less willing to accept them into the community-based program operating in conjunction with local schools. They were perceived as "less presentable" children, with a "lower cultural level," who had "difficulty in the use of language."[15]

Overt racism was no longer the principal factor in the failure of black urban schools. Rather, complex social and psychological problems bolstered assumptions about the limited ability of students of color. Depressed educational expectations about performance made students feel inferior so that they could not perform academically to their full potential. "It is no longer necessary to have specific techniques for gerrymandering schools and excluding Negro children from academic and other specialized high schools. These children are not prepared to pass the tests for these academic and specialized high schools. This is a most effective form of racial exclusion." For Clark, segregated schools were the crucial problem: "One cannot expect a group to attain the full status of equality of citizenship if the masses of the children of that group are being denied adequate education in their elementary and secondary schools." The public school system was guilty of depriving black and Puerto Rican children of the "ability to compete successfully with others."[16]

The psychologist reminded the public school system of its responsibility. By segregating levels of education for various races and social economic groups, it "becomes a force in solidifying undemocratic class cleavages, obstructs mobility and blocks the use of human intellectual resources." He did not accuse the board of conspiracy; there were societal causes. But those responsible for the education of the community had to solve the problems that were interfering with their effectiveness.[17]

Clark's charges embarrassed the Board of Education. While attention was focused on the South, Clark pointed his finger at the largest school system in the country and accused it of being segregated. Clark's remarks moved the Board of Education President, Arthur Levitt, to request that the Public Education Association (PEA), an organization created in the late nineteenth century to improve the public schools, conduct an investigation of blacks and Puerto Ricans in the school system. The Board of Education also declared that the Brown case was a "legal and moral reaffirmation" of its own principles. It agreed with the Supreme Court that racially segregated schools resulted in psychological harm to children. The creation of racially homogeneous schools, according to the board, "is socially unrealistic and blocks the attainment of the goals of democratic education, whether this segregation occurs by law or by fact." In spite of the challenges to integration, the school agency declared, it was determined to "accept the challenge" of the Brown decision. On December 23, 1954, the board unanimously passed a resolution establishing a Commission on Integration to suggest ways to bring about integration in the schools. The Commission was in turn divided into five subcommissions. The nine board members included educators and civic leaders.[18]

By February 1955, Mayor Robert Wagner had appointed a committee to survey the utilization of school buildings to relieve overcrowding. He noted that 225 of the 566 elementary schools were overcrowded, while the remaining 331 schools had 80,000 seats available. By the end of the year the Mayor had promised to pursue integration regardless of the obstacles. "Greater Integration of our school children," he declared, "leading to a more wholesome integration of our citizenry, is worth the cost of providing safe guard crossings, overcoming traffic difficulties and a proper adjustment of school time."[19]

In the fall of 1955, the PEA released its report detailing widespread segregation in the school system. There were forty-two de facto segregated elementary schools (a student body that was 90 percent or more black and Puerto Rican) and nine junior highs (85 percent or more) in the city. The PEA asserted that the board was not responsible for the segregation, but the agency did little to create racial balance.[20]

Although the left-led Teachers Union (TU) fought for integrated schools back in the 1930s, after the Brown decision more activists and civil rights organizations began focusing on New York's segregated school system. One such activist was Annie Stein, who attempted to force the Brooklyn NAACP to join the struggle for school desegregation in New York. Born in 1913 as Annie Steckler, she was the youngest of three girls born to Russian émigrés who fled after the unsuccessful 1905 Revolution. She grew up in a working-class home with few luxuries. Her father became a peddler barely squeaking out a living. When Annie Steckler was only a teen her father suddenly died of a heart attack, which of course made the bad family situation even worse. Eventually, Annie and her older sister decided to move out of their Brooklyn home and rent an apartment in Manhattan. Although Annie worked part time while going to school her oldest sister also helped to support her through high school and college.[21]

Around 1927 Steckler met Evelyn Weiner, a politically active young woman whose parents had been members of the Jewish Bund, a socialist organization. Following in her parents' footsteps, Weiner had joined the Communist Party at a young age. Weiner attempted to convince her friend of the social and economic injustices of capitalism and the logic of a socialist society. Although no date for the decision can be fixed, after many debates and arguments Steckler was eventually convinced and decided to join the American Communist Party. Both women became active in the Party's Youth League. Steckler went on to Hunter College and majored in math. While in college she met Arthur Stein, a Columbia University math major also active in the Party. They soon began dating, and in 1933 married.[22]

Like many leftists, Annie and Arthur were excited by the New Deal because it represented a new direction for the country. The issues championed by the Communist Party, the eradication of poverty and unemployment, adequate housing, and the right of labor to organize were being addressed by Roosevelt and his New Deal. For many leftists, the hopeful atmosphere in the nation's capital offered an opportunity to further their cause. The twenty-year-old Annie Stein and her husband decided to move to Washington in 1933 to work for the New Deal and push for a more progressive agenda; they wanted to help organize workers to mount a challenge to capitalist exploitation.[23]

Arthur worked for one of the New Deal agencies. Both Arthur and Annie became union organizers. Arthur became the co-founder of the United Federal Workers, the first federal employees' union. He later left his government job and became a full-time union employee. In 1938, Arthur Stein attended the first Constitutional Convention of the Congress of Industrial Organizations (CIO), representing the United Federal Workers.[24]

Annie Stein became an organizer for both the hotel and restaurant workers and the Women's Trade Union League. In the late 1930s she became chairperson of the League. She helped organize the lowest paid women workers in Washington, D.C., including laundry, domestic, restaurant, and hotel workers.[25]

During the Second World War, Annie Stein represented the Industrial Union Council (CIO) on the Office of Price Administration (OPA) price panel, working to see that grocery and restaurant owners observed ceiling prices. After the war Stein became chairperson of the Washington Committee for Consumer Protection and helped organize a city-wide strike against the stores that increased their prices on meat and milk. "Don't Buy Meat Over Six Cents a Pound" was the slogan of the strike. The boycott helped keep prices stable for several weeks by rallying 40,000 housewives to sign a petition. In 1949, Stein joined with Mary Church Terrell, organizer of the Black Women's Club movement, to wage a battle against segregated restaurants and other eating facilities in the Nation's capital. She helped organize hundreds of ordinary citizens, civic groups, labor organizations, and black ministers to successfully defeat Jim Crow practices in Washington, D.C.'s eating establishments.[26]

Stein's desire to stamp out racial discrimination stemmed from her radical politics and world view. Like many rank-and-file members of the Communist Party during the 1930s, the Steins were convinced that the Depression signaled that a revolution in the United States was not only possible, but might actually be imminent. Taking as a model the Soviet Union, they contended that it was possible to establish a "workers' State" and eliminate poverty and oppression. To accomplish this goal, the working class would have to unite. Racism, they argued, fragmented the working class. Racism was a form of exploitation used to divide workers. To help unify the working class, communists were waging an unrelenting campaign to eliminate all forms of oppression that divided workers.[27]

As time passed, Annie Stein's organizational skills matured. She learned how to lead nonviolent protests and build alliances. She would use these skills in the struggle to reform the New York school system. By the early 1950s the Steins had relocated to the Flatbush section of Brooklyn. Finding

herself longing for political activity, Stein wrote to Mary Church Terrell asking for suggestions. Terrell, with decades of experience, told Stein that she
should join the parent-teacher association. Stein was utterly shocked by the
suggestion. She saw the PTA as an organization made up of conservative
middle-class white women who baked cookies. Nevertheless, trusting
Terrell's judgment, Stein decided to join. Stein became president of the PTA
of Junior High School 246 on Veronica Place and Snyder Avenue, Brooklyn.
She soon joined the Brooklyn branch of the NAACP and turned her attention to education, a direction that would lead her into the struggle for school
integration in New York City.[28]

As the school integration movement gained momentum, Stein and other
members of the NAACP became involved in the fight around Junior High
School 258, located on Marcy and Halsey Streets. Although board officials
promised that the school would be integrated when it opened in 1955, on
opening day the school was over 95 percent black and Puerto Rican. According to board officials it was impossible to integrate the school because it
served a predominantly black community. Board officials had supported the
neighborhood school concept, the view that children should attend schools
in their own neighborhoods, and therefore rejected bussing children for the
purpose of integration. Leftist members including Annie Stein tried to get
the organization to take action in the 258 fight. For their efforts, they were
attacked within the organization. Stein was accused of exploiting the community in order to "cultivate relationships with Black men." A member of
the Brooklyn NAACP, Father Archibald McLees, had contacted Gloster B.
Current, Director of Branches, informing him that Stein had been a member of the National Students League, a left organization, and had been identified as a member of the Communist Party. "Father McLees said he had spoken about her to an ex-Communist who knew her during the 1930s and was
with her at Communist meetings in Washington during the 40s." Current
said he would have to check with the legal department of the organization
to see if it would be possible to leave her name off the ballot in the election
for executive board.[29] Clearly, the red-baiting did more than hinder the left
from taking command of the Brooklyn organization; it impeded the organization from moving to a more militant activist position.

Unable to mobilize the Brooklyn branch of the NAACP, Stein and Winston Craig, chair of the Education Committee, who was an ally of Stein, went
to Galamison, requesting his assistance. Galamison asserted that they came

to him because they knew he could provide an "umbrella" to leftist members of the civil rights group. Galamison's radical political views were probably well known. Despite Stein's political affiliation, Galamison was more than willing to work with her because her cause was a moral one. As he noted in his sermons, anyone, including communists, who fought against racism and other social injustices deserved the support of Christians.[30]

Galamison was no newcomer to the struggle for school integration. During the early years of his ministry at Siloam, he represented black employees of the Board of Education who accused that agency of racial discrimination. In 1954, he became involved in a heated exchange with school officials over the board's policy of promotion. That same year, Galamison sent William Jansen, Superintendent of Schools, a letter requesting that he look into two cases of possible promotion discrimination. The first involved Mrs. Catherine T. Alexander, who had worked for the board's Bureau of Attendance for a number of years. In 1953 Alexander had passed all parts of an examination except the written part for a promotion. She had taken another examination in 1954, and Galamison asked the superintendent to look into her case. The second case involved Mr. Francis A. Turner, an assistant director in the Bureau of Community Education. Turner complained that the board had failed to consider him for a position as an assistant superintendent although he met all qualifications. While not directly accusing the board of discrimination, Galamison concluded his letter: "I am most reluctant to accuse any agency of injustices, but in the light of irrefutable facts as presented in the cases of these two individuals, I am lost in my search for an alternative reason; and I respectfully request that these individual cases be examined in the light of merit and fairness."[31] John Conroy, assistant superintendent, responded to Galamison's letter. He argued that Alexander had taken and failed an objective examination used to measure all candidates for promotion and that Turner was not qualified for an assistant superintendent's position because he had trained himself for only a "specialized position" in the Bureau of Community Education.[32]

In a biting reply, Galamison pointed out that the oral examination or interview that Alexander had failed was not an objective test: "Intangible personality factors are present which rule out objective standards and it must be admitted that on any occasion when, let us say, two examiners orally examine an applicant that they will almost never record an equal scoring on any given question. You would know this much better than I." The

Siloam pastor noted that Alexander was a respected person in the community, and when a person of her ". . . calibre and ability is denied promotion
on the basis of an examination area which cannot, in all intellectual honesty,
be regarded as objective then the community and I have every right to
assume that an error has been made and the case is worthy of review."

In the case of Turner, Galamison correctly questioned the concept of a
"specialized position." Galamison argued that the "experience" argument
had been used to keep blacks out of high positions: "We have always been
told, 'because you have no experience you cannot have the position,' and
then because we never get the job we never get the necessary experience. It
adds up to a rather vicious and frustrating cycle." Galamison continued:

> And the very fact that, out of some 36 to 40 field superintendents,
> only one Negro holds this job, is a stench and a shame upon the City
> of New York which is commonly regarded as the most integrated city
> in the nation. The responsibility should not be placed on the citizen
> to prove discrimination; rather those in authority should be most
> zealous to protect the citizen, especially during these days of world
> crisis when we seek world leadership, and when we should be setting
> an example for our brethren in the South who face the problem of
> integrating their public schools.

He closed his letter by appealing to board officials to "stop defending the
existing situation," and take action to end discrimination. Although it is not
clear what happened to Alexander, Galamison's intervention on behalf of
Turner led to his promotion as an assistant superintendent.[33]

## Leadership and Organization

Galamison was ripe for action when Annie Stein and Winston Craig appeared in his office and asked him to join the struggle for school integration. His Christian radicalism and the view that any force struggling
against the evil of racism should be supported because it was morally correct linked him to the militant forces in the Brooklyn NAACP. The young
pastor's justification for working for integration was based on the welfare
of children. Throughout the years that he was involved in the struggle for

school integration, he continually used an appeal that crossed race lines; he contended in speeches that segregation hurt all children. "We contend that within the framework of segregated education both white and Negro children are crippled emotionally and mentally, irreparably and for life." Galamison argued that segregation psychologically damaged black and Hispanic children because it reinforced the notion that they were inferior. The Presbyterian pastor also contended that white children also suffered because it reinforced the notion that they were superior to people of color. Segregation was also anti-democratic because discrimination denies people their humanity and political freedom. Integration, on the other hand, would restore dignity to all children, provide them with an equal opportunity to succeed, and break down class barriers by giving them equitable access to educational resources. The struggle against segregated schools was one that could not be postponed because "every school day can make a difference in the lives and attitudes of tomorrow's generations."[34]

It was decided that the Siloam pastor would run for chair of the education committee of the branch. Along with Craig, he won the position in December 1955.[35] When Galamison took office, the Brooklyn NAACP's Education Committee had fifty-five members. However, it was not the committee that became the key instrument for the militant members of the civil rights organization. Taking Terrell's suggestion that she work with the PTA, and relying on her skills as a mass organizer, Stein, working with Craig, another ally by the name of Clair Cumberbatch, and Galamison, created a mass organization named the NAACP Schools Workshop (the forerunner of the Parents' Workshop). Before Stein approached Galamison, she had been encouraged by her mentor, Mary Church Terrell, to build a grassroots organization. In an April 2, 1954, letter to Stein, Terrell thanked her for working with the Brooklyn NAACP and hoped she would succeed in "getting colored teachers in the Brooklyn schools and in organizing colored women so that they can use their combined strength to promote the welfare of our group along any line that is useful and needed."[36]

Milton Galamison and Annie Stein did not build the school integration movement from scratch. They relied on previously established teacher-parent organizations to build the movement. A campaign to improve education for all children in New York City was already underway when the Siloam pastor and Stein arrived in Brooklyn. Parents in Bedford-Stuyvesant were working through the PTAs for change. Almost three decades after

Galamison had resigned as president of the Brooklyn branch of the NAACP
he was unable to specifically point to anything he had done to build a
parents' movement. He stated that there were just "good people around."
Galamison and Stein were able to build the Schools Workshop because of
the rich tradition of parent activism, especially in Bedford-Stuyvesant,
Brooklyn. For years, parents who were PTA members had campaigned diligently to improve the public schools of that community. One of the most
active PTAs was Public School 35. It consisted of community activists, concerned parents, and dedicated teachers. Organized in 1938, this association
was first led by community activist and *Amsterdam News* columnist Maude
Richardson. Under Richardson's leadership, P.S. 35's PTA fought for a kindergarten for the school, an evening school for the community of Bedford-
Stuyvesant, and a new building to replace the school's 64-year-old structure.
The parent-teacher group attempted to win support by networking with
church leaders, members, and civil organizations, going door-to-door can-
vassing for support, and by distributing flyers and other notices to children
for them to give to their parents. These tactics helped attract large crowds to
the numerous conferences the PTA sponsored at the First African Methodist
Episcopal Zion church in Bedford-Stuyvesant.[37]

In 1940, P.S. 35's PTA was led by Ada B. Jackson, who had strong ties to
the Bedford-Stuyvesant community. She was a member of one of the most
prestigious churches in the community, Bethany Baptist Church. Along
with her church affiliation, Jackson was a member of several civic groups
including the Crispus Attucks Community Council. Under Jackson's leadership, the PTA battled for greater educational resources and a new building. It also sponsored a series of conferences in order to foster good relations between teachers and the community. In the winter of 1942, she led a
delegation of parents to the Board of Education headquarters to protest the
poor conditions in P.S. 35 and demanded that the school agency build a new
building to replace the antiquated one.[38]

Other PTAs demanded that the board improve conditions in the public
schools. The parent-teacher associations of P.S. 3 and P.S. 93 insisted that
the board relieve overcrowding, assign experienced teachers to the schools,
and improve the physical plant. The PTA of P.S. 93 attempted to persuade
the Board of Education to integrate and relieve overcrowding of the elementary school, located on Amsterdam Avenue in Manhattan, by sending a
letter to the school agency's zoning committee.

As a result of a conference held at the First AME Zion Church in the Fall of 1943, sponsored by various PTAs of Bedford-Stuyvesant schools, the Bedford-Stuyvesant-Williamsburg Schools Council was established. Its executive board consisted of parents from almost twenty parent-teacher associations. The officers of the group were made up of parents and teachers. The Council had an interracial leadership. Its president, Ada Jackson, was an African American as were the first and third vice presidents. Morris Salz, the second vice president, and Mildred Flacks, the membership secretary, were white. Both Salz and Flacks were members of the Teachers Union of the CIO. With the exception of Salz, all the officers of the Council were women. The executive board was also dominated by women: of the 26 members listed in 1946, 22 were women. For the most part, it was women who stepped to the fore and struggled to improve the education of their children in the Bedford-Stuyvesant and Williamsburg communities.[39]

The major objectives of the Schools Council of Bedford-Stuyvesant and Williamsburg were regular licensed teachers for every classroom instead of day-to-day substitutes, all-day neighborhood schools, an end to "discriminatory zoning," construction of new school buildings to replace the old dilapidated ones, adequate supplies, textbooks, hot lunches, health and welfare facilities, and increased guidance activity. In order to win its objectives the Schools Council relied on various strategies including negotiation, publicizing conditions, demonstrations, and conferences. On several occasions, the Schools Council met with board officials. Through its various publications and press releases, the Council also revealed inadequate educational conditions in the various schools, including overcrowding, a shortened school day for children due to that overcrowding, and poor physical conditions in the schools. The group also held numerous demonstrations outside of the Board of Education's headquarters attempting to pressure the school agency to improve conditions. In addition the Council joined with other civic groups demanding the removal of teachers accused of racial and ethnic bigotry. Its annual spring conference attracted hundreds of parents, teachers, and administrators and served as a forum to express grievances about the schools in the community and adopt resolutions. Moreover, along with the militant teachers Union, the group demanded that the board desegregate the school system by building schools in fringe areas where black and white neighborhoods were in close proximity. This latter request would later be echoed by Galamison and the school integration movement.[40]

was part of a continuous struggle waged by parents and community activists long before Galamison arrived at Siloam. However, Galamison and Stein gave the movement a new thrust by presenting and articulating the objectives of the movement, the benefits of an integrated harmonious community and the detriments of a segregated school system, by organizing activists and concerned parents, and presenting aggressive strategies to accomplish the goal of integration.

Stein believed that "[d]esegregation became the number one civil rights issue of the day," and published the fact that the Board of Education had not kept its promise to open Junior High School 258 as an integrated school. Relying on the tactic of disseminating information to the public in order to help organize people (the same tactic used in the Washington campaign), Stein took the case for social justice to the people of New York. She believed that the more information people received, the more likely they would be to mobilize for action. The workshop contacted parents through the PTA, organizing them into a force that worked to integrate the New York City school system. Because the Workshop relied on PTAs for its membership, the vast majority of its members were mothers. It held meetings every six weeks, and claimed a membership of 400 parents, mostly women, including presidents and officers of sixty-four PTAs in Bedford-Stuyvesant and nearby neighborhoods.[41]

The NAACP Schools Workshop empowered parents by providing them the opportunity to negotiate with officials and even challenge the board's policies. Parents who became members of the Workshop wrote letters to the superintendent, expressing their discontent with board policy. They also selected representatives to meet with board officials to express their complaints. In one such case, Naomi Clark of the NAACP Schools Workshop presented a report from parents of children who were transferred to relieve overcrowding in Bedford-Stuyvesant. At that same meeting, Mrs. Athea Buckner discussed "bus problems" of Bedford-Stuyvesant children attending schools in the predominantly white area of Glendale, Queens.[42]

Through the Workshop parents could express their grievances and receive assistance, and deliver their complaints through their PTA representative. The Workshop handled individual complaints by visiting schools on the behalf of parents. Complaints included reports of racial discrimination: high school students alleged that schools segregated black and Puerto Rican children by placing them in "special classes" in integrated schools; black and Puerto Rican students complained that teachers arranged segregated seating in classrooms. From his own personal experience, Galamison was sensitive to the complaint that officials were tracking black and Puerto Rican students to vocational, not academic high schools, despite their wishes.[43]

Unlike many religious, social, and political organizations that were divided by race, ethnicity, and class, the workshop was an alternative social world that linked parents from different neighborhoods, racial and religious backgrounds, working for integration. Black, Latino, and white parents in Bedford-Stuyvesant, Brownsville, Williamsburg, Flatbush, and other parts of the borough came together because they had a vehicle for changing the school system. Minutes of a conference with Board of Education members demonstrated the strength and accomplishments of the Brooklyn NAACP Education Committee. Parents and teachers found themselves acting as leaders and spokespeople for their community. Besides Galamison, they included Claire Cumberbatch; Stein; Edna Cameroon, President of the PTA of P.S. 258; Anita Best, PTA President of Junior High School 93; William Fay, PTA President of P.S. 70; Thelma Hamilton; Edwin M. Best, who was affiliated with the PTAs of P.S. 93 and 258; Clarence Hoyt, who was associated with the PTAs of 93 and 258; and Sylvia Aronowitz, who was associated with the PTA of P.S. 24. Representing the board were Cecile Truth Sands, Charles H. Silver, Gardner C. Taylor, Dr. Jacob Greenberg, Dr. David H. Moskowitz, and Mr. Francis A. Turner.[44]

Galamison argued that the area designated for the building of public schools 304, 40, 305, and 309 extended the present pattern of de facto segregation in Bedford-Stuyvesant. The 309 site would reverse the pattern of integration achieved through transfers of children from Bedford-Stuyvesant to Bushwick schools, as would the projected zoning of P.S. 299 (then under construction). A delegation took the matter to the board, and the two sides agreed to meet again and work out alternative fringe sites for the schools. Galamison also suggested that all new schools be built as kindergarten to third grade (K-3) schools, if there were no fringe schools providing racial balance.[45]

During 1956, Galamison and the committee managed to persuade principals to establish intellectually gifted childrens classes in segregated schools. These principals tested students and discovered that there were substantial numbers of children who scored high marks and deserved to be placed in the program. Schools opened libraries and children received homework for the

first time because of the committee's diligence. School repairs were made,
thanks to pressure from the NAACP; renovations were made at P.S. 129; and
P.S. 168 received a new roof. Moreover, renovations were promised at two
other schools, and new schools were slated to replace at least seven old elementary school buildings.[46]

In its annual report, the committee listed goals for the next year. They
included continuing to press the board to desegregate Junior High School
258, working to desegregate all schools in Bedford-Stuyvesant, working to
bus the fourth through sixth grades "out of the box," extending its campaign
to Brownsville by parents' request, and improving teaching standards, as
well as math and reading scores. The report was signed by Galamison,
Craig, and Stein, who was the secretary of the Committee.[47]

Arguing that the predominantly black and Puerto Rican schools were
overcrowded and in some cases were a "few blocks away from half-empty
white schools on the other side of Broadway and also at Fulton Street," the
committee called for the board to do away with "the box," racially segregated schools in predominantly black and Puerto Rican communities, and to
send black and Puerto Rican children to underutilized schools. Moreover, it
called for building new schools where integration was much more feasible—in areas where blacks and whites lived close to one another, popularly
called fringe areas. This demand included the building of a new junior high
school on Eastern Parkway.[48]

## Ideological Conflict

Junior High School 258, which Galamison viewed as the test of the board's
sincerity, became a major focus. Galamison, in a letter to Superintendent
Jansen, accused the board of misleading the public. Noting that the board
had evaded its responsibility to integrate 258, Galimson asserted that claims
of progress were nothing more than ". . . an effort to exaggerate what little is
being done and . . . an attempt to distract the public from the Junior High
School 258 issue." The civil rights activist claimed that there were "20,000
children in the Bedford-Stuyvesant and nearby area attending seventeen
segregated schools. It is difficult to see how the limited proposals of the
board can affect more than a negligible minority of this vast number." He
noted that the 1954 Supreme Court Brown decision had outlawed segrega-

tion and that the board had committed itself before the school opened to end segregation in New York public schools.[49]

Galamison and members of the Education Committee maintained that the board had deliberately separated black and Puerto Rican students from white students. Although black and white children lived in the same neighborhood, black children were zoned for the "box" north of Empire Boulevard in Bedford-Stuyvesant, while the white children were zoned south of Empire Boulevard in schools with predominantly white student bodies. The Presbyterian pastor demanded that black children be zoned south and white students be zoned north. Galamison also requested a meeting with the Mayor to discuss 258. Despite the pressure from Galamison and the NAACP, Jansen stood firm and publicly supported the neighborhood school concept.[50]

What Jansen failed to realize was that parents and the NAACP were requesting more than an experiment in social engineering. For numerous parents in Harlem, Bedford-Stuyvesant, Brownsville, and other black and Puerto Rican communities, it was clear that their children were receiving an inferior education. Their children attended the worst schools, had the least experienced teachers, and received inadequate services. Race was a determining factor, and integration was a means of assuring their children better educational opportunities.

Jansen added fuel to the fire when he made a public statement that Junior High School 258 would be "impossible" to integrate. He predicted that if an attempt were made to integrate the junior high school, there would be violence on the part of resisting whites. Charles Silver, president of the Board of Education, reiterated Jansen's claim of the difficulty of integrating the junior high school. Instead, he promised to provide the school with additional services. The school system's leaders, backing the neighborhood school concept, ideologically were at odds with Galamison and the civil rights movement. Jansen's and Silver's offer indicated their belief that they could provide black and Latino children with a decent education in a segregated setting, thus ignoring Galamison's assertion of the urgency to end segregation because children could not properly learn under such conditions.[51]

When corresponding with Board of Education officials, Galamison did not pull any punches. His tone was at times hostile and direct. He portrayed board officials as people attempting to uphold segregation. The issue was

clear to him. Segregation was evil and it was up to those with power to eliminate it as soon as possible. Jansen's explanation of the difficulties of integrating the schools was nothing more than a stalling tactic. He told the
superintendent that his comments to the press were "inadequate, misleading," and "an attempt to evade" his responsibility to desegregate Junior High
School 258. He reminded Jansen that the NAACP had submitted a formal
memorandum to integrate the junior high school in February yet nothing
had taken place. He accused the board official of trying to distract the public and insisted that the only reason for the failure to integrate 258 had to do
with the board's opposition to integration. Attacking Jansen's argument of
the geographical difficulties of integrating 258, the pastor contended that
within a mile in any direction from the junior high school white communities could be found.[52]

Upset over Galamison's public letter, Jansen shot back by spelling out his
own views on integration. He asserted that integration meant not just black
and white children attending the same schools but also good human relations. In addition, it meant that the board provide services for students with
special needs. As far as J.H.S. 258 was concerned, the head of the school system claimed that the school had been built to relive overcrowding and provide the community with an evening center. He reiterated how difficult it
was to integrate the school because it was located in a "homogeneous"
community and added his own sarcasm: "It is important to remember that
in calculating distance[s] to a school building we must calculate them by
measuring the distance[s] that children have to walk and not distances as
the crow flies." He pointed out that the school was filled to capacity and no
more children could be admitted.[53]

In order to keep pressure on the board, Galamison announced that the
NAACP was launching a petition drive, demanding that Mayor Wagner request the superintendent's resignation. Galamison's action created a storm.
His letter to the superintendent revealed the major difference between the
national organization and those of the more militant members of the
Brooklyn local: while the Brooklyn pastor wanted to launch a frontal assault, John A. Morsell, assistant to NAACP President Roy Wilkins, informed Reverend Grant Shockley, president of the local branch, that the
national organization was concerned with the means as well as the ends.
Morsell argued that a distinction should be made between New York City
where officials had committed themselves to the NAACP goals and the

South where authorities had banded together to oppose integration. He criticized the Brooklyn branch for jeopardizing a nationwide effort to integrate schools by creating community opposition by its demand of rezoning. He claimed too much fanfare had taken place with Galamison's November letter to Jansen.[54] Morsell's letter to Shockley was a clear warning from the national leadership that the Brooklyn branch should adopt a less provocative endeavor.

Galamison's actions not only exposed the ideological split between the national and the Brooklyn NAACP but also revealed the division within the local organization. The Executive Committee of the Brooklyn NAACP, disavowing Galamison's call for Jansen's resignation, passed a resolution claiming that the call for the superintendent's resignation was a concern of the branch president, executive committee, and the national organization. Winston Craig, a close ally of Galamison, defended the call for the superintendent's departure by asserting that if the national had interceded nine months earlier there would have been no need for the Education Committee to have called for such action. For his part, Galamison admitted that it had not been decided whether his letter to Jensen represented the views of the committee or only of himself. Realizing he had little support from other New York branches of the civil rights organization he called for the national to conduct an appraisal of Jansen's record on school integration.[55]

Galamison felt that the major problems he faced came from within the Brooklyn NAACP, where opposition forces were accusing him of acting as a lone gun who had "overstepped" his authority when calling for the superintendent's resignation. The Presbyterian pastor's militant activism put him at odds with the more moderate among the NAACP who shied away from combative approaches. The episode also exposed another problem that would cost Galamison dearly in the future; he made public statements and took positions without any discussion with those it concerned. The eagerness to act without consultation was a weakness in Galamison. He was too quick to act alone, a fault that would later hinder the movement for school integration.[56]

Although Brooklyn and national NAACP's leadership argued that Galamison had "overstepped" his authority when calling for the superintendent's resignation, the Presbyterian pastor felt that the accusation that he was acting as a lone gun was a facade. He argued that his militant activism simply put him at odds with the more moderate with the NAACP leaders who shied away from combative strategies.

Years later, Galamison contended that the Executive Board of the Brooklyn branch had supported his action, but unfortunately one of the opposition members was chair of publicity—he never reported the executive board's vote. The Siloam pastor asserted that if Jansen had been aware of the support from the association, he would have integrated Junior High School 258.[57] Yet, even if Galamison had won support from the Brooklyn NAACP Executive Board, his notion that Jansen would have capitulated may be too simplistic. There are no signs that even with the public support of the Brooklyn NAACP, a small organization, Jansen would have caved in. From all indications, he was adamant in his belief in the neighborhood school.

To save himself from humiliation, Galamison informed the press that Jansen claimed that he had been misunderstood; he wanted to see Junior High School 258 integrated. On the basis of this explanation, the Brooklyn civil rights group decided to postpone its drive and give the superintendent time to come up with a plan for the integration of the junior high school.[58]

To make matters worse, the tension between Galamison and Wilkins would increase dramatically over the methodology of struggle. In the summer of 1957, Wilkins wrote an angry letter to Galamison complaining about the Siloam pastor's association with unknown groups. He had read a *New York Times* article about a meeting that had taken place among the mayor of New York, the NAACP, the Negro Teachers Association, and the Parents' Committee for Better Education. He contended that although the NAACP was listed, Galamison was the only speaker noted in the paper, inferring that the pastor was using the name of the NAACP without approval from the organization. He also demanded to know what the Negro Teachers Association and the Parents' Committee for Better Education were and why Galamison was associating with these groups.[59]

Galamison's anger could not be contained. He shot back at the leader of the national civil rights organization: "Your letter of inquiry of July 15th has been received, and in all fairness to us both," the young minister affirmed, "I should say that its implications cause me some perturbation. For 9 years, I have been the leader of a church congregation in Brooklyn which now numbers 2000 of the Borough's finest people, many of whom feel that the N.A.A.C.P. is fortunate to have my volunteer services. For as many years I have worked on national committees of my denomination. But never have I been subjected to the suspicion and distrust which has accrued around my labors in the N.A.A.C.P." He noted that the Brooklyn branch had been invited by the Education Committee of the Manhattan branch to the meeting with Wagner. He also noted that a spokesperson from each branch who attended the meeting had given a brief presentation.[60]

The Presbyterian pastor pointed out that the Negro Teachers Association was made up of members of the Teachers Guild and led by Richard Parrish, an executive board member of the American Federation of Teachers. In a bold fashion, Galamison answered Wilkins's question of why a Negro Teachers Association existed by contending that it was "for the same reason that a National Association for the Advancement of Colored People exists within the United States; or for the same reason that an Afro-Presbyterian Council would find it necessary to exist within the framework of the total Presbyterian Church." Racism made it necessary for black teachers, like blacks in other fields, to organize and struggle to alleviate the dreaded pathology. He also explained to Wilkins that the Parents' Committee for Better Education, led by Ella Baker, had been organized because of the "inactivity" of the Education Committee of the Manhattan NAACP.[61]

The tension between Galamison and Wilkins demonstrated not only a personality conflict, but also a division between the national leadership of the venerable organization and the the grassroots leadership. While community groups and other associations that worked directly with ordinary people were mobilizing for the fight for school integration, Wilkins, by his reluctance to affiliate with these groups and his stress upon negotiation among the "right" people, revealed that he was not in contact with the grassroots. Instead of seeing Galamison as a person who read the pulse of ordinary people and was willing to act, Wilkins, who had succeeded long-time NAACP Executive Secretary Walter White in 1955, saw the Presbyterian pastor as a person who was out of control. By refusing to follow proper procedure, he was threatening the organization's civil rights objectives. For Galamison, the national organization was an obstacle to the militant struggle to desegregate New York City schools.

In late November, the Brooklyn NAACP's Education Committee claimed a partial victory. The Board of Education declared that Junior High School

61 would open as an integrated school in September 1957 instead of as an all-white school, as originally planned, and that steps would be taken to integrate Junior High School 258 in the fall. The board promised to improve conditions at 258 by adding more "good" teachers and administrators. The board and the committee did not define what was meant by a good teacher and administrator, and it failed to list any criteria. The board also promised to reduce the number of students in the school—nothing was said about reducing class size—and to create an after-school reading program.[62]

While some moderates opposed Galamison's militancy, he did gain attention and support from other individuals and civil rights groups, among them Daphne Sheppard and James Hicks of the *Amsterdam News*, the Harlem Branch of the NAACP, the NAACP Legal Defense and Educational Fund, the Intergroup Committee of New York Public Schools (a coalition of twenty-eight civil and civil rights groups), and the Urban League of Brooklyn.[63]

The incident over the call for Jansen's resignation made the leftwing members of the Brooklyn civil rights organization aware that if they were going to move the NAACP into the fight for school integration, they would have to take over the leadership. They decided to create a slate with Galamison running for president, Annie Stein and Claire Cumberbatch running for the executive board, and Winston Craig serving as manager of the campaign.[64]

The opposition decided on the last day of nominations to present a slate challenging Galamison's group. James Powers, former president of the Brooklyn branch and arch opponent of Galamison, nominated C. V. Harris for president with Justice Myles A. Page and Reverend Archibald McLees as first and second vice presidents. McLees had earlier turned down an offer to run on Galamison's slate. The event made the public aware of dissension within the Brooklyn NAACP.[65] In spite of the challenge, Galamison won the election on December 13 overwhelmingly, defeating Harris 159 to 46. The victory can be attributed to the support he gained among the membership over his battle for school integration.

The election did not go uncontested. An election teller, Ruth Lewis, accused another teller of opening the sealed envelopes containing the ballots of executive board candidates, and of counting them before the designated time without another teller present. Lewis, who was appointed by Harris, lodged a complaint with the outgoing president, Reverend Grant Shockley, and the national office, charging improper procedures, and challenging the validity of the election for executive board. In a sworn affidavit, Lewis asserted that the envelope containing ballots for the executive board had been opened by teller William Thompson, who began counting them before the other tellers had arrived. Although the national decided to process Lewis's complaint, it later upheld the election because Thompson admitted he made an error in judgment and there was no evidence of erasures.[66]

Galamison and the progressives who were elected to the executive board eagerly took office in January 1957 with the clear objective of forcing the Board of Education to create a racially balanced school system. Despite Galamison's victory, not all were in support of his leadership; he was inheriting a divided NAACP. He did not have a mandate and could expect challenges.

## The Vanguard of the Movement

Milton Galamison did not operate in a vacuum. At the same time that the Siloam pastor became president of the Brooklyn NAACP, parents and community activists were putting greater pressure on the Board of Education to desegregate the school system. Galamison's leadership came at a time when there was intense community activism in New York City. This activism, along with Galamison's efforts, forced the school agency to take steps toward integrating the schools.

In February, the new president of the Brooklyn NAACP participated in a symposium sponsored by the Americans for Democratic Action. The focus of the gathering was Junior High School 258. Galamison criticized the Board of Education for not having lived up to its promise for integration: "The real question here is not whether the school was built in a Negro area, after the United States Supreme Court decision and the board's own pronouncements against segregation; the real question is the board's willingness to take positive steps to integration."[67]

At that same symposium, the Urban League of Greater New York pointed out that Junior High School 258 was like other schools in poor black and Puerto Rican areas. Out of seventy teachers only eighteen held regular licenses, and twenty-two were substitutes, with emergency licenses. The remaining came in on waivers from elementary schools. A league spokesman argued that this situation proved that a subcommission on integration teaching assignment recommendations, which would have called for trans-

ferring more experienced teachers to schools in predominantly black and
Puerto Rican neighborhoods, was vitally needed.[68]

Under fire for the lack of progress in school integration and not publicly
endorsing the recommendations of the subcommission on teacher assignments and personnel, which released its recommendations in December
1956, Charles Silver, president of the board, and Jansen issued a joint statement. They claimed that there had been a misunderstanding of several aspects of the integration program. Noting that five subcommission reports
had been issued and the board had approved three, they stated that the last
two would be acted upon by the end of the month.[69] Jansen and Silver attempted to appease both sides of the controversy, explaining that rezoning
would encourage integration but would not do away with the neighborhood
school concept. The officials did not say whether they endorsed bussing but
mentioned that the subcommission recommended that it only be used with
the parents' consent and if "conditions permit." They also contended that all
schools could not become desegregated, because of housing patterns.

As for rotation—the policy by which all schools were required to have the
same ratio of experienced teachers to substitutes—the board had approved it
the previous June, and some effort had been made. They reassured teachers
that volunteers would be transferred to ghetto schools; only if there were not
enough teachers would the board seriously consider an involuntary plan. The
board promised not to uproot teachers with twenty or more years experience
and would consider individual hardship cases.[70] The problem with the statement was that it lacked teeth. There was no firm commitment to a city-wide
integration plan and no commitment to a strong reassignment plan.

Despite Jansen's and Silver's attempts, the attacks on the board kept
coming. The Intergroup Committee on New York Public Schools, consisting of twenty-six civic, labor, and religious groups, criticized the board for
delaying action on the subcommission on integration and zoning recommendations. The group was justified in its criticism. The board had submitted a budget proposal that contained no request for funds to implement
the recommendations.[71]

Again in February a rally was held at Siloam sponsored by the Interde-
nominational Alliance, a group of ministers of various denominations who
supported school integration. The rally was in response to a report on
school crime released by the board, claiming that more crime was taking
place in schools in black and Puerto Rican communities. Galamison argued

that the board had released the report in an attempt to prevent white parents from supporting an integration plan that would send their children into nonwhite areas. Although the rally was expected to attract 1,500, it drew a crowd estimated at only 250.[72]

Galamison, refusing to let the JHS 258 issue die, issued another memorandum claiming that fourteen months after his first memorandum on 258, Jansen still had failed to make any progress on desegregating the school. He noted that feeders, elementary and junior high schools from which students were sent to the school on the next level within that particular zone, had been added to 258 almost assuring that the school would remain overcrowded. On behalf of the parents of JHS 258, he requested the withdrawal of additional feeders, the granting of full freedom of choice of high schools to 258 graduates, and the maintenance and improvement of remedial and guidance work and stability of teaching staff.[73]

After a long delay, the board approved the reports of the subcommissions on zoning and integration, but reserved to itself the "privilege of interpreting the meaning to be attached to certain terms and phrases, of further studying and exploring the merits of specific recommendations and of resolving the administrative problems which necessarily arise in carrying out any policy for a school system as complex as that of New York City."

Meanwhile, opposition to the board's integration plans was mounting among opponents of desegregation. The Queens Chamber of Commerce called the board's program ill advised and wholly unnecessary, denying that segregation had been a problem in New York City schools and throwing its support to the neighborhood school policy. Parent groups also joined in the attacks, calling the proposals forced integration.[74]

The board's endorsement of the subcommission reports was warmly greeted by civil rights groups. At a meeting of principals and civic organizations, however, Jansen pulled the rug out from under the pro-integration groups. He assured teachers that there was not going to be any compulsory transfer of teachers to schools in the black and Puerto Rican areas, areas that teachers referred to as the Siberia of the school system. Instead, the board would rely solely on volunteers. He also assured 700 representatives of parent and civic groups that white children would not be transferred to ghetto schools for integration reasons. Racially homogeneous schools in racially homogeneous areas would not be altered, and the neighborhood school concept was safe. Repeating a similar theme, the superintendent asserted:

"there are in New York City a few localities populated by Negroes which cover so large an area that it is difficult to provide an interracial population for those schools located in the heart of such areas. It is essential that we work for interracial housing to break up such areas." Jansen argued that a voluntary teaching transfer plan would draw considerable numbers, ruling out any consideration of an involuntary plan.[75]

Civil rights groups were in an uproar over Jansen's statements and the lack of progress in school integration. The Urban League charged that three and one half years of investigation, negotiation, and recommendations to correct de facto segregation had been "thrown out the window." The league accused the superintendent of cramming 1,150 newly licensed elementary teachers into Bedford-Stuyvesant's and Harlem's segregated schools, violating the board's own policy of rotation and the commission on integration's recommendation that experienced teachers be transferred into black and Puerto Rican communities. The league also noted that Jansen had made little effort to recruit volunteers among experienced teachers for ghetto schools, that he had delayed issuing a zoning plan ordered by the board, and that he had not established a central zoning unit.[76]

Not willing to lie idle, community people began to engage in a struggle for desegregation. When September rolled around, enraged parents in the black and Puerto Rican communities began to organize protests, asserting that the board had made little progress. About 500 parents belonging to Parents in Action Against Educational Discrimination—sponsored by several groups including the Negro Teachers Association, the Jamaica, Queens, chapters of the NAACP, and the Parents' Committee for Better Education—demonstrated at City Hall on September 8. The group demanded an equal share of experienced teachers in the black and Puerto Rican community, smaller class size, a standard curriculum in every grade, a full day of school for all children, more remedial teachers, and integration. Mayor Wagner appeared before the protesters and promised that he would arrange for them to meet with himself and Jansen.[77]

Feeling the heat, Jansen released a "Progress Report on Integration" just before the meeting with protesters. He contended that the board had integrated a number of schools and was providing more services to "difficult" schools than to schools with a predominantly white student body. He also promised to transfer more experienced teachers into schools with a predominantly black and Puerto Rican student body.

During the meeting, the superintendent came under fire. When requested, he refused to name schools where progress had taken place, claiming that "To publish the fact that these schools are being made more Negro and Puerto Rican might stir up some feeling that could hurt our effort." Fifteen representatives of the group attacked the superintendent for his refusal to set a time frame for sending experienced teachers into the black and Puerto Rican areas. He simply said that he was "working on that." Nor could Jansen cite one specific example of a case where more services were being rendered to "difficult schools." When parents pointed out that, for every dollar spent on black and Puerto Rican children, the board spent $7.60 for white children, Jansen did not deny it. He explained that spending on laboratories and noninstructional materials accounted for the differences. Jansen did cite progress in moving black children to white schools. When criticized for slowness in obeying the Supreme Court decision, he said, "better late then never."[78]

On the same day that Jansen issued his report on integration, Ella Baker, chair of the Education Committee of the New York branch of the NAACP, and member of the Parents in Action Against Educational Discrimination, met with the Mayor. Claiming to represent hundreds of parents, she asserted that the board had not issued a plan for integration in spite of several recommendations of the Commission on Integration. In fact things had gotten worse since she had last met with Wagner in July. Baker criticized Wagner for his "hands off" policy when it came to the Board of Education. Besides urging the Mayor to help bring about an effective teacher assignment plan, standard curriculum for all grade levels, and a transfer of children for integration, the civil rights leader called for Jansen's resignation.[79]

Lester Granger, executive director of the National Urban League, charged that New York City teachers were in collusion with district superintendents to avoid serving in schools in the black and Puerto Rican communities. Speaking to a group of social workers and civic organizations, Granger said that the teachers' avoidance of duty was a disgraceful abdication of professional responsibility: "My contention is that there are few difficult schools, but there are many difficult teachers. Colored children who go to their classrooms from a background of poverty, disorganized family life and unwholesome neighborhood conditions are not different because of their color or language habits from the children of immigrant families who, in an earlier New York day, moved from exactly the same types of homes and neighborhoods."[80]

Teachers Guild President Charles Cogen defended the position of his group, which would become The United Federation of Teachers, by arguing that integration and difficult schools were separate problems. He noted that the guild supported integration efforts but opposed forced transfers of teachers because it "will not remedy the basic difficulty." Cogen was attempting to protect what was clearly a privilege for teachers. Because teachers were city employees, the Board of Education should have had the right to assign them where they were needed. The leadership of the city school agency had therefore failed to take serious steps to end an unfair distribution of experienced teachers.[81]

While protest activities were heating up, Galamison and the NAACP continued to press for integration through various avenues, including testifying at Board of Education and other public hearings. On January 7, 1957, Galamison sent a letter to Morris Warschaver, secretary of the Board of Education, requesting that the NAACP be allowed to testify at the public hearing on the subcommission report on teacher assignment and zoning. The request was granted. At the hearing Galamison praised the subcommission: "These reports address themselves eloquently to the errors of the past, to the present need for substantial adjustment and to the hope we have for tomorrow." He also thanked Mayor Wagner, Kenneth Clark, Arthur Levitt, and Charles Silver for their "vision and faith." They had created a new era in public education. Galamison declared that it was never easy to break ties with tradition, but it was wrong to perpetuate "ancient practices that time has made evil."[82]

According to Galamison, it was a tragedy that the students with the greatest need in the system got the least experienced teachers because of the way teachers were assigned. The Presbyterian pastor criticized a school system designed to protect the privileges of teachers while neglecting the needs of children. "We must determine whether the New York City school system exists for the benefit of the children of New York City or whether it exists for the benefit of the professional staff." He supported the recommendation for training teachers in human relations to help eradicate racist views of children. Galamison also supported the subcommission's recommendation for a zoning policy to promote integration, the creation of a central zoning unit, and the creation of a representative advisory council on zoning.[83]

At a City Planning Commission public hearing on the 1958 capital budget, Galamison congratulated the framers of the budget proposal because it contained serious proposals on construction of schools where racial balance could be achieved, reversing the old policy of building schools in areas where segregation would persist, such as Junior High School 258. However, he expressed his disappointment at the proposal that P.S. 257 be replaced by P.S. 24. The latter school, built in 1871, although mostly black and Puerto Rican, had an experienced teaching staff and hired extra persons under a special pilot program from the Ford Foundation. Thanks to the program, smaller classes were created, resulting in higher reading scores, the highest in Bedford-Stuyvesant. Galamison admitted that the building was dangerous. Another school, 257, was needed to prevent the breakup of the teaching staff and the shifting of students to overcrowded schools in Bedford-Stuyvesant. The site chosen for the school would also allow integration, because a new project, Bushwick and Hylan House, could create an integrated population. It was up to the city to assure that the housing project would not be segregated.[84]

Galamison noted that three years had passed since the board and the Mayor said that steps would be taken to desegregate the schools, yet segregation had grown in Bedford-Stuyvesant. There had been in the three-year period an increase in segregated junior high schools. Segregated schools decreased the self-esteem of children of color. He urged all present to appropriate funds for building new junior high schools to end segregation.[85]

In 1958, Jansen retired and John Theobald, former president of Queens College, became the new Superintendant of Schools.[86] To his embarrassment, parents kept seven black children out of P.S. 93 on New York Avenue and Herkimer Street in Bedford-Stuyvesant because the school was segregated, and therefore inferior. Superintendent Theobald met with the parents and agreed to rezone the children to P.S. 138 at Prospect Place, near Nostrand Avenue. Theobald noted that rezoning was supposed to take place in March when a new public school at Prospect Place and Albany Avenue, P.S. 289, was completed. Apparently the parents did not take him at his word.[87] The incident marked the growing frustration and anger of parents over the board's lack of will to move on the issue of integration.

Parents were not the only ones losing patience with the board. Despite Galamison's optimistic note at the 1957 capital budget hearing, the Presbyterian minister sounded harsher at the October 1958 hearing. The Brown decision was just four and a half years old, and it had been four years since the Board of Education had pledged to "put into operation a plan which will prevent the further development of such [segregated] schools and would integrate the existing ones as quickly as practicable." Despite the appoint-

ment of a commission on integration to develop a plan, Galamison asserted, segregation had increased. Since 1953, the number of segregated public
schools had increased from seventeen to twenty-five. Moreover, five schools
proposed for construction in the capital budget were doomed to segregation because of the proposed site selection.[88]

Galamison once again proposed K-3 schools in segregated areas, a compromise between those who argued for the neighborhood school concept
and those who argued for immediate integration of all grades. The children
would then be sent to integrated schools so that their skills would not suffer. Segregated schools meant inferior education. Galamison declared that
he and the committee had asked the board to use underutilized schools
near Bedford-Stuyvesant. The NAACP estimated that there were more than
5,300 children in Bedford-Stuyvesant and an underutilized capacity of
8,000 seats in schools within a mile and a half of the perimeter of that
north central Brooklyn neighborhood. Admitting that his figure on under-
utilization might not be exact, Galamison reasoned that, even if it were cut
in half, it represented the possibility of providing an equal and integrated
education for 4,000 of the 5,283 children in the Bedford-Stuyvesant area,
many of them receiving only a part-time education. What little had been
done to relieve overcrowding was due to parents' initiatives. In a determined tone, Galamison asserted that this gigantic problem could not be
handled by a piecemeal approach. What was needed were "long range,
overall plans for the equalization of our educational system."[89]

## Keeping the Public Informed

Similar to the movement to integrate restaurants in Washington, D.C., the
Brooklyn NAACP publicized its activities and its struggle for school integration in reports and newsletters and distributed these throughout the
city. "Discriminatory Practices in the Public Schools of Brooklyn, New
York" charged that there were nine segregated elementary schools (over
85% black and Puerto Rican) and two segregated junior high schools (nearly 100 percent black and Puerto Rican). In Bedford-Stuyvesant fringe areas,
there were six segregated elementary and six integrated schools between
Fulton Street and Eastern Parkway, an area divided evenly among white and
black schoolchildren.[90]

The civil rights group accused the board of gerrymandering, sending black children in fringe areas north to J.H.S. 258 and white children who lived in the same area south to J.H.S. 61 and J.H.S. 210, which had a predominantly white student body. Giving other examples of blatant gerrymandering to uphold segregation, the report pointed out that white parents living south of Eastern Parkway sent their children to P.S. 241, located in the northern zone on Sterling Place, and ninety percent white. Black children were sent to P.S. 42 (95% black) in the southern zone. The report noted that P.S. 241 was considered an excellent school, while P.S.42 was considered a poor one. The report noted a number of other schools in which children were zoned according to race; the black and white children living in the same apartment building were often assigned to different schools.[91]

In April 1959, the Brooklyn NAACP delivered its most stinging attack to date on the Board of Education. In "Progress of the Integration Program," the civil rights group gave a critical analysis of the board's integration program. Although Galamison is listed as the author, Stein's statistical analysis is evident throughout the work. The NAACP contended that urban areas suffer from de facto segregation and inferior education because they have the least experienced teachers and an inferior physical plant. In 1954 the Public Education Association reported forty-two de facto segregated elementary and nine junior high schools in New York City. By 1959, the number of segregated schools had risen to seventy-two elementary and twelve junior high schools. (A segregated elementary school was defined as a school with a 90 percent or greater black and Puerto Rican student body. A segregated junior high school had an 85 percent or greater black and Puerto Rican student body.) In 1954, Brooklyn was home to nine segregated elementary schools and one junior high school. However, by 1959 there were twenty-five segregated elementary and four segregated junior high schools. Between 1957 and 1958 segregated schools increased by 11 percent, although the black population increased only by 6 percent. The report attributed the increase in segregation to zoning and school and housing building programs which perpetuated de facto segregation. Black and Puerto Rican students received an inferior education, while white students received quality education thanks to experienced teachers, newer buildings, and superior services.[92]

"Progress of the Integration Program" alleged that black and Puerto Rican parents had to endure daily attacks on their children, who were labeled as culturally inferior and as being from broken homes. Pushed into nonacademic programs, these children did not achieve adequate reading and math skills.

The NAACP's report accused the board of hypocrisy. In 1954 the board passed a resolution proclaiming that "Public education in a racially homogeneous setting is socially unrealistic." The board, according to the civil rights organization, declared that its policy was to create and "put into operation a plan which would prevent the further development of such schools and would integrate the existing ones as quickly as practicable." In spite of the board's resolution recognizing its obligation, the appointment of a commission on integration which recommended desegregating the schools, and the board's adoption of those recommendations, segregation increased. In fact, Superintendent Jansen made statements upholding the status quo by defending the neighborhood school concept, which, according to the Brooklyn NAACP, was nothing more than a glorification of de facto segregation.[93] The only reason, the report alleged, that some black children had been assigned to integrated schools was the intense community pressure from parent groups who petitioned, picketed, took legal action, and launched school strikes.

The board did adopt permissive zoning (permission to attend a school other than the one the child was assigned to). However, when Dr. Jansen issued his comprehensive zoning plan in September 1957, it limited permissive zoning. The superintendent wrote that it should be deferred to high schools and that schools must have room to accept students. According to Galamison, in September 1958 nine parents of children who attended school in a segregated junior high school in Harlem refused to send their children to the assigned school, charging that the schools were inferior. They requested permissive zoning, but were denied. On March 30, the *World Telegram and Sun* reported that a restricted permissive transfer plan had been worked out by the board's central zoning unit for junior high school children. However, over a three-year period the board had repeatedly demonstrated its insincerity. Few permissive transfers had taken place below the high school level.[94]

Galamison claimed that permissive zoning was used to permit white children to escape from predominantly black schools: "This practice is now in effect for children of Navy Yard personnel who are transported many miles to an all-white elementary school in Bay Ridge, P.S. 102." The report also noted that white elementary school-aged children living in Fort Greene were "gerrymandered to escape P.S. 67 and P.S. 287, both with a predominantly black and Puerto Rican student body."[95]

Although the commission on integration recommended the use of bus transportation for integration, Jansen's comprehensive zoning plan contested bussing. Claiming it should be used only to relieve overcrowding, Jansen added that the transfers could take place only with the permission of the parents. This was a crafty move on his part. He was throwing a stumbling block in the way of integration.

The Brooklyn NAACP contended that, after three years of working to assist parents in achieving transfers to promote integration, because of the obstinacy of the board, by September 1958 only ninety students had been transferred to integrated schools. P.S. 287 exemplified the board's resistance. A segregated school, it had 487 children without seats, and students received less than a full day of instruction. Five hundred parents signed a petition to have their children transferred to underutilized schools but were turned down by both the field superintendent and the assistant superintendent of central zoning, Francis A. Turner. Turner instead offered them another segregated school. Through appeals and negotiation, the children were transferred, but it took parents and the NAACP to get the board to live up to its policy.[96]

"Progress of the Integration Program" argued that although Jansen and the commission on integration had recommended achieving racial balance in junior high schools by establishing zone lines in fringe areas, the superintendent's plan for J.H.S. 258 proved that he was not serious. The school had 1,495 black children and only five white children. Although the school was not far from fringe areas—it was less than a mile and a half away—no effort was made to integrate the school. The NAACP submitted a memorandum demanding that J.H.S. 258 and the predominantly white J.H.S. 61 be integrated; nothing was done. Jansen protested that, if integration were implemented, white parents might get violent. Jansen hypocritically apologized for having failed to integrate 258 but noted that integration meant more than black and white children going to school together. It meant providing services within "budgetary limitations to schools where students have special needs." As the NAACP noted, "Even Dr. Jansen's separate but equal definition of integration is sharply qualified by budgetary limitations and statements that Negro pupils are children with special problems."[97]

The board claimed that it had opened several fringe schools in Bedford-
Stuyvesant and in Harlem. But the NAACP report argued that some of these
schools were segregated, including J.H.S. 33, opened in a predominantly black
and Puerto Rican community and over 90 percent black and Puerto Rican.
Moreover, P.S. 289 in Crown Heights was scheduled to open as a segregated
school. Of the eight new schools that were opened, only two were integrated.
White and black children living in the same neighborhood were gerrymandered to different schools, blacks to P.S 11 (90 percent black and Puerto
Rican) and whites to schools with a greater white student body miles away.
Thus the only progress in integration was being made through permissive
zoning—14,000 transfers of black children to predominantly white schools.[98]

Realizing that it could not just attack the board, the Brooklyn NAACP suggested ways of solving the problem, especially in communities like Harlem,
which was almost totally segregated and had almost no fringe areas. It proposed bussing black children to white areas and white children into Harlem.
Segregated schools were in black and Puerto Rican areas. Eighty-five percent
of the de facto segregated schools were overcrowded, one-third had 300 children more than their official capacity. Galamison claimed that within a 1.5
mile radius of Bedford-Stuyvesant there were 7,950 empty seats. At the same
time, children in black areas were receiving less than a full day of instruction.

The report contended that de facto segregated schools could be eradicated by challenging housing patterns. The federal housing authority could
have assigned multi- racial and class groups to projects, putting an end to
its homogeneous class and race policy.[99]

"Progress of the Integration Program" pointed out that reading scores in
predominantly black and Puerto Rican areas were far below that of children
in predominantly white areas. Galamison attributed this to the mis-educa-
tion of black and Puerto Rican children. The board was denying black and
Puerto Rican children what white children were receiving, forcing children
of color into a life of destitution, and continuing the cycle of poverty in the
black and Puerto Rican communities.


## Community Activities

Although the major concern for Galamison and the Brooklyn NAACP was
school integration, it was not the only one. The local chapter addressed nu-

merous civil rights issues facing the nation and New York City. At Siloam, New Yorkers could get first-hand reports on southern civil rights campaigns. In May of 1958, Galamison informed the executive board of the Brooklyn NAACP that Daisy Bates, president of the Arkansas NAACP state conference and spokesperson for the nine children known as "the Little Rock nine," who were fighting to integrate Central High School in Little Rock, were coming to Siloam to report on the struggle.[100]

The Brooklyn NAACP continued to monitor police brutality in New York City. The legal redress committee met to discuss the shooting of a black man, Al Garrett, by a white patrolman, John Cuzzo. Galamison released a statement calling the shooting of Garrett police brutality: "It is difficult to conceive of any circumstances under which a patrolman would be justified in shooting an unarmed man, under arrest, in a police precinct." He expressed disappointment with a preliminary investigation by police inspector George H. Redding which, without consultation with the victim, absolved Cuzzo. Promising that the NAACP would seek justice for victims of police brutality, the Presbyterian minister informed his fellow clergy that the NAACP would hold a rally on May 19.[101]

The NAACP printed thousands of flyers and distributed them throughout the community. The flyer compared lynching in Mississippi and the rape of a black woman in Florida to police brutality in Brooklyn, noting that Garrett died on May 6. On May 8, a 14-year-old was kicked and beaten by a police officer. This "new wave" of police violence could not be separated from the violence in the South. Both were attempts to "halt the fight for civil rights." The flyer featured drawings of a black man being lynched, a black man in police custody being beaten, a black child being beaten by a police officer and a black women with her hands clasped, under a caption that read "They killed my boy." The bottom of the flyer was captioned: "Stop police brutality! Defend your civil rights." Speakers for the rally included an attorney for a Vicksburg, Mississippi, lynch victim, a witness in the Florida rape, and the attorney for the family of Al Garrett. To assure a large turnout, Galamison asked his fellow clergy to announce the rally.[102]

Galamison also wrote a letter to Governor Nelson A. Rockefeller requesting a state investigation, but the state declined to investigate the shooting, arguing that the district attorney's office of Kings County had conducted a proper investigation.[103]

In addition to police brutality, the NAACP reported that it was dealing

with several cases in housing, education, and labor. It acted as a referral
agency, directing people to lawyers and welfare agencies. The Brooklyn
group noted that "a great many persons turn to the NAACP for help, and no
one is turned away without receiving the best information we can give."
Galamison worked diligently to increase the membership and raise money
for the NAACP. Besides launching an annual membership drive, he established a church committee consisting of community ministers, requesting
that they put the NAACP in their budgets.[104]

In addition, the Brooklyn NAACP supported a strike of hospital workers
in the summer of 1959. The strike was not just an issue of class exploitation
but racial exploitation. Galamison claimed that since "98 percent" of the
strikers involved were black and Puerto Rican, it was vital that the civil
rights organization support them. "We must always regard the exploitation
of our people," Galamison declared, "as a discriminatory practice."[105]

On June 5, 1959, the Brooklyn branch reported a total membership of
2,834; 1,464 were from the churches of Brooklyn. To help increase the membership, the NAACP solicited in subways and held an NAACP "Night at a
Theater" fund raiser. It had also hosted a "Night of the Stars" in 1957. At that
time, Harry Belafonte and other black artists had entertained for the Brooklyn branch, raising more than eight thousand dollars.[106]

Under Galamison's leadership, the NAACP had become Brooklyn's leading civil rights organization. It had been transformed from an inactive organization with little contact with the grassroots to an agency that struggled on
behalf of ordinary people. Moreover, through its Schools Workshop, it had
given working-class parents the vehicle to address the educational needs of
their children.

## Exit From the NAACP

The Brooklyn NAACP tried to promote integration by continuing to request meetings with board officials. Galamison informed Silver that the
parents of children attending P.S. 287 and the NAACP were petitioning
the board, requesting transfers to underutilized schools. The Brooklyn
NAACP head requested a meeting with Silver and board member Gardner
C. Taylor, who supported the objectives of the civil rights groups, to discuss the "broader issues" of the board's policy.[107]

Attached to the letter was a memorandum used to pressure the board. The minister expressed his pleasure at the meeting on June 9 about the board's decision to transfer children out of the overcrowded schools into underutilized schools. The memorandum reminded Silver and Taylor that Cecil Sands had assured them that the central zoning unit had authority to arrange the transfers and that the matter "had been acted upon by the Board of Education and would be brought up again." The superintendents affected by the decision would be asked to present a plan for the transfers. He expressed his disappointment at the lack of progress for school integration: "The school year has begun with more overcrowding than ever in the schools in the Bedford-Stuyvesant and Fort Greene areas."[108]

To halt the mounting criticism, the board declared it would transfer 400 children from overcrowded schools in Bedford-Stuyvesant to underutilized schools with a predominantly white student body in Glendale and Ridgewood, Queens. New Superintendent John Theobald insisted that the transfers were to relieve overcrowding and not for integration purposes. Galamison expressed his gratitude to Theobald for his decision in the Glendale controversy. To gather support for the board's decision, Galamison held a rally at Siloam. Reverend Adam Clayton Powell Jr. was the featured speaker and a recorded message from Jackie Robinson was played at the rally.[109]

Parents in Glendale, furious at the board's decision, launched a boycott of Chock Full O' Nuts coffee because its major spokesperson, Jackie Robinson, publicly supported the transfer of children. To counter the boycott, Galamison called on churches to double their purchases of the coffee. Glendale and Ridgewood parents also organized taxpayer groups to protest integration. On June 17, speaking before a group of Glendale civic organizations protesting the transfers at his office at 110 Livingston Street, Theobald attempted to walk the fence. He asserted: "By permitting parents of these children who are on doubled session, getting only four hours of instruction a day, to send them to schools within a 3.1 mile radius from their homes in Bedford-Stuyvesant, the Board of Education is not contradicting the concept of neighborhood schools in which we have always believed." He continued: "I have said from the beginning that the transfer of these children would continue only until places were provided for them in new buildings planned for that Brooklyn area." He explained to the irate group that, after the board ran out of space in Brooklyn schools, it turned to Queens: "We haven't skipped any underutilized schools in Brooklyn as we fanned out in

a radius from the Bedford-Stuyvesant schools. After finding room for about
699 pupils in these schools, we need to place about 400 in the next adjacent
areas," Glendale and Ridgewood. Despite his reassurance, about 300 parents
from Glendale picketed City Hall. The mayor refused to intercede in the
Glendale dispute, noting that the superintendent was justified.[110]

Spokespersons from the First Presbyterian Church of East Williamsburg
supported transferring black and Puerto Rican children to Glendale, thus
challenging the view that the entire community opposed integration efforts.
Twenty clergymen representing Protestant and Jewish leaders of Glendale
and Ridgewood endorsed the letter.[111]

The commission on intergroup relations commended the board for having upheld its decision to transfer black children from overcrowded elementary schools in Bedford-Stuyvesant but requested a clarification on the
board's statement that the transfers were a temporary emergency act until
more schools could be built in the area.[112] The children were transferred
without much fanfare. Annie Stein, who visited every school where children
were transferred in Glendale, reported that on opening day of school, there
were picket lines at three elementary schools where the children were transferred. She noted that two of the picket lines were large but there were no
incidents. The worst episode Stein reported was a woman who spat on a
child at P.S. 68. "We reported this to the police captain because the cop standing by did nothing about it." Stein also reported that a boycott by white parents resulted in only one school having full attendance. "Boycott about 2/rds
effective but not uniform." Besides the boycott, thirteen parents from Glendale took Theobald and the board to court. Justice James J. Crisona ordered
the superintendent to explain why he and the board should not rescind
the transfers.[113]

To assure the success of the Glendale project, Galamison, Stein, and a
third member from the Brooklyn branch met with a board assistant superintendent and five Glendale principals of schools where Bedford-Stuyvesant
children attended, and parents of all schools except P.S. 68 in the Glendale
community. The NAACP representatives complained about black and
Latino children being called "bus children," clearly an insulting and deroga-
tory expression. All agreed to stop using the phrase. Galamison raised concerns about the lack of matrons on the busses and noted that some of them
were not arriving at school on time. The school officials agreed to provide
matrons, inform parents of changes in bus schedules, and demand a 9:00

arrival. The group also agreed to request that more teachers be assigned to Glendale. The group agreed that parents should work together through class conferences, grade conferences, and special assemblies.[114]

Despite Galamison's success as president, he disappointed those close to him by deciding not to seek a second term. Decades later, the Siloam pastor would assert that he had left the NAACP because he had trouble getting the organization to become involved in the school integration struggle. This seems doubtful, since the organization under his leadership had become extremely active in school integration. A more feasible answer was given by Galamison in a 1970 interview:

> [o]ther interests which sometimes took preceden[ce] over what I thought ought to be given priority. Running membership campaigns, raising money, having time-consuming fund raising affairs and, you know, carrying on in order to keep an organization like that going. But I wasn't interested in these time consuming procedures which got in the way of what I felt should have been the purposes of the agency. So I decided to come out, and my friends Annie Stein and Claire Cumber-batch decided to stay in, and they didn't think I should come out.[115]

There is evidence that the Brooklyn civil rights group under Galamison was having organizational difficulty. In April 1959, Eunace Woodson, special campaign director, was dismissed by the national organization because she was not successful in the membership campaign. Neither she, nor anyone else from the Brooklyn branch, bothered to show up at the kickoff meeting at the national office. Gloster B. Current, director of branches, asserted that the Brooklyn campaign was not "very well organized and does not look as if it will be successful under its present direction."[116] Although Woodson lost her position, Current's letter was an indictment of Galamison's leadership. As president, he should have been concerned about the growth of the organization and should have assured that people from his branch would come to the kickoff meeting. Apparently, Galamison was not interested. Moreover, there is some indication that the group was having financial trouble. Current informed Galamison that Carita Roane, who was appointed as a special campaign worker, was nearing the end of her four-month assignment. Current acknowledged that the national office would extend her term two weeks especially in view of the branch's "present financial situation."

The number of political activities did not lead to growth of the organization. In its campaign proposal for 1959, the Brooklyn branch reported that between 1956 and 1957 it lost 1,000 members.[117] Although it gave no reason for the decline, the battle for control between the leftwing forces and the more moderate members in 1956, along with the red-baiting that conflict generated, may have taken their toll and caused the decrease in membership.

The Brooklyn branch's financial difficulty was due partly to mismanagement on the part of its officials. In 1959 it had submitted membership reports without checks covering the share to the national office. In April 1959, Woodson reported that the Brooklyn organization had $720.99 in the bank but had a debt of $1,295.05. It owed the national $531.83 and Con Edison Electric Company $727.86. Roane complained to Gloster Current that Galamison mishandled money. She noted that the benefit for Willie Reed, a victim of police brutality, had been fumbled. Although forty people attended, only $49 was collected. The event itself was poorly organized. Galamison gave little time for organizing the event and he unnecessarily had thousands of leaflets printed at a cost of $125. According to Roane, most of the leaflets were discarded.[118]

It should be noted that Roane was not a neutral party in the battle between the left-leaning and the more moderate forces in the Brooklyn NAACP. In her letter to Current, she complained that the left wing of the branch had acted in an undemocratic fashion in order to maintain control. She asserted that at a membership meeting at Siloam, the left planted themselves throughout the audience and they "controlled the election" of the Nominating Committee. "George Fleary tied with Claire Cumberbatch, chrman of the Ed. Com—dominated by Anna Stein—and on the run off, Claire got 2 more votes than George so that eliminated him." She went on to argue that "Unless something is done, the commies . . . will take over the Bklyn Branch."[119]

Not all of the Brooklyn NAACP's financial difficulty with the national organization was purely an economic predicament. The battle over money with the national was at times a political encounter. While Wilkins and Current constantly demanded that the Brooklyn branch submit its portion of membership dues and money from fund raisers, Galamison consistently contended that the money owed to the national should be used by the local for its various campaigns and other needs. For instance, when Current requested that Galamison pay the national's share from the "Night of Stars" fund raiser, the Brooklyn branch president requested that at least $1,000 of the national share be withheld and that the local be given permission to raise $10,000 to hire adequate staff. According to the Siloam pastor, the entire $10,000 should go the local. By requesting that money be withheld from the national, Galamison was claiming that the political work of the Brooklyn branch took precedence over its financial obligations to the national and that the parent organization should throw its support behind the branch's campaigns.[120]

In spite of his work in other areas of civil rights, Galamison was concerned primarily with education. He was fully aware of how schools can hinder children and even ruin their lives. He wanted to dedicate his time to eradicating segregation and not to dealing with fund raising, membership drives, and the other tasks required of the president of the NAACP.

To the dismay of his associates, Galamison decided not to seek reelection in October of 1959. But it would not be long before the civil rights leader would step forward to lead a more intense struggle for school integration.[121]

# chapter four

# THE PARENTS' WORKSHOP FOR EQUALITY IN NEW YORK CITY SCHOOLS

In 1960, a new phase began in the struggle for school integration with the creation of an independent parents' organization. Unlike the Brooklyn NAACP's Schools Workshop, the Parents' Workshop for Equality in New York City Schools would aggressively fight without fear of opposition or hindrance within its own ranks. Relying on parent-teacher associations for members and support, and unlike the other civil rights groups that had little contact with the grassroots, the Parents' Workshop adopted a more inclusive approach. It continued to nurture leadership skills in parents and allowed them to become speakers, writers, negotiators, and organizers for the parent group. The new organization helped instill in ordinary people a strong belief that they could reform the New York City school system for the benefit of their children.

The Parents' Workshop took a combative tone when confronting the Board of Education. Developing a faith in its ability to change policy, it was unwilling to accept anything less than city-wide integration. The growing militancy of the grassroots organization reflected its vision of itself as an agency for change. It was the vision of the Parents' Workshop for Equality in New York City Schools and the reluctance of the Board of Education to take serious steps to desegregate the entire school system that would eventually lead to a major city-wide confrontation.

## Origins and Structure of the Parents' Workshop

One of Galamison's first acts, once he had freed himself from the duties of the NAACP leadership, was to openly associate with leftist forces. On December 7, he notified Rose Russell, legislative director of the Teachers Union, that he was stepping down as the president of the Brooklyn branch of the NAACP; he would be free to address the annual meeting of the Teachers Union.[1] Delighted, Russell requested that he speak on April 9 at their 24th annual educational conference. The minister spoke and received glowing reviews on his performance.[2]

Galamison's relationship with the Teachers Union had become a very close one. Besides occasionally speaking at some of the union's major functions, he publicly praised the organization's leadership. He was not afraid to identify with those accused of being communists; in fact, he took pride in associating with militant activist groups. On October 21, 1960, the Presbyterian pastor offered a tribute to three leaders of the Teachers Union, Rose Russell, Abraham Lederman, and Lucille Spence. Galamison contended that the hope of the world "lies in the calibre of militant minority leadership exemplified by the honorees of this occasion."[3] He forged an alliance with the Teachers Union, although it had been labeled a subversive organization and decimated by Cold War hysteria. He wanted a radical change, something outside the scope of the anti-communist Brooklyn branch of the NAACP.

Galamison decided to create his own organization and was soon joined by Annie Stein and Clair Cumberbatch, who first argued with the Presbyterian pastor about his decision to leave the venerable civil rights organization, which they saw as a good platform for social justice. The NAACP brought a "certain amount of dignity and support to the struggle."[4] It did not take long, however, for both women to decide that the NAACP was not the vehicle for mobilizing people to challenge segregation in the school system. In

the election of officers in 1960, Stein lost her seat on the executive board.
Although Cumberbatch had been elected chair of the education committee,
she and Stein were red-baited. The two women decided they would be better off organizing an independent group with the sole purpose of desegregation. Stein and Cumberbatch soon left the NAACP, joining Galamison in
his efforts to establish an independent parents' workshop.[5]

In March 1960 Galamison proposed the formation of a city-wide committee for equality to work for the integration of public schools. Its objectives were to explore the possibility of resolving the existing obstacles to
integration, to sponsor workshops for parents, and to "assist in the day-to-
day struggles carried on within the framework of the existing situation."
The young pastor asserted that he was creating a new organization because
after serving three years as President of the Brooklyn NAACP, the administrative work was interfering with his pursuit of integration, and members of
the NAACP Parents' Workshop urged him to create an organization independent of the civil rights groups. Moreover, he noted that formidable advocates of integration had been removed from the Brooklyn NAACP board
during the last election, assuring that the organization would not be a militant front for school desegregation.[6]

The details are not clear, but organizing meetings began at Siloam in
early 1960. The former NAACP leaders began recruiting by contacting PTA
members and informing them of the new independent group. In addition,
parents from the NAACP School Workshop left the venerable organization
to join the new workshop. Although the workshop was a city-wide organization, its most active members came from the Bedford-Stuyvesant, Williamsburg, Fort Greene, and Brownsville sections of Brooklyn, the most
active areas for the Brooklyn NAACP School Workshop. Other people who
joined heard by word of mouth. Thelma Hamilton, a mother of eight who
had been active in a PTA, joined because she was upset with deteriorating
conditions in the New York school system. Told by a friend that a parents'
group was meeting at Siloam, she went to the church and was delighted to
see ordinary people taking charge.[7]

To assure that working-class parents would be able to join the organization, annual dues were set at one dollar. The payment of this nominal fee
allowed people to become voting members in the Parents' Workshop. The
new group also attempted to entice students and organizations. Students
could join the youth council for fifty cents. Entire families could become

involved in the struggle for integration. According to the constitution, any association that paid an annual fee of ten dollars could join the Parents' Workshop as an affiliated organization, allowed two voting delegates and two alternates. Each affiliation could cast a maximum of two votes.[8]

The administrative structure of the organization was democratic, giving every member a voice. The structure also guaranteed that parents would help lead the organization. It consisted of a general membership body, executive board, area unit, and officers. The general membership was the "highest governing body of the Parents' Workshop," making policy and determining the type of action the organization should take to achieve integration. Made up of "all members and representatives of affiliated organizations attending a regular or special meeting of the membership," the general membership had the power to grant charters to local workshops upon the recommendation of the executive board. It also elected the city-wide officers and members of the executive board annually.[9]

The executive board was the second most important decisionmaking body of the Parents' Workshop. This body, which could not exceed thirty-five members, decided policy and tactics between meetings of the general membership. It was made up of city-wide elected officers, the chair, and one other officer of each chartered Parents' Workshop. It also included one representative, one alternate from each area unit, one representative from the youth council, and three people elected at large. The area unit consisted of the members of the organization in neighborhood areas. Its major function was to give members an opportunity to meet whenever they wished and discuss local school problems. Allowing people to meet as a collective, it established strong community ties.[10]

Besides these bodies, the Parents' Workshop had a president, vice president, administrative secretary, recording secretary, treasurer, and director of organization. Only paid members who were parents or guardians of a child in a public school in New York were eligible for office. All officers were elected at an annual general membership meeting in June by a majority vote of the members in a secret ballot process. The officers took office on the first of July.[11]

The Parents' Workshop's constitution called for at least four city-wide general membership meetings during a school year, at least two a semester. The president had the power to call a special meeting of the general membership. The executive board met at least six times a year, at least three times a semester. The organization also had several committees, including membership, research and school budget, curriculum and standards, grievance, public information, and legislative. The various committees gathered information and prepared reports in their respective fields.

However, despite the organization's democratic structure, Galamison was president; he always ran unchallenged for the position. In part, this was an indication that the members recognized how vital his leadership was to the movement. It also revealed that the new organization relied on a conventional model of leadership. Galamison would serve as a major spokesperson who would articulate the concerns of the group to the media, at meetings, and to city and Board of Education officials. He was the symbol of the Parents' Workshop. This was undoubtedly a comfortable position for Galamison who, as a pastor, had been trained to lead a "flock." His domination of the presidency gave the group stability. But it did not guarantee it flexibility when negotiating with the board.

But the conventional model of leadership shared space with a more collective model. Galamison was not just leading a "flock," but was also involved in building a movement with people, some of whom had experience in grassroots struggles. The provisions of the Workshop's constitution, Annie Stein's emphasis on allowing ordinary people to step to the forefront, and the parent-teacher association's tradition of activism assured that parents would play a leading role. They would be spokespersons, officers of the organization, have direct contact with school officials, negotiate, and organize.

The reliance on PTA members gave the new workshop a membership that had experience in organizing, conducting meetings, and contacting other parents throughout the city. Unlike the NAACP, the new organization would focus solely on the issue of school integration. Its constitution contended that school integration was the most important issue facing people of color. Integrated schools provided black and Puerto Rican children an equal opportunity to succeed in society, thereby breaking the cycle of poverty.[12]

The founders of the new city-wide organization wanted members to be people whose children attended the public schools. They, more than anyone else, were aware of the adversities of a segregated school system. Because of this decision, the organization, like the NAACP School Workshop, became primarily a women's group, reflecting an activist women's culture. The workshop gave women across race and ethnic lines the opportunity to work together to build a school system that provided for all children, regardless of race and economic position. They planned strategy, wrote position papers, led demonstrations, negotiated with board and city officials, cultivated their speaking ability, and raised money. Most of the officers and members were women; most of the activities of the organization were carried out by women.

Similar to the NAACP School Workshop, the Parents' Workshop had become a unique women's social world with an oppositional subculture that stressed radical activity. They organized parents, held rallies, voiced opposition to the board's policies, and carried out militant action. As a child, Eleanor Stein, the daughter of Annie Stein, remembers attending meetings and witnessing women working together with very few men present. Although Galamison had reached out to notables such as Dr. Kenneth Clark for help in organizing the new organization, the Parents' Workshop relied heavily on the PTAs. The most active members of the new group came from these associations. Because of their involvement in the parent associations they had first-hand knowledge of political, as well as the educational, events in schools. Some were used to confronting school officials about their children's education and conditions in the schools. These parents were not just shaped by Galamison but also helped mold the Parents' Workshop into a grassroots organization that addressed their concerns. At a rally for the new organization, the PTAs' presence was evident. Several PTA presidents were recognized by the workshop; parent association members from Bedford-Stuyvesant, Williamsburg, and Brownsville addressed the audience, giving first-hand accounts of conditions in the schools of those Brooklyn communities; and parents participated in a discussion on the issues facing the school system.[13]

Not willing to accept a visible leadership role, Stein became Galamison's "advisor." But she was clearly more than an assistant to the pastor; she was the organizer of the Parents' Workshop. She made the contacts with parents involved in the various PTAs throughout the city, took and kept the minutes of meetings, prepared and gave reports at the Parents' Workshop gatherings, and organized fund raisers for the Parents' Workshop. Eleanor Stein recalls people coming to her mother's home for meetings and fund raisers for the grassroots organization.[14]

To be sure, Annie Stein's greatest contribution to the parent organization was her ability to help develop leadership skills in parents, especially women. She constantly urged black parents to take the initiative by going to

their child's school to learn about their progress of their children's education, to meet with teachers and school officials, and to demand to know
what steps school officials have taken to improve educational standards.

Thelma Hill's story was a fine example of Stein's ability to cultivate leadership. Hill recalled going to Siloam and becoming involved in the Parents'
Workshop: "I became one of a group of dedicated parents who had involved
ourselves in the struggle to revolutionize education." Soon after Thelma
Hamilton joined the parents' organization, Stein encouraged her to run for
office. She was elected director of organization, traveling to public schools to
assist parents in their struggle with school teachers and administrators. On
several occasions she traveled with Stein, sometimes alone. She noted that
many parents involved in the workshop went to schools, "but Annie and I,
we took the tough ones. We often went into enemy territory." Hamilton also
wrote for the newsletter and became executive secretary of the organization.
According to Hamilton, because of her involvement in the Workshop and
her close connection with Annie Stein, she became secure in her ability to
organize. She also helped arrange Parents' Workshop speakers for organizations and developed a reputation as a superb speaker. On one occasion,
Esther Linder, president of the Education Committee of Executive Board P.S.
289, requested that Hamilton send a speaker from the speakers' bureau to
discuss Open Enrollment. On another occasion, Clara Krell, a secretary of
the Fort Greene Houses East Tenants Association, wrote to the Parents'
Workshop: "I have heard that Mrs. Hamilton spoke to tenants at Red Hook
Houses a while back and was very well regarded. Since our circumstances are
similar, perhaps Mrs. Hamilton would be willing to come to Fort Greene."[15]

Galamison and the activist parents wasted little time in joining the battle
for school integration. In an open letter to Mayor Wagner, dated March 1,
Galamison expressed his disappointment with the city planning commission's decision to build Junior High School 275 at Rockaway and Riverdale
Avenues, a predominantly black and Puerto Rican neighborhood. Galamison
pointed out that it was a violation of the board's policy, asserting that it was
"disastrous and reactionary." Despite complaints, the school agency went
ahead and built two more junior high schools in predominantly black and
Puerto Rican areas, J.H.S. 33 and J.H.S. 265. In addition, soon after the board
promised that another school, P.S. 289, would be integrated, it decided integration was not feasible. The Board of Education. had shown "indifference to
the possibilities of integration."[16]

Galamison told the Mayor that he regarded the site for J.H.S. 275 as "an affront to the democratic forces of our community life." The decision to build the school at Hegeman and Rockaway Avenue was "indefensibly reprehensible and a manifestation of absolute disregard for the welfare of all the children of New York City." City officials, according to the minister, were refusing to comply with the Brown decision. Quoting the board's promise in December 1954, to come up with a plan to prevent further segregation and to integrate the existing schools, Galamison warned that citizens would not endure the city's official actions.[17] The threat of action reflected a growing militancy on the part of the grassroots revealing a growing frustration among parents and others over the board's inability or unwillingness to live up to its early promises to do away with segregation.

Despite the transfer of children from Bedford-Stuyvesant and Fort Greene to Glendale, the Parents' Workshop argued that little progress had been made in transferring children from overcrowded areas to underutilized schools. In a letter to PTA presidents, the head of the Parents' Workshop noted that the progress made in school integration through transfers was being eradicated by new rules and regulations created by the board: "Instead of progress in relief of overcrowding, only a minimum number of children are being offered transfers to underutilized schools." Instead, children were being offered transfers to segregated schools, keeping some schools "lily white."[18]

The Parents' Workshop demanded a meeting with Superintendent Theobald. When Theobald agreed to meet with the group on April 25, 1960, organizers sent a letter to PTAs encouraging them to attend the meeting for moral support and offering them the opportunity to participate in the meeting. Galamison urged the presidents to show up at the meeting and speak for their schools. He also announced that the new organization would hold a rally on April 21.[19]

Galamison made an appeal that would become an ongoing theme for the Parents' Workshop: "The Parents' Workshop for Equality in NYC Schools is organized to help you and the children in your school by combining the efforts of all parents in search of full equality desegregation and a better education for all children. We urge your support and participation." The Presbyterian pastor was making two arguments. The first was that of self-interest: parents should become involved because it benefited their children. The fight for school integration would lead to a school system that provided services and quality education for all children. Gwendolyn Timmons, a member of Siloam, recalls Galamison using this theme when speaking to white parents about integration. She asserts that he argued that integration would provide their children with quality education. "He was at his best," she asserted, "when attempting to convince white parents that integration would lead to better education for white as well as black children. A united parent front would assure that all children received the best the school system had to offer."[20]

The second argument appealed to the notion of social justice, a theme Galamison consistently made throughout his public life. The phrase "full equality desegregation," was directed toward a sense of fair play. How could American citizens allow fellow citizens to be denied the opportunity of equality? The notion of separate meant inequality. Galamison contended that the concept of separate but equal "is fallacious and that no educational atmosphere, however comparable the physical equipment, can provide an equal education if it is separate." Both black and white children are crippled emotionally and mentally. It creates a feeling of inferiority in black children while fostering a false notion of superiority in white children. The Presbyterian pastor argued that it is the obligation of moral people to obliterate segregation. This moral argumentation was similar to the argument Galamison used in his sermons. Instead of appealing to just Christian virtues, however, he appealed to the American value of equal opportunity, a theme that crossed racial, religious, and class boundaries.[21]

All parents were invited to the rally on April 21. Galamison also asked parents' associations to contribute to the Parents' Workshop and attempted to build unity: "The Parents' Workshop for Equality in New York City Schools is organized to help you and the children in your school by combining the efforts of all parents in search of full equality, desegregation and a better education for all children. We urge your support and participation."[22]

To the surprise of the superintendent, who expected only a handful of people, two hundred parents from Bedford-Stuyvesant, Williamsburg, and Brownsville attended the session, which lasted three hours. Several parents spoke to the Superintendent, including Georgia Wyche of P.S. 168, chairperson for Williamsburg; Vivian Woodruff, president of the parents association at J.H.S. 33; Charles Turner of P.S. 168; Shirley Beasley of P.S. 297; Mr. J. Goldstein of P.S. 59; Hilda Haesberg, president; and Hilda Brugeras of the parent association of J.H.S. 126. The parents protested the zoning policies of the board and the inequalities of teaching staff in segregated schools. The irate parents attacked the board official because he refused to transfer more children to Glendale and Ridgewood. According to a press release issued by the Parents' Workshop, Theobald said the city was not ready for integration "and that he could proceed only by gradual, imperceptible degrees." Beatrice Wordlow, speaking for parents of children now in Glendale schools thanks to transfers, claimed that Theobald was more concerned about the racist attitudes of bigots in New York City than about the rights of black children to an equal, integrated education.[23]

According to Galamison, the board had not moved forward; "whereas previously children were permitted to by-pass nearer schools with available space, under the present plan children are funneled into the nearest empty situation without regard for ethnic composition, consequence or unreasonable walking distances. These restrictions have resulted in all kinds of undesirable consequences." Galamison continued: "By refusing to transfer for overcrowding, we have effected the further containment of Negroes in their segregated schools. By taking away even the minimum reasons that contributed to accidental integration, we now have our zoning unit engaged in detailed planning to bus for segregation in the best Georgia tradition."[24] The group demanded voluntary transfers for integration without regard to overcrowding, and a program with a timetable for the desegregation of New York City schools. Theobald made no commitment but said he would study the data submitted.[25]

As in the NAACP School Workshop, Stein's influence on the independent organization was evident. Stein and the Parents' Workshop conducted several studies, published results of meetings, and distributed materials to parents, including critical examinations of the board's integration policy. Informed parents, they contended, would support the efforts of the Parents' Workshop. The Board of Education wanted to keep people ignorant.

In "Bill of Particulars on Zoning," the grassroots organization informed parents that it feared that the board planned to use 200 segregated schools instead of underutilized schools in Greenpoint. The board planned to end all transfers to J.H.S. 126 in Greenpoint and rezone children from Marcy Houses to a junior high school in Williamsburg. The parents complained that ending voluntary transfers to J.H.S. 126 (apparently an underutilized school) and sending children to P.S. 110 was "tantamount to busing for segregation."[26]

The parents requested the continuation of voluntary transfers to J.H.S.
126 and to other underutilized junior high schools in Brooklyn, and full relief of P.S. 59 (but not by transfer to P.S. 110, which was already unbalanced
ethnically, compared to surrounding schools). They supported voluntary
transfers for integration and a plan for the desegregation of the schools. In
addition, the three-page document gave statistical data on the schools under discussion. In 1959, P.S. 59, located on Marcy and Sumner Avenues, had
an overload of 486 children and no empty rooms. It was 95 percent black
and Puerto Rican. The average reading level for a sixth grader was 4.8
grade. In contrast, P.S. 31 had twenty empty seats, and P.S. 34 had eleven
empty seats. P.S. 31's student body was 25 percent black and Puerto Rican,
while P.S. 34's was 5 percent. The reading level for sixth grade students at
P.S. 31 was 6.9; it was 5.4 at P.S. 34. The group also warned that if 200 children were transferred to P.S. 110, the percentage of blacks would rise from
54 to 73. The Parents' Workshop also noted that the board proposed to stop
transfers to Ridgewood and Glendale school districts from segregated
schools in Brooklyn.[27]

In June, the Parents' Workshop reacted bitterly to the board's adoption
of a capital budget that would hinder integration. In a press release, the civil
rights group noted that there had been an increase in the number of black
and Puerto Rican schools in Brooklyn since the Supreme Court decision in
1954: the city had gone from nine to thirty-eight segregated junior high
schools. The group predicted that segregated schools would increase to
forty-seven due to the capital budget proposals of the Board of Education.
The group declared: "So this Board of Education continues to build and to
propose to build monuments to inequality and separation to the shame and
disgrace and injury of our city." It continued: "For five years now we have
been bringing education equality by the teaspoon and throwing it out with
a bulldozer." Three of the four elementary schools scheduled for construction would be segregated when they opened. The budget proposed to
reduce school capacities in the neighboring white communities by closing
down underutilized schools. Approximately 3,400 seats would be sacrificed,
which would prevent future transfers out of segregated communities and
"eliminate the potential for integration." The Parents' Workshop also announced that it would hold a public rally at Siloam on June 9 at eight in the
evening to "decide on a strategy for achieving the desegregation of the public schools."[28]

Tensions between the Workshop and Theobald were running high by June. Apparently the leader of the Parents' Workshop had requested a meeting with the superintendent and was refused. Galamison informed the Superintendent, "we are disturbed by the continuing refusal of the board to remedy the inequities against which we have complained." He asserted: "we are annoyed by the indifferent treatment we have received because we consider it our responsibility to protest these injustices." In a threatening tone, Galamison declared it was "just as well that you have no time to meet with my parents again, since meetings seem to have availed us nothing."[29]

In his response, Theobold noted: "You are fully aware that I have given rather extensive time both to you and to the problems which you have raised." Apparently still angry about the April 25 meeting, where he felt that he had been under attack by 200 parents. Theobald complained it had been arranged for himself and two or three members of the Parents' Workshop. Instead, it turned out to be a gathering so large that they were forced to use the Board of Education meeting hall. The superintendent said that this type of meeting was not constructive.[30]

By the middle of June, Galamison and the Parents' Workshop had decided to force the board to execute a plan for desegregation. They decided to initiate a sit-out. Probably influenced by the Harlem parents who had kept their children out of school, eventually forcing the board to transfer them to underutilized schools, workshop leaders realized that the method would generate media coverage and embarrass the board. The group asked its area captains to bring mailing lists of organizations, churches, and leaders in their communities. They would mail leaflets and set up distribution committees to reach all the people, informing them of the boycott.[31] To house children who would be participating in the sit-out, Galamison contacted pastors, asking them for the use of their churches on September 12.[32]

Fearing a massive boycott and its consequences, Theobald announced on August 31 a pilot program called Open Enrollment, allowing the parents the opportunity to voluntarily transfer their children from black and Puerto Rican segregated schools to predominantly white schools. The program included sending and receiving schools. Sending schools had in excess of 85 percent black and Puerto Rican students; receiving schools had predominantly white student bodies and were underutilized. Parents with children in sending schools could apply for transfers for their children to receiving schools. If the program were successful, it would be protracted.

In making the announcement, the superintendent reiterated the December 23, 1954 statement on integration, declaring that integration in the city schools was an essential and imperative element of a democratic education. He said the school agency was determined to act on two fronts: first, to continue improving services in schools with minority concentration; second, to secure better ethnic distribution in the city schools. Galamison refused to call off the boycott because Open Enrollment was limited to the junior high schools. When Theobald included sixteen elementary schools, the sit-out was suspended.[33]

Galamison admitted that Open Enrollment was a compromise, but he still wanted to push for a city-wide integration plan. The threat of mass action made the board adopt a program that had the potential to desegregate a large portion of the school population. Moreover, the parents had proven that they were able to move the board to address their concerns. In "An Analysis of the Board of Education Open Enrollment policy," the president of the Parents' Workshop commended Mayor Wagner and the board for publicly announcing the program, which represented a "giant step forward in the direction of equalizing education."[34] Galamison even defended the program from critics who claimed that blacks who supported the integration program lacked race pride. He asserted children should be prepared to live and function in the "whole of society," not a corner of it.[35]

Although the sit-out was called off and the Parents' Workshop proclaimed victory, Galamison was nevertheless critical of the Open Enrollment program. He pointed out that the board had not taken leadership in assuring desegregation, instead placing the burden on the backs of black and Puerto Rican parents. Open Enrollment was nothing more than a voluntary program that relied on parents taking the initiative. Even though elementary schools were involved, there was no assurance that their school would be selected as a sending school. Sending schools on a junior high school level had to have an 85 percent black and Puerto Rican student body. However, there were several schools just under 85 percent that should be considered as sending schools. He also claimed that only seventh graders were eligible. Moreover, the board refused to pay transportation costs for the transferees. Through negotiations with the Parents' Workshop, the board decided to provide free transportation for children traveling a mile or more to school.[36]

Another problem with the Open Enrollment program was the system of notification. Instead of the board notifying parents directly, letters announcing the due dates for application were distributed in schools to children, increasing the possibility that the letters would go astray.

Despite its many flaws, Open Enrollment was a vehicle that allowed some children to experience a desegregated environment. This endeavor by the Board of Education came about only because of the militant steps taken by people struggling for integration.

## Spreading the Word

The Parents' Workshop published and distributed fact sheets to inform parents when transfer forms would be distributed and the date by which they had to be returned. They listed receiving schools, sending schools, and the reading levels of each grade in both. The fact sheets also provided information on free bus transportation, noting the miles between schools and other vital information.[37] In one fact sheet entitled "Questions and Answers on Open Enrollment" the Parents' Workshop informed parents that schools must provide free bus passes and offer maps and tours of the schools.

The grassroots parents organization affirmed that the school integration struggle was part of the larger civil rights movement. "By helping to integrate the schools of our city, you are breaking down the walls of segregation and discrimination here in New York, just as our sisters and brothers are doing in the South."[38]

The Parents' Workshop also informed parents about Open Enrollment and the struggle for integration through its monthly newsletter. Like the NAACP parent workshop newsletter, the independent Parents' Workshop newsletter consisted of a message from Galamison, reports on meetings between the workshop and board members, an analysis of board policy, progress reports on integration, letters from members, and the political and social activities of the workshop, as well as notes on the personal accomplishments of members and friends of the organization. The paper was operated by women members of the workshop who wrote most of the articles, printed the copies, and distributed them throughout the city. In order to recruit members, the newsletter contained a membership application and the office hours of the organization. The group kept its doors open to allow parents to raise problem issues and complaints and to help them mobilize for action. Parents could discuss their battles and accomplishments and ex-

press their thoughts and feelings on the struggle they were waging for integration. One example is Daisy Modeste, an active member of the workshop,
who wrote in the February 1961 issue of the newsletter that it was the information given on reading scores that had convinced her and her husband to
allow their children to be part of the Open Enrollment program. In fact, she
helped convince parents of seventy children attending the neighborhood
school to participate in the program. The newsletter also revealed that parents played a leading role in the operation of the Parents' Workshop and listed personnel to contact, including area chairpersons in Bedford-Stuyvesant,
Williamsburg, Fort Greene, Brownsville, and Crown Heights.[39]

The Parents' Workshop newsletter described the activism of women in
the Parents' Workshop, making it clear that Galamison did not always direct
the actions of the members. They collectively took militant steps to improve
education for children. Members of the Workshop used the newsletter to
inform parents about the mistreatment of their children. For instance, the
group notified parents that several children were not receiving bus passes.
In one case, an assistant principal at P.S. 221 refused to give free transportation passes to children; they were forced to walk, arriving home at four and
five in the afternoon. After parents protested, the principal promised a free
bus service to take the children home.[40]

The newsletter informed its members about demonstrations, forcing
principals and other school officials to take action to protect the safety of
children. In December 1961, Margaret Stepherd of Corona, Queens, reported that children attending P.S. 125 in Woodside under the Open Enrollment
policy were forced to wait 45 to 50 minutes after school for a bus. The parents saw this as a way of undermining the program. Despite complaints to
the principal, district superintendent, and the bureau of supply, nothing was
done. Finally, the parents called an official at the board who arranged emergency bus service. In another case, parents of P.S. 136 in Queens, under the
leadership of Mrs. Josh Booker, PTA president, Mrs. G. James, and Mrs.
Anthony Timpone, led a protest demanding a crossing guard near the
school. Mothers and fathers with baby carriages and preschoolers closed the
street, picketing for three days. The city responded after the third day and assigned a traffic cop to the street.[41]

The newsletter reported important political campaigns, such as its 1961
drive to get Galamison appointed to the Board of Education. It managed to
collect more than 4,000 signatures in the petition drive, with endorsements

from such celebrities as Ossie Davis and Ruby Dee; the famous African American historian John Hope Franklin; Dr. Hugh Smythe, professor of sociology at Brooklyn College; and Dr. Abraham Eisenstadt, professor of history at Brooklyn College. Other endorsements came from doctors, lawyers, PTA presidents, and the Brooklyn branch of the NAACP. Although he was unsuccessful in his bid, the campaign demonstrated Galamison's and the Parents' Workshop's growing popularity across race and class lines.[42]

The newsletter carried articles written by the leadership of the organization noting the failure of the board to educate children. In one such article, "The Reading Crisis," Annie Stein maintained that Theobald had admitted that 10,000 seventh graders were reading below a third grade reading level and 38 percent of junior high school students were two or more years behind. But the board did not admit that the system was racially segregated. Although the superintendent had proposed hiring new teachers, Stein contended that this would not stop the decline in schools. There must be a complete turn around in attitude among school personnel; teachers must realize that their job is to reach all children and not give in to prejudice. She claimed that the best way to achieve this goal was through integration, transferring experienced teachers into black and Puerto Rican areas.[43]

The newsletter also carried articles and reports from less well known members of the Parents' Workshop. Mrs. Phyllis Bowman's piece, "City Budget Hearing," is an example. She argued that parents should not have to beg for school funds; it was shameful that there was a dual system. A child's right to an education, which would prepare them for the future, should be guaranteed. The newsletter honored heroes of the civil rights movement in New York City, including the Harlem 9 and others who conducted a boycott, the children who faced and conquered opposition in Glendale, the "first" children to be bussed under the overcrowded-underutilized school plan, and children who were "first" in the Open Enrollment program.[44]

Articles such as "What To Do if Your Child Is Suspended" advised parents on how to deal with problems faced in the schools. The article suggested that parents should see the principal immediately to discuss the validity of his action and bring a Parents' Workshop representative with them. If there was no satisfaction with the principal, the parent should set up a meeting with the assistant superintendent within ten days along with a representative from the group. It also informed parents that they could appeal their cases to the Bureau of Child Guidance.[45] An article by Doris Graves gave parents helpful tips on how to prepare a child for college, making students aware that the credits they receive make up "units" they need for graduation.[46]

The February 1961 newsletter announced that the Parents' Workshop had established the Jefferson Avenue Education Center to ensure successful adjustment of students who were transferred in September under Open Enrollment. For a fee of six dollars a week, children were offered help in reading and math, with classes on Mondays and Wednesdays for an hour and a half.[47] The newsletter alerted parents to the fact that children were supposed to bring home applications on January 24. The applications, which had to be returned by February 7, contained a list of schools from which the parent had to choose.

To help parents with their selection, the newsletter listed a number of receiving schools, the percentage of black and Puerto Rican students in each school, the average reading scores, and the nearest bus and subway stations. The newsletter also included percentages of black and Puerto Rican students in the schools children would be sent to if they were not transferred. These schools ranged from 82 to 100 percent black and Puerto Rican. Reading levels from the eighth grade students ranged from 5.4 to 6.2 grade. Expected reading scores for eighth graders should be 8.6 years, the newsletter revealed, while the average reading score for children in the receiving schools ranged from 7.2 years to 9.6 years. In the segregated schools, 44 to 63 percent of eighth graders were reading three years or more below grade level.[48]

The newsletter made an urgent appeal to parents to participate in the Open Enrollment program. "The Board of Education has taken a giant step forward to integrate and improve the schools of New York." It contended that "children attending segregated elementary schools need no longer go on to segregated junior high schools, sixth grade children may now go to high achievement, integrated junior high schools."[49]

As the Parents' Workshop approached its first anniversary, Galamison reflected on the accomplishments of the organization: "One year ago we were up against the proverbial stone wall in our effort to integrate the city schools. Today, we find the entire city in motion toward desegregation, while we search out countless possibilities to make New York City the most integrated public school system in the nation." While this was certainly an exaggeration, the organization had managed to bring to the attention of the city the obstacles that children of color faced in the public school system. Despite his optimistic note, he warned members that they could not stop struggling: "At any cost we must avoid this snare into which many organizations have fallen." No doubt he was referring to the Brooklyn NAACP. He asserted that the Parents' Workshop should not let fund raising and other activities consume its efforts. To remain effective, it must continue to struggle for children.[50]

## The Battle Heats Up

According to the March newsletter, parents expressed their enthusiasm for Open Enrollment at the membership meeting, although they still felt that the board needed to take certain steps. Principals of sending schools should call meetings to guarantee parents that their children would receive adequate transportation, to reopen enrollment registration for those who missed it, and to extend open enrollment to elementary school grades not included in the original program. There were 3,600 students who had applied for junior high school Open Enrollment transfers, a clear indication that parents wanted to take advantage of the program.[51]

The newsletter reported that the Parents' Workshop was negotiating with the board to extend Open Enrollment to the high schools. Galamison and the Parents' Workshop were becoming frustrated with the lack of success of Open Enrollment and the board's slow action. The Presbyterian pastor argued that the Federal and local governments were failing to enforce the Brown decision not just in Louisiana, but also in Englewood, New Jersey; Chicago; and New York City. Only through threats would New York respond to charges that it was creating "one-way desegregation on a limited basis." Those in power would have to be forced to change through "social action."[52] The message was meant to capture the attention of board officials, signaling a move to a more militant position.

The Urban League of Greater New York agreed with the Parents' Workshop's assessment of Open Enrollment. According to the league, there were twenty-two sending junior high schools with 85 percent or more black and Puerto Rican students, while there were only eight receiving junior high schools with 75 percent or more white students. There were 12,000 eligible students entering the seventh grade in September and only 3,000 available seats. Two high schools were included in the program: Girls' High, at Nostrand Avenue and Halsey Street in Bedford-Stuyvesant, a sending school;

and Franklin K. Lane, a receiving school, at Jamaica Avenue and Dexter
Court in Brooklyn. On the elementary school level there were sixteen sending schools and thirty-one receiving schools in the pilot project. However,
there were 7,883 eligible pupils with only 4,000 available seats.[53] The league
pointed out that children from the third to the fifth grades were permitted
to transfer in the pilot, with applications being accepted from January 3 to
January 18, a short period for a crucial decision. In all, there were 95 sending schools and 124 receiving schools participating in the project. With
50,000 children eligible for transfer, there were only 15,000 available seats.[54]

By late March of 1961 the relationship between the workshop and
Theobald had deteriorated to the point where the superintendent refused
to share information that would assist the group in assessing the board's
desegregation policy. Rejecting Galamison's request for information on
school segregation, he argued that such data needed to be interpreted
"only by experts."[55]

By April the enthusiasm expressed a month earlier for Open Enrollment
had faded. An article in the April newsletter, "The End of the Rope On
Junior High School Open Enrollment," complained that applications for
junior high school Open Enrollment had been rejected. Francis Turner,
assistant superintendent in charge of the zoning unit, contended that while
his office had received 4,000 applications, there were only 2,000 seats in
underutilized schools; therefore, 2,000 children had to be rejected. The
Parents' Workshop proposed its own study to determine whether there was
a scarcity. If so, the organization promised parents that it would find a way
to achieve integration. A meeting with Francis Turner on Open Enrollment
in the junior high schools was described as "fruitless."[56]

More telling about growing disappointment with the board was the article entitled "Setting our Sights," which charged that the board had gone
back on its promise to build schools where integration could take place.
Max Rubin, who was then President of the Board of Education, disregard-
ed the wishes of parents on Long Island, who requested that their new
school be located in an area where racial balance could be reached; instead,
the school was built in a segregated area. "We are convinced," the group
asserted, "by this time that he has little to voice but despair on the most significant educational issue of our time, integration."[57]

When the board decided to rent eight unused classrooms in one school
on a temporary basis to a yeshiva, the Parents' Workshop saw the decision

as a sign of bad faith. While parents were attempting to get the board to re-lieve overcrowding and provide adequate educational services to their children, while school officials were telling them they were unable to help, the school system had decided to rent underutilized classrooms to a private agency. Galamison was furious and requested an explanation. In a letter to the Presbyterian minister, board president Charles Silver brushed off the complaints, contending that he had checked with Theobald, who had assured him that this was not unusual. He stressed that it was a temporary situation with a separation of public from private functions and would not interfere with Open Enrollment.[58] How could the board expect parents and the civil rights community to accept this explanation at the same time parents were being rejected for transfers because there was "no room"? As could be expected, Galamison shot back by asserting that the use of public schools by private religious institutions was a violation of the separation of church and state, and a misappropriation of public school facilities. Galamison argued that the public school is an "indispensable pillar of a democratic society. It is built and supported by public tax funds; dedicated to public purposes and maintained for an education free from sectarianism and other private interests." Public education is for everyone; those who want a private education should pay for it. The fact that the school was a yeshiva was incidental. If it were Protestant or Catholic, the group would have taken the same position. The Parents' Workshop voted at its April meeting to protest the board's decision to grant eight rooms at P.S. 103 to the yeshiva.[59]

By May, defiance and pessimism had taken hold of the Parents' Workshop. Galamison contended that the problem of the lack of space in junior high schools for Open Enrollment was not going to be solved by September. Noting that more than 2,000 students had been turned down for transfers, he urged the board to consider new possibilities. In a cynical tone, the minister blasted the board for considering only schools with 15 percent blacks and Puerto Ricans or fewer as receiving schools. Why not 20 or 25 percent? Since the board had refused to share racial data, it was impossible to confirm how many seats were available by "a simple change in the arbitrary percentage figure." He argued that, by changing the arbitrary number, the board could find room for all 2,000. He urged the parents not to give up hope, even though the board had given many apologies and offered few solutions: "The parents must press for the swift solution of this problem before we are told it is too late." He warned that parents might refuse to send their children to segregated schools.[60]

According to the May newsletter, Theobald had publicly offered to create an Open Enrollment program for the high schools by September 1962. A meeting had been held on February 27 to confirm his public commitment, but by May he had not come forward with a program. The organization made it clear that it would be a "bitter disappointment to parents who have hoped for this program if some excuse is offered for its not being implemented" by the fall. Although the workshop had submitted a plan to the board, nothing had been done. The plan called for students designated for Boys' High, Eastern District, Franklin K. Lane, Prospect Heights, and Wingate to select Midwood, Madison, Lafayette, Fort Hamilton, or John Dewey. Proposals for Manhattan and Queens were also submitted. Elected schools were based on available space, with sending schools chosen because of a disproportionate black and Puerto Rican population. The civil rights group argued that the majority of senior high schools were segregated white schools, making it impossible for them to become receiving schools.[61]

The Board of Education reacted by issuing its own progress report, under the direction of John King, associate superintendent of the division of elementary schools, praising the pilot program. The board claimed that in a one-year period it had moved 20,000 children, mostly black and Puerto Rican, to underutilized schools.[62] However, it admitted that most of the overcrowded schools with short-time sessions were in black and Puerto Rican communities. A result of the program was greater ethnic distribution in the schools. Under the pilot program, 7,883 applications were distributed to children going into the third, fourth, and fifth grades in sixteen sending schools, and 212 children were transferred. King spoke to principals of receiving schools on May 21, 1961. An Open Enrollment committee was organized and in-service courses exploring ways of improving community relations were offered. These courses were conducted by field superintendents and school and community coordinators. At least one staff member from each school took the courses.

Although the in-service workshops were organized with the assistance of the Commission on Intergroup Relations, the National Conference of Christians and Jews, and the Migration Division of the Department of Labor, Commonwealth of Puerto Rico, not one community organization was involved. The principals discussed with sending school staff the purpose of

Open Enrollment. Presidents of PTAs received copies of circulars, letters, and forms that dealt with Open Enrollment.[63]

The board claimed that it had distributed 50,000 applications for September 1961. Yet only 3,078 applications were received. Of these, the board authorized 2,831 applications. Although the report asserted that every child from grades two through four in the sending schools had been given an application to take home, the report never mentioned how applications were distributed, or whether the board could have done more to get the word out to parents. By sending the applications home with the children, the board had chosen the worst way of distributing the applications. Children that young could easily have misplaced them or forgotten to give them to their parents. The board could have mailed applications with a detailed explanation of the program and its importance to parents. The number of applications returned to the schools may indicate the flaw in the board's method of distribution. Perhaps deliberately, the procedure assured low returns. The board was finding it hard enough to place the few children who applied. If thousands applied, and the board could not find room, it would have been a fiasco.

To the credit of the board, it directed principals of receiving schools to prepare their staff and the PTA for the potential candidates. Unfortunately, the parents involved in the pilot program had to provide transportation for their children. However, by 1961, thanks to pressure by the Parents' Workshop, the board was providing transportation for children a mile or more away from the receiving school. The report did little to cool the tempers of parents whose children were rejected. The Parents' Workshop thus organized a boycott for September. On September 7, hundreds of parents, organized by the workshop, kept their children out of school, refusing to send them to segregated facilities. Three separate groups of parents were involved in the boycott, from the Brevoort Project in Bedford-Stuyvesant, Williamsburg, and the Manhattanville project in Harlem. Although parents had warned they would conduct civil disobedience actions if their children were sent to segregated schools, and although the workshop had offered the board alternative proposals to desegregate, the school agency had ignored them.[64]

By September, the Board of Education had a new president, James Donovan. Galamison sent him a letter of congratulations but wasted little time in "acquainting" him with issues. The civil rights group had come to the conclusion that Open Enrollment was not going to desegregate the schools, although it was a "step in the right direction." Yet 700 children had not returned to school because their parents were dissatisfied with their neighborhood school. The board must go beyond Open Enrollment and come up with a plan and timetable to desegregate the schools. Open Enrollment had failed to desegregate the schools in minority communities, placing the burden of integration on blacks and Puerto Ricans. Galamison warned the board official that the agency must move with speed.[65]

Donovan thanked Galamison for his letter but cautioned him he was preoccupied with other matters of reform. He looked forward to the time when he could address the issues Galamison raised and promised to do so soon.[66] The correspondence between Galamison and the board suggests that both sides were closing doors to compromise and negotiation.

After a five-day sit-out, Manhattanville parents were permitted to send their children to the school of their choice, and 600 Bedford-Stuyvesant parents were allowed to send their children to underutilized schools after October 2. Once again, the board's concession, brought about by protesting, left the message that the best way to get the school agency to take action was through protest.[67]

To diminish criticism of its lackluster role, the board announced the introduction of the Higher Horizon Program offering students in the third grade and beyond special services, smaller classes, remedial services, extra counseling, and greater parental involvement in an attempt to upgrade ghetto schools. Galamison attacked the board for having tried to divert attention from the issue of integration. He claimed that nationalist sentiment among blacks would lead to their support of the Higher Horizon program: "Those who are in favor of segregation have helped promote the separation of the Negro by appealing to a false pride and a sense of nationalism, making the Negro feel that any desire on his part for integration indicates an absence of race pride. . . . The desire for integration is not at all a reflection on the race pride of the Negro; rather, an expression of our desire for equality and the fulfillment of the democratic dream of America."[68] Galamison's critique of nationalism revealed that he had not changed his early position reflected in his sermons.

The struggle for school integration went beyond the goal to improve education for black and Puerto Rican children. It was a campaign to save the city's schools. Galamison and others argued that denying children an adequate education, as well as an equal distribution of service and staff, posed a danger to the entire system. If children suffered because of race, other children could suffer because of another excuse, such as lack of funds. The real solution was to unite people and struggle for a system that provided all children a decent education. For this to happen, people had to fight to do away with unfairness.

By the winter of 1962, the relationship between the board and the Parents' Workshop had all but deteriorated, and its February newsletter strongly suggests that it was moving on a course that would paralyze the entire system. The civil rights group had run out of patience and was threatening massive action. A letter had been sent to the superintendent to assure him that the group supported Shirley Rector's suit against the school agency. Rector was first cited for libel because she refused to send her children to what she claimed was a segregated high school. She in turn filed a suit maintaining that the board had deliberately violated the Fourteenth Amendment by segregating up to 20 percent of the high schools. The Parents' Workshop had attempted to negotiate this issue with board officials, but the agency refused. The newsletter issued a threat not given since the board announced Open Enrollment: "If the problem cannot be resolved, we will take social action. We will request that parents who are related to the workshop demonstrate and sit out until the Board of Education grants unlimited high school choice to Negro children, and makes a firm commitment on the issue of desegregation in our city schools." It concluded "we are rapidly losing patience with the expressed indifference of the Board to the problems of minority groups in our schools."[69]

In his column, Galamison declared that the Parents' Workshop had moved to a purely adversarial role with the Board of Education. "Our present situation is clear cut," Galamison asserted. "We know that we can expect no help from this Board of Education and this Superintendent in the area which concerns us most. We know, therefore, the size of our battles. No one will fight it for us. We must fight it for ourselves."[70]

In 1961 a state investigation uncovered a major scandal in the headquarters of the Board of Education, including misspending of funds in construction as well as payoffs. Theobald also confessed that vocational high school students had built a boat for him. A new board was appointed in 1961 and Theobald retired in May 1962.[71] In 1962 the board appointed Dr. Calvin Gross, from the Pittsburgh school system, as superintendent of New York City schools. Gross's relationship with the Parents' Workshop and civil

rights groups seemed no better than that of his predecessors. Galamison
was extremely critical of the new superintendent because of his comments
on school integration. Responding to questions from reporters, Gross said:
"Segregation is essentially undesirable. School systems have an obligation to
do nothing that will promote segregation. However, this is a community
problem, and not solely a problem for the schools." He referred to the transferring of children to underutilized schools as a good step but a side factor;
open enrollment was good as long as it did not lead to overcrowding. These
kinds of remarks, according to Galamison, added up to the "same old double talk" used by other city officials, such as Mayor Wagner and outgoing
Superintendent Theobald.[72]

One major problem the Parents' Workshop faced was lack of money. It
used creative ways to raise funds, including listing boosters and contributors
in the newsletters, but the cost of operating the organization, printing, and
mailing drained the workshop. In late 1962, members were asked to become
boosters and urged to seek contributions from local businesses.[73]

The militant protest movement grew out of a change in consciousness and
behavior. As political scientists Richard Cloward and Francis Fox Piven note,
there are at least three reasons why people become involved in militant protest movements: an institutional ruler loses legitimacy; people who are ordi-
narily fatalistic begin to assert their rights; people who once saw themselves as
helpless begin seeing themselves as powerful and able to make change.[74]

The board and its officials lost legitimacy by failing to take serious steps
to desegregate the school system. Parents involved in the grassroots organization saw themselves as agents for change. Through the threat of protest
they won some victories but not the ultimate prize, a city-wide program for
integration. Fueled with confidence in their ability to bring about change
through protest, and confronted by the board's inability or unwillingness to
make major changes, by 1963 they were ready for a major confrontation.

# chapter five

# THE FIRST CITY-WIDE
# SCHOOL BOYCOTT

In 1960, 37 percent of the 986,679 pupils in New York City schools were black or Latino. A special census taken on October 3, 1960, pointed out that 212,006 blacks accounted for 21 percent, and 153,967 Puerto Ricans accounted for 16 percent of the student body. By 1964, blacks accounted for about 26 percent or 264,600 of the total and Puerto Ricans about 17 percent or 177,544 of the student body in New York City's 860 public schools. There were close to one million children in the system.[1] But after numerous studies, policy statements, as well as commission and committee recommendations, little had been accomplished. The number of segregated schools had increased.[2]

Part of the increase was due to the increase in the number of blacks and Latinos in the city and a decrease in the number of whites. Housing segregation, white flight to the suburbs, and the shift of white children from public schools to private institutions all contributed to the increase in segregated schools. Board of Education policy was a major factor for segregation,

however. The board failed to implement its own commission's rezoning recommendations, including changing feeder patterns and building schools in
areas where desegregation would be possible; that is, in fringe areas that THE FIRST
bordered black and white neighborhoods.³ Instead the Board of Education CITY-WIDE
built schools where segregation would be assured, in the heart of black and SCHOOL BOYCOTT
Puerto Rican neighborhoods. While this would relieve overcrowding, it
would not address problems associated with segregation, such as the quality of teaching staff, instruction, and student services.

By January 1963, nothing had been done to diminish the cynicism of
Galamison and the activist parents struggling for school integration. In the
January newsletter, Galamison criticized the acting superintendent, Bernard
Donovan (Theobald had resigned), for appointing yet another "committee
to study ways of furthering integration in the schools." The Siloam pastor,
sounding exasperated, pointed out that numerous committees had been
created before to "study" ways of desegregating the schools. Despite competent recommendations, the board had refused to implement them. Sending
a clear message to board officials, Galamison declared "the acid test of our
sincerity does not lie alone in the appointment of committees and the cat-
aloging of recommendations. The test of our sincerity lies in the doing of
what needs to be done. For this no study is necessary. The problem is segregation. The answer is desegregation."⁴

In 1963 the civil rights movement was at its peak, with numerous campaigns, including Birmingham, Alabama, in early spring and the celebrated
March on Washington in the late summer. CORE (the Congress of Racial
Equality) had moved north and launched a fierce campaign to eradicate
ghettos. In the summer of 1963, Brooklyn CORE initiated a protest at the
construction site of the Downstate Medical Center, demanding assurances
that blacks and Puerto Ricans make up at least 25 percent of the construction workers building the medical center. Almost none of the construction
workers were people of color. When CORE's demands were ignored, the
organization turned to the ministers of Bedford-Stuyvesant for support for
a protest campaign. Galamison and thirteen other ministers from Bedford-
Stuyvesant not only agreed to join CORE but also led the demonstrations.
For two weeks, they brought their parishioners to the construction site, lay
down in front of bulldozers, and chained themselves to the fence in an
attempt to stop construction. By the end of the second week thousands had
participated in the campaign, and more than 700 people had been arrested.

Unfortunately, Governor Nelson Rockefeller and Peter Brennan, head of the construction trades union, did not bend.[5]

The number of protesters decreased and violence erupted. As the protests dragged on with no end in sight, the ministers, without the input of Brooklyn CORE, decided to work out a deal with Governor Rockefeller. The agreement included a promise by the Governor to enforce anti-discrimination laws and to establish hiring halls in Bedford-Stuyvesant. There was no mention of a quota or any change of the union practices that had led to the exclusion of blacks and Puerto Ricans from the ranks of construction workers.

Once the deal was made public, CORE accused the ministers of selling out. Galamison, who attempted to explain the settlement to protesters at the construction site, was called an "Uncle Tom" and a "sellout" and shouted down. Frustrated and angry, Galamison vowed that he would not be put in that situation again.[6]

The civil rights movement was not without its critics in the black community. Nationalist sentiment had been evident in urban black neighborhoods since the 1920s, when the nationalists had called for self-determination, economic independence from white America, and political autonomy. The messianic-nationalist group, the Nation of Islam, under the leadership of Elijah Muhammad, was in the forefront of the nationalist movement. The Nation of Islam was founded around 1930 by Wallace Fard, who taught that the true religion of blacks was Islam and that they were "Asiatic." Labeling whites as "devils," he asserted that God would eventually punish them for their subjugation of blacks. When Fard mysteriously disappeared around 1934, the movement split between those who taught that Fard was a prophet and those who believed that he was God incarnate, the latter group led by one of Fard's close followers, Elijah Muhammad.[7]

By the 1950s, Malcolm X, the young charismatic spokesman for Elijah Muhammad, had become the most outspoken critic of the civil rights movement. In numerous speeches and TV appearances Malcolm launched a frontal assault on national civil rights leaders and their tactics, often referring to them as Uncle Toms who did not represent the interests of black America. Malcolm argued that whites had no interest in integrating; integration would subjugate blacks to white control. The most viable solution to white racism and the best avenue for black progress, Malcolm contended, was black nationalism, black control of their own land, businesses, and institutions.[8]

Galamison had to defend integration as a goal against both racist whites and black nationalists. On one occasion he noted that blacks had fought in the War for Independence and the Civil War. African Americans, through their hard work, were responsible for building the nation into an industrial power. Blacks were "woven into the pattern of American life." According to the Presbyterian minister, "We have paid the fare. The question is whether we shall fight for the ride."[9]

Criticizing separatist schemes advocated by black nationalists, Galamison suggested that black nationalists were just as "arrogant" as the white supremacists. They were just imitating the "buffoonery" of white racists. The Siloam pastor said: "I cannot see black arrogance as an antidote for the negation of white arrogance. The cure resembles the illness." He declared integration must work because "nothing else can" and called for a common front against bigotry. Galamison rejected nationalism because it isolated blacks, dividing them from those with whom they had a great deal in common. On March 27, he debated Malcolm on the issue of integration. Galamison remembered that the debate, which was televised, drifted from the issue of integration to a debate about Islam versus Christianity. The Presbyterian pastor and integrationist did not recall that either he or his debating adversary expressed any faith in American institutions as the saviors of blacks.[10]

Despite their differences, a respect between Galamison and the fiery young Muslim minister developed. During the Downstate campaign, Malcolm made an appearance at the construction site. While he did not join the protest, because he felt that its objective was not in the best interest of blacks, his arrival demonstrated respect for the demonstrators and their efforts. According to Galamison, Malcolm expressed his respect and admiration during this diligent campaign. Malcolm's attitude reflected an ideological switch. In 1962 he had wanted the Nation of Islam to become actively involved in the civil rights movement, but Elijah Muhammad had ruled against it, leaving Malcolm frustrated. Circumstances would later draw Galamison and Malcolm X closer together.[11]

In 1963, James Allen, State Commissioner of Education, ordered school boards throughout the state to report on action taken to achieve racial balance, noting that, if a school was more than fifty percent nonwhite, it was to be considered racially unbalanced. It was the job of school districts to correct the problem because such schools were inferior. What Allen demanded was difficult for New York City, where the black and Hispanic school population was increasing. As the minority population grew, the number of segregated schools increased, making the goal of a racially balanced school system difficult.[12]

In spite of the difficulties, Allen's request was the best alternative in a system that had created separate and unequal facilities and had made little attempt to remedy the condition over the years. In New York City, the assumption that predominantly black and Hispanic schools were mediocre was well founded, due not just to slum conditions but to the Board of Education's lack of effort as well. It was apparent to civil rights leaders that the board had failed to make the change—unacceptable behavior in a period when civil rights militancy had led to gains in the South and elsewhere. Ordinary citizens and grassroots organizations, such as Parents' Workshop; the Harlem Parents Committee, founded in 1963 by parents upset with the lack of leadership in New York NAACP chapters and led by Isaiah Robinson and Thelma Johnson; and Brooklyn CORE, were taking a stronger stance. Because of these pressures (and probably fearing a loss of clout), the NAACP and the Urban League in New York took a more militant position in the school integration struggle and were ready to take stronger action. In 1963 the NAACP, CORE, and the Urban League decided to join the Parents' Workshop and the Harlem Parents Committee (HPC) to work for school integration. The decision meant that there was a major force for school desegregation.[13]

But why would the conventional organizations work with grassroots groups? Probably because these community-based organizations had gained strength and notoriety. Grassroots organizations such as the Parents' Workshop and HPC were leading the struggle by relying on an organizing tradition and consistently challenging Board of Education and city officials. For the older civil rights groups to remain viable, they would have to join forces with the groups that had taken the lead in the school integration battle. Hence the NAACP and the Urban League decided to take a more confrontative position in the New York City school integration struggle. It should be noted that many branches of CORE had relied on militant tactics, including mass demonstrations, sit-ins, and rent strikes in support of tenants in ghetto areas.[14]

The Parents' Workshop, HPC, and other groups that made up the militant wing of the school integration campaign should not be given full credit for bringing together both factions of the school integration struggle. The

Board of Education's recalcitrance and unwillingness to present a city-wide school integration program angered civil rights groups. Nine years after the Brown decision and the board's statement pledging to do away with segregated schools, no serious steps had been taken by the school agency to desegregate the school system. The NAACP and the other older civil rights groups came to the conclusion that some type of coercion seemed to be the only viable solution. By the summer of 1963, the radical wing of the school integration movement that relied on grassroots organizing, collective assertiveness, and mass action joined with the more mainstream civil rights groups that had in the past relied on negotiation and cooperation, and was distrustful of left forces.

In the summer of 1963 the New York Citywide Committee for Integrated Schools was organized. The group consisted of the six New York chapters of the NAACP, several chapters of CORE, the Parents' Workshop, and the HPC. The Urban League of Greater New York was only an observer; while participating in decisionmaking, it did not join in street demonstrations, claiming it was not a protest group.[15]

Galamison was reluctant to discuss why he had been chosen as leader of the new organization, although he did mention that he was probably selected to lead the City-Wide Committee because the NAACP and CORE were rival organizations. The leader of the Parents' Workshop was not nationally known and did not, at that point, represent a threat to either organization. Moreover, as a pastor he had time to devote to the organization. His years of struggle for school integration may have helped. Whatever the reason, in a private session of the coalition it was decided he would lead the City-Wide Committee.[16]

Besides giving greater acknowledgment to the fight for integration, the City-Wide Committee for Integrated Schools also assisted Galamison in broadening his base. It enhanced his reputation as a civil rights leader; he was no longer the head of a grassroots organization but of a powerful coalition of prominent civil rights groups. Although a leader of the New York City civil rights community, he found he would have to share the spotlight with others and work in a coalition. Since he would be speaking not just for his own organization but for several civil rights groups as well, he would have to reach a consensus on issues, tactics, strategies, and negotiations.[17]

By this time Galamison was publicly calling the Board of Education obstructionist, using rhetoric espousing the goal of integration in order to placate civil rights forces. Angry at the lack of progress in the battle for integration and the insincerity of the board, Galamison warned that pronouncements and meetings would not solve the problem: "Let us not be fooled by shallow counterfeit efforts to create the illusion of good intention." The newsletter urged parents to attend the June meeting because "we are about to become engaged in a big struggle."[18] A city-wide boycott must have been seriously contemplated. Suggesting that the City-Wide Committee would initiate some type of action, Galamison declared that Commissioner Allen had done an about face when he recanted on his characterization of a school that was 50 percent or more nonwhite as segregated. What Galamison saw as Allen's bad faith solidified his belief that a protracted city-wide boycott was needed.[19]

The fact that Galamison felt confident enough to issue threats to the board indicates that his organization was ready to launch a offensive strike. The only thing at this time that would have satisfied the civil rights community of New York was a plan and timetable for city-wide integration. In a letter addressed to Bernard Donovan, now executive deputy superintendent of schools, Galamison expressed great disappointment with the slow progress in school desegregation. He bitterly complained that the "most we have to look forward to is a scheduled series of conferences between the new Superintendent and various civic groups on a subject that has been under discussion since the appointment of the initial Commission on integration." Speaking on behalf of the Parents' Workshop, the Siloam pastor cautioned that anything that fell short of a plan to integrate the entire school system and that did not include a timetable for doing so would be insufficient.[20]

Parents could not endure another year of the "kind of deprivation children are suffering in the segregated schools without commitment on the part of the Board to change it." In a blatant threat, the civil rights leader proclaimed: "We can no longer permit the public school system to function while the needs of our children are not being met." He gave the board until the ninth of September to come up with a plan and a timetable. There was no mention of what would happen if the board did not submit a plan by that date.[21]

A late August meeting with new Superintendant of Schools Dr. Calvin Gross and civil rights leaders failed to produce an involuntary transfer plan of white and black children for integration. Gross said he could not support involuntary transfers nor come up with a timetable. The City-Wide

Committee announced that it would carry out a city-wide boycott of public schools.

Although the Parents' Workshop and the Harlem Parents Committee were pushing for a boycott because they felt that board officials were insincere, the older civil rights groups also went along with the idea. The board's programs had failed miserably. Permissive Zoning, Higher Horizons, and Open Enrollment had made only minimal progress in integrating the schools and improving conditions for children in the ghetto. The time for action had arrived, since the board did not seem willing to move beyond this point.

Once the civil rights groups had decided on a boycott, the length of the protest had to be discussed. There was disagreement, which reflected the different views on approaches to the struggle. Galamison, members of HPC, and other militants contended that prolonged mass action was the only sure solution to move the board. They argued that the boycott should be a protracted one, carried out until the Board of Education presented a serious plan with a timetable for integration. Galamison believed that the board would not react unless it was seriously wounded financially. Keeping children out of school over a period of time would cost the board a huge amount of money in state funds. A long boycott would also demonstrate a commitment to the struggle. The more moderate groups in the coalition, among them the NAACP, argued for a one-day boycott, which would embarrass the board and force school officials to consider the consequences if they failed to respond. They were hoping that such a boycott would force board officials to the bargaining table. Galamison and others argued, however, that a brief boycott would not be as effective as a sustained one and might actually backfire, giving the board a chance to regroup and build support. After a prolonged discussion the group decided on a one-day boycott if the board did not come up with a plan and timetable for integration.[22]

Galamison, who wanted to assure that hundreds of thousands of people would take part in the demonstration asked Bayard Rustin to help organize the boycott. In the 1930s Rustin had organized the Young Communist League and campaigned against racism in the armed forces. He became disillusioned with the Communist Party and left when the party moved away from passivism and backed the United States war effort during Word War II. But Rustin continued to fight for social justice, working closely with the African American socialist A. Philip Randolph. Rustin helped organize CORE in the early 1940s and carried out numerous nonviolent demonstrations. An aide to

Martin Luther King Jr. during the Montgomery Bus Boycott, Rustin organized the 1963 March On Washington, which drew 250,000 people. The Presbyterian pastor welcomed Rustin's expertise.[23]

To prepare for the boycott, Galamison extended his coalition to include
ministers through ministerial networking, a tactic used in the civil rights
movement. Although the ministers did not take a leading role in the boycott, as they had in the Downstate Medical Center campaign, many pledged
their support by opening their churches and sponsoring rallies. A group of
twenty Brooklyn ministers announced on September 1 that they were prepared to open their churches as "freedom schools" if the board failed to
come up with an integration plan and timetable.[24]

Borrowed from the Southern civil rights campaigns, freedom schools
were makeshift classes held during regular school hours and taught by professional and nonprofessional volunteers. The schools would be open to both
black and white children. The twenty ministers, who met at the Stuyvesant
Christian Church on Tompkins Avenue and McDonough Street in Bedford-
Stuyvesant, told reporters that they would also call for a mass rally to support
the boycott. To pressure the board, the Reverend Gardner C. Taylor, chairman of the meeting at Stuyvesant Christian Church, declared: "I plan to be
the first one on that picket line if this integration issue isn't satisfactorily set-
tled by next Monday." Because of his prominence, it was decided at the meeting that Taylor would be the main speaker at the rally at 9 P.M. at Cornerstone
Baptist Church.[25]

Board officials worked desperately to avoid the boycott, recognizing that
it could have grave consequences. They agreed to prepare a timetable, to
provide the civil rights organizations with an analysis of the techniques involved in the integration plan, and to create a policy integration council. In
spite of their efforts, civil rights groups saw the board's agreement as a
stalling tactic, a way of avoiding coming up with an affirmative plan for
racial balance. They refused to call off the strike.[26]

In a last-minute effort to prevent the mass demonstration, the board met
for four and a half hours with civil rights groups at the City Commission on
Human Rights office. It agreed to the civil rights groups' demands and announced that it would come up with a tentative plan that included a timetable for integrating the schools by December 1, 1963. Stanley Lowell, chairman of the commission, told the press that the board would consult with
civil rights groups and specify the effects of various techniques used to inte-

grate the schools. The board also agreed to come up with a final plan in
February 1964. Lowell said that the school superintendent would include a
provision for a substantial, realistic, and workable program of integration
for every school district by September 1964. By threatening a city-wide boycott, the Committee was able to force the board to the negotiating table.
Galamison would later write that the civil rights group had pressured the
board to come up with a tentative desegregation plan by December 1, 1963,
which would accomplish "substantial integration," and allow civil rights
groups to review the plan. The board also agreed to grant "professional and
advisory representation in the development of the plan."[27]

Although Galamison warned the agreement would have to be approved
by a meeting of the full City-Wide Committee, he was confident that the
entire body would agree to the suspension of the planned demonstration.
However, if the board did not live up to its promises, a new date would be
set for the boycott.[28] Galamison's warning may have been used to build a
consensus within the City-Wide Committee. As was acknowledged at the
press conference, the Harlem Parents Committee did not want to call off
the boycott, while more moderate elements such as the NAACP were probably relieved that the demonstration had been postponed. Galamison had
to appeal to both factions, and his statement that announced a postpone-
ment while adding a militant warning probably did the trick in satisfying
both factions.

When December 1 rolled around, however, Gross had still not presented a plan, stirring an angry response from the head of the Parents' Workshop. Galamison claimed that the superintendent had not kept his commitment to the City-Wide Committee for School Integration. Moreover,
Max Wolff, a prominent educator, had been selected by the Committee as
their professional representative. Galamison claimed that when the Committee agreed to call off the boycott, the board dismissed Wolff. Galamison
threatened: "We will answer this breach of faith in due time."[29] The boycott
was on.

The United Federation of Teachers (UFT) entered the fray by offering its
own plan for integrating the schools. While the UFT did not support the
demands of the City-Wide Committee, it called for city-wide school integration of pupils and professional staff. Specifically, it asked the board to reduce
class size in selected or difficult schools to no more than twenty-two students
and to provide additional guidance counselors, remedial and psychological

services, supervisors, and teachers. The Teachers Union called for the selection of seventeen schools in the first year, ten elementary, five junior high schools, and two high schools; thirty more the second year, and sixty more the third year. To reduce class size in the selected schools to twenty-two, it called for the transfer of 12,000 to 15,000 students over the three-year period from segregated black schools to predominantly white schools. Although the plan did not call for transferring white children into black neighborhoods, UFT officials argued that when white parents saw the improvements in the selected schools, they would want to send their children to them. They also asserted that reducing class size to twenty-two would result in transferring many black and Puerto Rican children to schools with a predominantly white student body.[30]

The plan also advocated increased construction of schools in black communities and in areas that would promote school integration with a minimum of bussing. The UFT called for teacher to teacher recruitment; the board and the union would cooperate to set up examination centers outside New York to recruit black and Hispanic teachers.[31] The plan also recommended creating a preschool nursery plan, supervised by licensed Board of Education professionals, giving preschoolers preparation and early identification of psychological problems impeding learning. The UFT doubted that mass student bussing could effectively bring about a racially balanced school system, but it recommended the board adopt the "buddy school" or Princeton plan for "mass pupil transfer."[32]

Although the UFT asserted that they supported city-wide integration, their plan was limited to "selected schools," involving at the most the transfer of 15,000 students over a three-year period. The burden for integration would fall on the backs of black and Hispanic children. Moreover, by advocating a recruiting effort in cities with large numbers of black teachers, it implied that the scarcity of black and Hispanic teachers in New York was due not to racism, but simply to the lack of qualified blacks and Hispanics in New York. There was no discussion of the plan to recruit from other areas, such as private industry. There was no mention of increasing salaries to attract people, nor was there a call for examining the criteria used for hiring. The UFT plan stressed providing guidance and psychological services for children in black and Hispanic neighborhoods, leaving the impression that these children were failing because they were psychologically impaired. It did not acknowledge that thousands of black and Hispanic children did not receive a full day's instruction or that they had the least experienced teachers. CORE noted that seventy percent of the math teachers in predominantly black and Hispanic schools were unlicensed.

In spite of the UFT's position, a number of teachers joined ranks with the civil rights organizations. One such group was the New York Teachers for Quality Integrated Education, which organized meetings, handed out leaflets, and spoke out for the boycott. At one of its meetings, Milton Galamison was the guest speaker. It would also help organize the demonstration at 110 Livingston Street on February 3. A few days before the boycott the teachers' group organized another meeting in conjunction with the Greenwich Village-Chelsea Branch of the NAACP. Galamison, Isaiah Robinson from the Harlem Parents Committee, and Fred Jones of the New York State NAACP spoke. The group asserted: "It is the teacher's professional responsibility to lead the fight for integrated quality education for all children."[33]

## Breakdown and Grassroots Protest

Instead of presenting a plan for city-wide integration along with a timetable for its implementation, Superintendent Gross issued a progress report and called for more Open Enrollment. The City-Wide Committee rejected Gross's plan, calling it a breach of faith, and issued an open letter accusing him of procrastinating. Brooklyn CORE immediately called for the superintendent's removal and the replacement of the entire board with a new one that was forty percent black and Hispanic. Arnold Goldwag, community director of Brooklyn CORE, said Gross was "willing to grant the same equality to Negro children gradually and eventually. We are tired of this."[34]

In a show of defiance and anger, the City-Wide Committee held a demonstration at the headquarters of the board at 110 Livingston Street. An all-night vigil was held at Siloam by black and white supporters of school integration. In addition, Galamison and twenty-five others were arrested for trying to stage a sit-in at the offices of Superintendent Gross, James Donovan, president of the board, and other Board of Education officials. Galamison's goal was to "disrupt the school system," he told reporters, demonstrating that parents were willing to "go to jail" to gain civil rights.

While marching outside Gross's office, members of Brooklyn CORE announced that the organization was preparing a sit-in at the governor's and mayor's offices shortly after New Year's, to kick off the February 3 boycott. Galamison, Thelma Johnson, and Isaiah Robinson, leaders of the Harlem Parents Committee, also demonstrated with CORE and were among forty-four arrested. Galamison explained that the new assault on the board was a protest against Gross. At 11:40 A.M. the first group of "jail birds for freedom" recruited for arrest by Galamison was taken out of the building. The demonstrators went limp; police had to carry them away. Two hundred pickets jeered the police as the first group was brought out and put into the police wagon. Most were women. Attempting to link the struggle to the civil rights struggle in the South, demonstrators shouted that the police were like those in Birmingham.[35]

To reaffirm the civil rights groups' claims, the Urban League of Greater New York issued a report declaring that segregation was getting worse in New York City. The number of elementary and junior high schools with an 85 percent or more black and Puerto Rican student body had increased, the report pointed out, and out of 5,424 teachers in 105 predominantly white schools, 31 were black. In the 109 predominantly black schools, there were 2,930 white, 1,483 black, and 77 Puerto Rican teachers. Thus, the league accused the school system not only of discriminating by not hiring people of color, but also of segregating the existing few professional staff.[36]

Frederick Jones, State Education chairman of the NAACP and representative of the thirteen New York City branches, contended that a "gap" existed between the board's stated official policy and implementation of that policy. The school agency, according to Jones, had issued a progress report instead of a plan and timetable. Jones claimed that the NAACP had offered ways of integrating the schools to the board, including revising the Princeton Plan to include large groups of schools, reorganizing grades by creating central fourth-to-sixth grade schools, reducing the grades of elementary schools, and converting secondary schools to specialized schools. Jones concluded that the New York City NAACP chapters had no choice but to mobilize for the school boycott.[37]

Roy Wilkins offered a less than enthusiastic response for the boycott. The national executive secretary of the organization, he noted that there might be times for a boycott. He said he supported the decision of the New York City branches (although he did not mention Galamison or the City-Wide Committee) but concluded, "We felt that children should go to school while adults argued the issue but that where parents decided upon a boycott we

would aid." Just three weeks earlier, the national had warned its Brooklyn
branch about participating in a sit-in at the Board of Education. Gloster
Current claimed that the branch was attempting to grab headlines instead
of evaluating proper tactics. Thus, at the height of militant activism among
civil rights advocates, the leadership of the NAACP was still reluctant to
participate in demonstrations at the grassroots level.[38]

## Attempts to Spread the Northern School Integration Struggle

While the City-Wide Committee for Integrated Schools prepared for the boycott, other cities in the North were initiating civil rights struggles, including
Chicago, Boston, and Cleveland. In an attempt to coordinate the school integration struggle in the north, thirty-two civil rights leaders from various
organizations met at the Manhattan Hotel on January 12, 1964. They included John Lewis from SNCC, James Bevel from SCLC, Albert Raby from the
Chicago Council of Community Organizations, Galamison, and Annie Stein,
who was the recording secretary for the gathering. There were representatives
from Cleveland's Citizens' Committee to Support Our Schools, United
Freedom Movement, Chester, Pennsylvania's Committee for Freedom Now,
Boston Freedom Schools, Massachusetts Freedom Movement, the Brooklyn
Ministers' Committee, Brooklyn CORE, and the Harlem Parents' Committee.
Galamison served as chairman of the meeting.[39]

John Lewis of SNCC (Student Nonviolent Coordinating Committeee)
gave his support for a multi-city boycott of schools, calling on people
throughout the country to make February "Stay away from school Month."
The Chicago delegation contended that 87 percent of the public schools
were segregated in that city. They carried out a boycott in the fall of 1963
and reported that 224,000 blacks and 10,000 to 15,000 whites had participated. However, boycott organizers admitted that little was accomplished
and there was no equivalent to Open Enrollment in Chicago. Still, the Chicago boycott made people aware of the problems, gaining more support for
the struggle. Because the Chicago School Board refused to consider most of
their demands, boycott leaders created the Chicago Freedom Day Committee to contact other civil rights groups nationwide and bring national pressure on local communities.[40]

Delegates from Chester, Pennsylvania, claimed that 1,200 black children had been forced to attend a segregated school built for 500 students more than fifty years before. Students were attending classes in a basement coalbin, and some were forced to take classes in a nearby housing project near a boiler room. There were only two toilets in the school. Pressure from the Chester group forced the school board to transfer 200 students to another predominantly black overcrowded school. While the school board also built two new schools, there was no attempt to desegregate.

The situation was no better in Cleveland, according to activists. Ninety-three percent of the children attended segregated elementary and junior high schools in that city. Despite picketing, the school board backed the neighborhood school concept. The civil rights movement in Cleveland did not have the support of black churches; only two black ministers were involved in the movement.

Delegates from Boston accused the black bourgeoisie of being apathetic toward the movement. Black ministers voted against the boycott, urging students to go to school. The delegation also contended that the school board had reneged on its promise to integrate schools and hire black teachers. Out of 3,000 teachers in Boston, only thirty-nine were black. It was reported that Gary, Indiana, Philadelphia, Hartford, Connecticut, Indianapolis, and Cambridge supported taking some type of action.[41]

The meeting produced mixed results for a multicity boycott. Cleveland delegates voiced support but warned that they would not participate in a February action, due to an extremely conservative "power structure." Representatives from Boston, Chicago, the Cleveland chapter of CORE, SNCC, and the National Lawyers Guild supported the formation of a permanent organization to end segregation in public education. A national representative from CORE argued against a permanent organization, however, and advocated exchanging ideas and plans. The delegates agreed that an informal organization could not address the numerous civil rights issues in these cities. They needed permanent groups that could challenge a well-organized "power structure" set on upholding the status quo. It was moved that members support a multicity boycott of schools on February 11. Galamison and the New York delegation argued for February 3; others gave no specific date in February.

In the end, the group voted to create a "Temporary Freedom Day Committee," naming Galamison as its chair, and to meet again on January 25, urging those who were present to invite others. The "loosely knit" organization

would support a school boycott in February, meeting in Chicago on January
25. Showing great enthusiasm for the Freedom Day Committee, Galamison
sent out a news release, informing the public that thirty persons representing
urban civil rights groups had "voted unanimously to support a multicity boycott of public schools" sometime in February.[42] In spite of Galamison's ex-
citement, too many questions at the meeting were left unresolved, such as the
date for a multicity school boycott. There was insufficient time to plan a
coordinated effort for February and no solid commitment. At least, the meeting had reassured northern civil rights leaders that they were not isolated.

## On the Eve of the Boycott

On January 16, New York CORE chapters issued a statement accusing the
board of defaulting on its promise to the City-Wide Committee to submit a
plan for integration by December 1, including a timetable. The state of education in New York, according to the groups, was dismal. The schools were
segregated, understaffed, and overcrowded; buildings were dilapidated, and
teachers improperly trained. Segregated schools had high numbers of sub-
stitute teachers. There were 165 segregated elementary schools and 239
school buildings built before 1910. CORE asserted that the city government,
through its City Planning Commission, helped perpetuate de facto segregation. CORE called for the board to come up with a timetable for city-wide
integration, reduce class size, arrange to maximize integration, select new
sites for schools, and work closely with the Board of Higher Education to recruit thousands of teachers. The board of Examiners, responsible for ad-
ministering tests for school professional staff, should stop excluding people
because of southern drawls or Spanish accents. The board should increase
teachers' salaries as an incentive to attracting new people, actively recruit
teachers from "every walk of life and ethnic grouping," and offer courses for
people to become supervisors.[43]

If there were any doubts about the cohesiveness of the coalition in
New York, the board's continued failure to live up to its agreement only
helped solidify the committee. By blatantly refusing to come up with a
serious plan, the board angered moderates as well as radicals. Fred Jones,
state education chair of the NAACP, asserted: "we have a series of bad faith
experiences with the Board of Education and there is absolutely nothing

at present which would make us call off the boycott." Jones argued that the "Board has simply proposed the same plan of voluntary free transfers that we rejected last August as piecemeal." He argued that the plan was "completely inadequate to meet the urgent problems of de facto segregated and unequal schools."[44] All the groups in the City-Wide Committee, agreeing that the board had failed to provide for "substantial and meaningful school desegregation throughout the City," supported a boycott.[45]

On Sunday, January 19, appearing on the WCBS television program *Newsmakers*, Galamison justified a boycott by arguing that it would show the public the "Negro's resentment to segregation and inferior schools." Contending that the school boycott was part of the black revolt in the United States, he hoped it would cause enough embarrassment to force the board to take action.[46]

In spite of Galamison's determination, the program revealed that some national civil rights leaders were not in full agreement with the boycott. Reporters on the television program noted that Roy Wilkins and Whitney Young had criticized the young minister. Wilkins contended: "We are not committing ourselves to a spread of boycotts. Our organization believes it is better for children to go to school than to stay home." Whitney Young lashed out at Galamison, implying that he had taken a shortcut to leadership by getting involved in civil rights.

Unwilling to attack these leaders on television, Galamison said only that it was necessary to keep children out of school to bring pressure on the board. The minister remarked that "those who are fighting for the rights of the Negro people—and there are countless people involved in this besides the ones who have achieved any national distinction—go pretty much unsung."[47]

Wilkins's and Young's complaints about Galamison were not new. When Galamison was head of the Brooklyn NAACP, he had come under criticism from the executive director of the national organization for his militancy. National leaders were unable to control Galamison. In a sense, they had become rivals, fighting for the loyalty of, and legitimacy among, African Americans.

Galamison's comments about violence may also have provoked fear in more moderate civil rights leaders. Although he said he was committed to nonviolence, the Presbyterian pastor let it be known that blacks were questioning the usefulness of the tactic. Noting that nothing had been gained at the Downstate protest the previous summer, Galamison declared: "Nobody wants violence, but once we turn a group of people loose in a demonstration, nobody can be responsible for everybody's conduct, and this must be realized."[48] This type of language may have contributed to the uneasiness of national leaders, and disturbed some within the coalition.

Galamison's dislike for James Donovan, President of the Board of Education, also became apparent during *Newsmakers*. Accusing Donovan of attempting to divide and conquer by inviting some civil rights leaders for a discussion and excluding him, Galamison insisted that Donovan resign because he had displayed neither the sympathy nor the understanding it took to be board president. Armed with statistics, Galamison refuted the view that segregation was caused by the increase in black and Puerto Rican student enrollments. He noted segregated junior high schools had increased from nine to thirty-one between 1954 and 1964, a "300 percent" increase that did not match the 7 percent growth in population. He blamed the board for segregation.[49]

On January 22, 1964, the City-Wide Committee criticized the school agency's suggestion that the public should decide on an integration plan. Such a plan, the committee asserted, should not be held up for public referendum: "Were the people ready for integration the Supreme Court decision would not have been necessary in the first instance." The proposal, according to the committee, did not provide desegregation of Harlem and Bedford-Stuyvesant, and the Princeton Plan was too limited. The board needed to extend the program from individual schools to the entire city.[50] The City-Wide Committee proclaimed that it must proceed with its announced plans to boycott on February 3 and to repeat this boycott as often as necessary until a specific plan and timetable for city-wide school desegregation was presented with all the necessary guarantees.

Galamison worked diligently to spread the word of the boycott. With Siloam as headquarters, meetings were held with representatives of civic and civil rights groups to plan the demonstration. Galamison held orientation and organization meetings at the church, attracting representatives from twelve groups. He addressed several meetings attempting to gain support for the action. In late December he addressed a public meeting in St. Albans Plaza in Queens, arguing that churches, civic, and civil rights groups should work together for civil rights.[51] A few days later he attended a "cocktail meeting" at the apartment of Norma Becker, a member of Teachers

Action for Integrated Quality Education. The New York organization asserted: "It is the Teacher's professional responsibility to lead the fight for integrated quality education for all children."[52]

Galamison revealed plans for a children's march on the day of the February boycott. Using the 1963 March on Washington as a model, he said children participating in the boycott would line up in designated areas in Bedford-Stuyvesant and march to board headquarters. He urged people not to be distracted by misleading comments and to try to recruit people for the march to 110 Livingston Street. Galamison asked those who could not march to call the board demanding an end to Jim Crow schools. Lists would be given out in front of schools directing people to the nearest freedom school.[53]

Ordinary people played a major role in organizing the boycott. Volunteers worked in boycott centers, producing thousands of pieces of boycott literature and distributing the materials throughout the city. One such flyer urged parents to keep their children out of school on February 3, and to instead send them to the supervised freedom centers in their neighborhood. It also urged parents to join picket lines and attend the City Hall demonstration. Volunteers worked on committees to direct the various demonstrations at school sites; they ran off a twenty-page guide for freedom school leaders. Preparing to operate the 500 freedom schools, scheduled to open at 7:30 A.M. and close at 5:00 P.M., they created lessons for children on the origins and nature of the civil rights movement. Some volunteers, including licensed teachers, college students, and parents, served as teachers, while others answered the telephones at headquarters. Many attended rallies, giving both moral and financial support to the boycott. People stenciled posters, made peanut butter and jelly sandwiches, and swept the floors of boycott headquarters, working well into the night. The movement saw parents rise to leadership positions. A new militant movement had come to life, thanks to the efforts of a coalition of traditional civil rights and grassroots groups, ministers, parents, and people concerned about the education of black and Puerto Rican children.[54]

The opening of freedom schools on the day of the boycott solved the problem of children who did not attend school and whose parents had to go to work during the protest. It was a way of gaining support from parents who feared that their children would be out on the streets, unsupervised. On the other hand, it disclosed the perception New York City school integrationists had of their movement. In Mississippi, civil rights activists established freedom schools in order to challenge Jim Crow and its effects on African Americans living in that state. They learned reading and writing, black history, and the history of the civil rights movement.[55] New York civil rights activists argued that the school integration movement was part of the larger black freedom movement. Similar to the freedom schools of Mississippi, New York City freedom schools challenged racism by redefining teaching and education. People who served as teachers were those who did not necessarily have teaching certification from the state or experience. They were people who were dedicated to freedom. They were willing to sacrifice their time in order to educate children for the day. Although science, mathematics, and English were taught, emphasis on black history, black literature, and the history of the civil rights movement were included in the curriculum. Hence, education was not just a means to individual success. It became an avenue for making children aware of the struggle for social justice and American democracy being waged by many people. Schools were redefined, not as stifling conventional classrooms, operated by an untouchable central body, but as places where children were cared for by dedicated professionals and nonprofessionals willing to sacrifice their time.

The creation of freedom schools also uncovered the reliance on a community-organizing tradition. Not only teacher-volunteers came to the fore, but ministers, pastors, and those who operated community organizations contributed their time for school integration. Boycott leaders appealed to community organizations and churches to open their doors for the day and serve as freedom schools. To help organize, the committee asked ministers to list their names, the address of their church, and whether they would be willing to set up a freedom school or lead a picket line. Dozens of pastors, mostly in Harlem and Brooklyn, agreed to establish freedom schools. A partial list of Brooklyn freedom schools contained thirty-four churches; a partial list of Manhattan schools listed fifty churches across denominational lines. Gardner C. Taylor of Concord Baptist church in Brooklyn volunteered to house 1,000 children in his freedom school. Newman Memorial Methodist pledged to seat 500. Others promised to seat from 30 to 300.[56]

On January 29, four days before the planned boycott, the board submitted a plan for integrating the schools. The plan offered nothing new. Attempting to deny its responsibility in the struggle for school integration, the board asserted: "[t]he moral commitments and democratic beliefs which bind the people of New York City are clearly much stronger than the differences which divide them. The differences involve primarily not ends, but means; not the values of an integrated education, but how best to bring it about; not whether the school system has a positive responsibility with regard to integration, but the extent to which the school system, as one institution of society, can aid those who have been wronged by the society."

The board blamed de facto segregation on housing, claiming it "could not possibly produce racial balance in all schools without wholesale shifts of school populations," a move the board argued would lead to "chaos." It could not solve the problem of youth unemployment. Instead, the board called for the creation of a city council on integration to address obstacles to school integration, such as housing changes, and a large-scale attack by city, state, and federal governments on the problems of slums.

Specifically, the board declared its policy was to institute common zones for elementary and junior high schools. Elementary school students should not have to travel each way more than two and one half miles, and junior high school students more than four miles to school. The schools should not be racially homogeneous. Although the board noted that 134 elementary schools had a racial makeup of 90 percent or more black and Hispanic and thirty-one junior high schools with an 85 percent or more black and Hispanic student body, it identified only twenty sets of elementary and ten sets of junior high schools that met the criteria for pairing. The plan called for the closing of Girls High School, an old, inadequate school with a 95 percent black and Hispanic student body, and for improving Benjamin Franklin High School, which had an 89 percent black and Hispanic student body.[57]

The board admitted that large numbers of elementary schools were on short-day schedules, practically all of them black and Hispanic. It also admitted that there were thousands of unused seats, mostly in predominantly white schools. It claimed that it would bus children to eliminate short days, provided that the traveling time did not exceed forty-five minutes. The plan also called for reducing class size, increasing special services in the schools, building improvements in ghetto schools, supplying additional regular teachers, examining existing zone lines on a school-by-school basis for integration purposes, equitably distributing black teaching staff, attempting to attract more black and Hispanic teachers and providing more in-service training for teachers. The board declared that it would initiate its plan in September 1964 and the process of pairing would be completed in September 1966.[58]

The board's admission that it was not providing a full day's education for thousands of black and Hispanic children was an admission of guilt, underlining what parents and community activists had been saying for years: the board was providing unequal education for black and Hispanic children.

The City-Wide Committee rejected the board's last-ditch effort, reaffirming that the boycott was still set for February 3. Both the Urban League of Greater New York, which had not originally given its support to the boycott, and the National Association for Puerto Rican Civil Rights, an organization created in late 1963, announced that they would support the February 3 demonstration. Criticizing the board's proposal, the civil rights groups maintained it was not a city-wide integration plan, since 114 out of 134 predominantly nonwhite elementary schools would remain segregated, only ten junior high schools would be integrated, and no specific plans had been offered for the high schools. The City-Wide Committee also claimed that the city's construction budget would result in an increase in segregated schools.[59]

In a final effort to win teachers' support for the civil rights demonstration, and as a show of determination to carry out the boycott, the City-Wide Committee issued "An Appeal to the Conscience of Teachers." Galamison asked union president Charles Cogen and the membership of the UFT to respect the boycott because they believed integrated schools would give teachers the opportunity to function effectively in the classroom. Galamison appealed to teachers to "participate in this lesson in citizenship which will enable us to more effectively put your knowledge to work through integrated education which reflects the real world in which our children live and grow." He urged teachers not to cross the picket line. Despite the appeal, the UFT did not publicly endorse the boycott. Instead, it asserted that it would protect the rights of any teacher who decided not to cross the picket lines. Without the support of the union, the threat of disciplinary action from board officials was too great.[60]

Bayard Rustin announced to the press that the objective of the boycott was to keep as many children out of school as possible. Picket lines would be mounted from 6:30 A.M. until noon at designated schools and at the board's headquarters. Demonstrators from Brooklyn and Queens would march to 110 Livingston Street, demonstrators from Manhattan would march to City Hall, and protesters from the Bronx would march to Governor Rockefeller's office at 20 West 55th Street. Rustin claimed that 5,000 pickets would be on the streets by 6:30 A.M. The targets would be segregated schools.[61]

Although Galamison was seen as the leader of the boycott, Rustin was clearly the organizer. Participants in organizing the boycott recall the organizer of the March on Washington's efforts in the New York protest. Leon Modeste asserts that Rustin mapped out every detail of the boycott. He created maps and charts, printed instructions to boycotters and spoke to demonstrators at the church about the boycott. Modeste remembers coming to Siloam and seeing charts plastered all over the basement listing sites of picket lines and times when demonstrators were to appear and leave. Gwendolyn Timmons also recalls seeing Rustin at Siloam giving instructions and creating charts. In order to assure large turnout for the event, Rustin created a form for ministers throughout the city requesting their support for the boycott. The ministers who had been asked whether they would be willing to participate in the demonstration and use their churches as freedom schools for the day responded in overwhelming numbers. Dozens of ministers agreed to rally their church members for support and open their churches as freedom schools on February 3.[62]

In a last attempt to avoid the boycott, board officials met with members of the City-Wide Committee. The meeting was a disaster. According to Stanley Lowell, who attended the session, the two sides could not even agree on the purpose of the meeting. Realizing that it could not avert the one-day boycott, school officials announced that they did not plan any other moves to stop the demonstration. However, to reduce support for the boycott among board personnel, Dr. Bernard E. Donovan, the executive deputy superintendent acknowledged in a radio message that there would probably be a boycott but warned teachers and supervisors that they must report to work on February 3. If there were any unauthorized absences, the board would regard them as neglect of duty. Appealing to parents to send their children to school, James B. Donovan, president of the board announced that all schools would be open.[63]

Rustin accused the board of unduly pressuring teachers. If they supported the boycott, teachers would not only lose a day's pay, but would also be charged with neglect of duty. This could disqualify any teacher from a future administrative position.[64]

As the boycott drew near, demonstration leaders attempted to allay public fears about violence. Bayard Rustin told reporters that he expected 200,000 pupils and their parents to participate in the demonstration. Rustin also met with top police officials, promising that the participants would not initiate violence. Police officials in turn assured him that they would not interfere in peaceful picketing. Galamison was less reassuring, asserting that "violence is always possible," and it might be wise for parents to keep their children home. In part, Galamison was being honest. It was impossible for him or any other civil rights leader to guarantee that violence would not erupt at the demonstration. On the other hand, the civil rights leader may have been trying to scare many parents into keeping their children out of school, thereby increasing the numbers of absentees.[65]

Civil rights groups accused Mayor Wagner of doing nothing to help the situation. Two days before the boycott they implored the Mayor to use his office to help create a plan and timetable for desegregating the schools but to no avail. Wagner would not interfere.[66]

To win support for the board, James Donovan called the boycott a "lawless course of action." He swore he would not give in to pressure and would hold the Siloam pastor personally responsible if any child were hurt during the demonstration. Donovan accused Galamison and others of conducting a campaign of intimidation, keeping children out of school by mentioning the possibility of violence.[67]

The boycott became a test of strength. Galamison wanted to demonstrate that the civil rights movement (which he characterized as "his movement") was able to keep enough kids out of school to cripple the board, forcing it to come up with an extensive integration plan. On the eve of the boycott, however, one burning question went unanswered. Were the civil rights leaders putting too much faith in the one-day demonstration? If the board did not give in to their demand for a city-wide integration plan and timetable, what next? The civil rights groups proposed holding one-day boycotts at intervals, but how would they maintain their support among the masses?

As the day of the boycott neared, it became apparent that the major objective of the City-Wide Committee—a plan and timetable for integration of all city schools—was dividing the conventional interracial coalition for better education, as well as liberals in New York City. Not everyone saw similarities between New York and the South. Some liberal groups asserted that school integration was impossible as long as de facto segregation and ghettos existed and the nonwhite student population increased while the white population decreased. They feared a mass exodus of white, middle-class families to the suburbs or of white children into private schools, if they were forced to attend ghetto schools. What was needed was improvement and integration without extreme methods. According to the United Parents Association, "goals cannot be achieved by keeping children out of school but only by unremitting day by day effort by government, by school officials and by parents." It called the boycott "destructive." The American Jewish Committee and the Catholic Interracial Council also opposed the boycott. Kenneth Clark, an outspoken critic of the board, also rejected the boycott, instead calling for school improvement as the best means to integration.[68]

In spite of criticism, boycott organizers geared up for February 3. Leaflets and flyers were issued to mobilize people for the event. The Parents Action Committee for Equality, one of several parent groups supporting the boycott, asked parents in Harlem to support the demonstration, making both an existential and self-interest appeal: "Won't you now insure for yourself and your family that sense of pride and that unique feeling of satisfaction that comes with knowing that you expressed your interest in a meaningful way?" Not acting, according to the group, allows others to speak for you.[69] The Astoria-Long Island City NAACP chapter held a mass school meeting on January 31 at the Jacob Riis Queensbridge House community center, where speakers gave final instructions for the boycott and freedom schools.[70]

A few days before the event, the City-Wide Committee issued a manual to civil rights, fraternal, and religious organizations, suggesting the best way to mobilize for "Freedom Day" was by distributing leaflets and contacting people by phone. Local groups were urged to print leaflets encouraging people to boycott and directing them to freedom schools. The group, targeting women, suggested that leaflets be handed out near beauty parlors, laundromats, and grocery stores. Ministers were given leaflets to hand out to their parishioners and were encouraged to speak about the boycott the Sunday before the event.[71]

The City-Wide Committee issued an elaborate question-and-answer flyer making a moral appeal to New Yorkers. Major civil rights organizations, parents, and church groups were working to end "inferior segregated education of our children." Noting the evils of segregation, the City-Wide Committee asserted the American ideal that "all men are created equal" and, therefore, all are entitled to equal education. The Committee wanted "to wipe out the last vestiges of de facto segregated schools in order that our children no longer be disadvantaged by a system that is not only contrary to the law of the land but robs our children of the right to their place in tomorrow's world."[72]

The committee contended that the board should integrate because of the

1954 Brown decision and its own statements: "they have no choice but to provide a complete education for all children and this will only be achieved through the integration of all our schools." Declaring that the board had accomplished nothing in a ten-year period to integrate the schools, the City-Wide Committee pressured it to take action. Placing black and white children in the same school was not integration; it was the first step. The board must be ready to provide a "meaningful integrated educational experience." Claiming that the neighborhood school was legally and morally wrong (it was not provided for in the Constitution or state laws), the committee urged parents to boycott inferior schools.[73]

To assure a successful nonviolent protest, instructions were issued to picket captains, who were given the responsibility for maintaining order at picket sites. Picket lines should be "carried out in a quiet and orderly fashion." Pickets were encouraged to sing freedom songs to "maintain spirit." Captains were also allowed to speak to the press when no representatives of the five organizations that made up the City-Wide Committee were present. Captains were to carry a list of freedom schools and to direct people to them. They would survey the area on arrival to locate entrances and telephones. The picket line should be at the front of the main entrance, with other picket lines being formed as enough people became available. The stress was on order and nonviolence.[74]

At a rally held at Concord Baptist Church the night before the boycott, an estimated crowd of one thousand sang "We Shall Not be Moved" and heard their leaders denounce the Board of Education. The crowd of blacks, Hispanics, and whites heard Rustin, Galamison, and Gardner C. Taylor speak on the significance of the demonstration. Taylor excited the crowd when he declared that the real troublemakers in the city were "the slick-talking, foot-dragging, excuse-making mass segregationists."[75] Although rhetoric that night was indeed flamboyant, a burning question remained to be answered. Would the efforts of boycott leaders and countless foot soldiers yield the dividends they so desired?

## The Day of Reckoning

The answer came on February 3, when the Board of Education estimated that 464,361 pupils, or about 45 percent of the total enrollment of 1,037,757, did not attend classes. There was peaceful picketing at 300 schools throughout the city, and 3,500 demonstrators braved the 20-degree temperature and sang freedom songs as they marched to the Board of Education for a noon rally. Moreover, 3,537, or eight percent of the 43,865 teachers stayed out of school; the normal absentee rate among teachers was three percent. After learning the results of the boycott, Bayard Rustin claimed a "tremendous success," asserting that it had been the largest civil rights demonstration in the nation's history. It showed that blacks and Hispanics could come together and work for common objectives. Boycott leaders claimed that 90,000 to 100,000 children had attended the freedom schools, although most parents probably kept their children home. The schools most affected by the boycott were in the black and Hispanic communities, Harlem, Bedford-Stuyvesant, the South Bronx, and South East Queens. At Junior High School 139 in Harlem only 100 of the 1,350 students reported and at Benjamin Franklin High School, out of 2,300 students, only 350 attended. Districts 10 and 11 in Harlem reported a 92 percent absentee rate, some schools in the Bronx, an 82 percent absentee rate. Three-quarters of the students attending school in Bedford-Stuyvesant were absent. High schools were hit hard by the boycott; close to 61,000 out of 204,000 in the academic high schools missed classes. Schools in predominantly white areas suffered little. Rustin estimated that one-fifth of the demonstrators were white.[76]

Extremely happy about the boycott, Rustin declared: "I think we are on the threshold of a new political movement." Predicting an end to discrimination in housing, jobs, and schools, he said that "winds of discontent are about to sweep over our city." He told reporters: "The boycott and the rent strike are fair warning that the civil rights revolution has reached out of the South and is now knocking at our own door."[77]

James Donovan had a different opinion of the boycott. Appearing on a television program with James Farmer, the head of CORE, the board president called the boycott a "lawless course of action" and vowed he would not "react one inch" to the demands of the protesters. Donovan repeated that he would hold Galamison "personally and criminally" responsible if any child were hurt during the boycott and that black leaders had conducted a campaign of intimidation by referring to the possibility of violence.[78]

Donovan later referred to the boycott as a "fizzle," claiming that it was easy to get children to take a holiday and that boycott leaders had intimidated and frightened parents into keeping their children out of school.

Farmer sarcastically responded: "if this is a fizzle we want more fizzles like this. . . ." Rustin called for the resignation of Donovan, declaring that he did not have the insight for the job.[79]

Despite his bravado the board president could not disregard the numbers. From all accounts the boycott was an enormous success. Although the national civil rights organizations supported the boycott, it was the grassroots people who were responsible for its success. The less celebrated people involved in the protest took few breaks, sneaking naps at headquarters. Oliver Leeds and Arnold Goldwag, both of Brooklyn CORE, dispatched picket captains to ninety-four top-priority schools (elementary schools with ninety percent or better black and Hispanics); second-priority schools (junior high and high schools with a majority of black and Hispanic students); and third-priority schools (schools with a 50 percent minority student body). Women played a key role. Some, giving up a day of work, began marching on picket lines while pushing baby carriages at 6:30 in the morning. Teachers, risking disciplinary action by the board, joined demonstrators carrying signs that read "Fight Jim Crow Schools" and "We Demand Quality Education."[80]

Freedom school volunteers—college professors, clergy, social workers, parents, and students—were racially mixed. Arnold Buchheimer, a professor at City College of New York, became a freedom school teacher for the day.[81] William Washington, a senior at William Taft High School in the Bronx, was a teacher in a freedom school at the Joseph Kennedy Community Center at West 135th Street and Lenox Terrace. He told his young students that the boycott was part of the civil rights movement. Other volunteer teachers discussed the struggle for civil rights. A freedom school at the New York Society for Ethical Culture on 64th Street in Manhattan gave students a mix of academics and recreation. Fifty-five students were registered and given name tags. First told why they were there, they had lessons in African-American history, held discussions on the meaning of freedom, and sang freedom songs. Students also wrote letters of protest to Mayor Wagner and James Donovan. Volunteers prepared lunch for the students. In the afternoon, the students played various sports and games.[82] Lee Davis, who had no children but who had nieces and nephews attending a school in Harlem, said she demonstrated at the school because something needed to be done.[83]

Elana Levy, a member of Downtown Manhattan CORE, had been involved in the Rutgers Housing Construction protest, demonstrating for jobs for blacks and Puerto Ricans in the construction trades. She began teaching at Junior High School 71 in 1963. Levy, a 22-year-old math teacher, had graduated New York University that June with a degree in math and had only taken four education courses that summer. She contended that many teachers assigned to the junior high school located on the lower east side with a predominantly black and Puerto Rican student body, were young and inexperienced. Levy worked diligently to make the boycott a success in her school, passing out leaflets to students and teachers, speaking to her classes and colleagues about the significance of the demonstration and spray-painting sidewalks with a stencil that read "Support the boycott on February 3." Levy recalls that her efforts paid off. On the day of the event, 80 percent of the student body and 50 percent of the faculty at her school stayed out.[84]

The boycott brought together blacks and Hispanics. Unlike the Downstate Medical Center campaign, where Hispanics had been absent from the demonstration, an estimated 100,000 to 150,000 Hispanic students stayed out of the city's schools on February 3. Gilberto Gerena-Valentin, head of the National Association for Puerto Rican Civil Rights, was a visible force, appearing at rallies along with Galamison. Even before the boycott, there was euphoria. Irma Vidal Santaella, Deputy Corrections Commissioner, received a standing ovation at a rally Sunday night when she shouted: "This is the beginning of the partnership between the Puerto Ricans and our sisters and brothers."[85]

Stanley Lowell, head of the Commission on Human Rights, attempted to bring together the boycott leaders and board officials the day after the boycott. The board officials refused mediation by the commission but said they would meet with the "right leaders" who could present "specific, constructive proposals," only if the board needed advice from such leaders. James Donovan also announced that teachers who had taken the day off would be docked a day's pay: "We don't pay people to march around buildings." Teachers' actions would be taken into consideration if they applied for promotions, he added.

Responding to Donovan's statement that the boycott had been a fizzle, and the board's refusal to meet with boycott leaders, Galamison told the press: "We have no alternative but to go ahead with plans for ' "fizzle" number two.' " The Presbyterian pastor said that while he would have to meet with the City-Wide Committee to decide the next course of action, it was a "foregone conclusion" that there would be unanimous support for a second

boycott.[86] Galamison, and Frederick Jones of the NAACP joined Adam
Clayton Powell, congressman from Harlem, in demanding Donovan's resignation. Jones said the board president had shown racial chauvinism.[87]

Soon after, it became clear that there were deep divisions within the board.
Although the board president acted as the agency's spokesperson, taking a
hard line, many inside the agency objected to his comments. Other board
members argued that Superintendent Calvin Gross was the person who
should be taking administrative action, not Donovan. Some accused Donovan of speaking out without the board's support; others accused Gross of
removing himself from the controversy. (He was recuperating in California
from an illness and was not accessible.)[88] The disunity within the board benefited boycott leaders, who found themselves in a position of strength.

Galamison emerged as the most important civil rights leader in New York
City. He had become the head of a coalition that crossed race and class lines.
Through a grassroots effort, thousands of people were recruited for picket
lines, rallies, and working behind the scenes at boycott headquarters. Martin
Luther King Jr. gave his "moral support" to the New York boycott. Even Roy
Wilkins, national head of the NAACP, who had attacked Galamison in the
past, did not criticize the boycott.[89] The New York Times referred to the Presbyterian pastor as the leader of the New York civil rights movement because,
as leader of a grassroots organization, he had been able to pull off a significant civil rights demonstration.[90] Galamison's status had increased so dramatically that he was invited to speak at rallies in other cities where school
boycotts were planned. In fact, he began discussions about a joint boycott on
February 25 with leaders of Boston and Chicago boycotts.[91]

However, Galamison's success was due partly to the era. The civil rights
movement appealed to the moral consciousness of the nation. Galamison
exploited this feeling by linking the fight for integration in New York to the
goals of the larger movement, comparing the New York struggle to the
Southern battle and modeling their demonstrations on Southern civil rights
campaigns. Galamison appealed not only to social justice but also to the self
interest of New Yorkers, noting that the struggle benefited all children, regardless of race. As he celebrated the day after the boycott, little did Galamison know that within a few days his movement would crumble to pieces.

# chapter six

# THE SECOND SCHOOL BOYCOTT AND THE END OF THE MOVEMENT

On February 3, Galamison was in a jovial mood; he had managed to carry out one of the largest civil rights demonstrations in the nation. At Galamison's church Rustin and others danced and sang the religious song "A-Men." The 53-year-old civil rights organizer proclaimed to the press: "I think we are on the threshold of a new political movement. . . . It is going to change the face of New York in housing, in jobs and in schools."[1] Galamison, full of confidence, proclaimed that the next boycott could be held on February 25, to coincide with similar demonstrations planned in Chicago and Boston. He also announced his plans to go to Chicago for a rally in support of the planned demonstrations. Lawrence Landry of Chicago's Coordinating Council of Community Organizations told the press that "working papers" detailing the strategy of the February 25 boycott were being distributed in the North and South.[2]

It must have been a surprise to many in the coalition that a February 25 boycott was in the works, since none of the conventional civil rights groups from New York had been involved in the planning sessions. To be sure, Galamison was reacting to the success of the New York demonstration and what he saw as his right to act as spokesperson for the City-Wide Committee. He also demonstrated his firm belief in militant action as a means of winning integration.

At the same time some who claimed to be sympathetic to the plight of African Americans were at best unsure of the objectives and tactics of New York civil rights leaders. June Shagaloff, special assistant for education of the NAACP, noted a lack of support among white liberals for the boycott. Some objected to mass transfers of white children to predominantly black schools and blacks to predominantly white schools. Some argued that what was needed was to upgrade the schools in black communities. Some white liberals viewed integration as a one-way street. For them, it meant bussing black children into predominantly white areas, hence, the burden for desegregation falling on the backs of people of color. Those who argued that the focus should be on upgrading the schools in the black community did not support the view that segregation led to inequality. Instead of blaming structural inequality in the school system, they pointed their fingers at the "disadvantaged child." The Anti-Defamation League of B'nai B'rith was on record as opposing mass transfers of children, as were the United Federation of Teachers, the New York Liberal Party (a minor party that usually endorsed liberal candidates for city office and that tried to influence the political process by making public its position on issues), and members of the New York Civil Liberties Union. George Backer, a member of the board of the New York Civil Liberties Union, argued that integration was not the solution to the problem of education in New York City. "This idea is hindering the possibility of a real educational solution. The disadvantaged Negro has to have not just what the white child has but much more—many extra services to compensate for his past handicaps." Some liberals argued that mixing disadvantaged children with privileged children could psychologically damage those they were trying to help. Moreover, they asserted that massive bussing was not practical. Others, such as Norman Podhoretz, editor of *Commentary*, a journal published by the American Jewish Committee, had supported the boycott "as a sort of ritualist gesture of protest," but said he would oppose similar actions in the future.[3]

For those in the civil rights movement, especially the more militant wing, it appeared that white liberals talked a good game but were unwilling to become active in the struggle. To Galamison, white liberals were upholding the status quo. He would later claim that they were only interested in controlling him and the civil rights movement.

To make matters worse, Galamison and the militant wing of the New York civil rights movement faced opposition from within. On several occasions representatives of national civil rights organizations accused the minister of acting unilaterally. The day after the boycott, at a meeting of the City-Wide Committee, CORE representatives urged that Galamison be removed from the leadership because he was making statements to the press that the group had not endorsed, including the threat of a second boycott.[4]

On February 9, Galamison announced that the City-Wide Committee had decided on another one-day boycott sometime between March 9 and April 17. According to Galamison, the period had been selected to economically penalize the Board of Education. The school year is divided into eight attendance periods, and the board picks four of the best attendance periods to apply for state aid. The greater the number of children attending school, the larger the state package. Galamison also announced that the National Association for Puerto Rican Civil Rights had been given full status on the City-Wide Committee and that the Urban League of Greater New York would participate in all policy discussions.[5] The apparently increasing role of the NAPRR was an indication of the group's success in keeping 150,000 Puerto Rican students out of school on February 3. The committee was also attempting to make up for its mistake in not having granted the group full status so it could participate in the decisionmaking process.

Not everyone on the City-Wide Committee agreed on a second boycott. At the February 9 meeting some argued that another boycott would not be as effective as the first; other tactics should be explored. The meeting was described as "bloody." According to Galamison, the NAACP and the more moderate elements of the coalition reacted strongly to his calling for a second boycott because they were not serious about using militant tactics to move the Board of Education. On the other hand, moderates in the coalition claimed that Galamison had no idea of what he was doing. In his book *110 Livingston Street*, David Rogers quotes a critic of Galamison:

A number of us raised questions when Milton was charging ahead with the second boycott. There was nothing like the organization that went into the first. He just went charging off with the bit in his teeth, and when we asked about the organization, the money, the community backing, whatever, his response was something like, "of course, of course, let's move ahead." But there was no thinking it through at all.[6]

To be sure, there were differences between the radicals and moderates of the civil rights coalition. The moderates had little taste for continued militant acts and were more comfortable at a bargaining table negotiating than on the streets protesting. Just two days after the boycott, Frederick Jones sent a telegram to Wagner begging him to intervene because of Donovan's rigid position. Jones's actions demonstrated that he would rather rely on his contacts with city officials than on the actions of the movement.[7] On the other hand, the militants, including Galamison and the Parents' Workshop, HPC, and several branches of CORE, came to the conclusion that the board was not serious about integration and that protracted coercion was the only way to make the board act. Moreover, the first boycott had given the militants momentum and had mobilized a large number of New Yorkers. To delay action would only cost them support and give the board the upper hand. The militants also were opposed to closed-door negotiations because they excluded the grassroots, the very people the militants relied on for support. To exclude them meant to alienate them.[8]

Galamison's public statements and actions revealed not only his trust in militant grassroots action and his distrust of the older civil rights organizations in the coalition, but also a desire to dominate the movement. He referred to the New York City school integration movement as "my movement," an indication of how he treated other civil rights leaders. Objections at the meetings of the executive committee of the organization were seen as "stalling tactics." Although Galamison claimed that he was "bending over backwards to demonstrate that [he] was capable of working democratically with others," he admitted he used some undemocratic measures: "There are two unsurpassed methods of improving neurotic meetings, that is to stop inviting those who keep the group moving in a neurotic cycle or to stop having meetings altogether. I elected the former course of action." Leon Modeste, an ally of the pastor whose wife was an active member of the Parents' Workshop, even described Galamison's tactics as "authoritarian."[9]

In contrast to the discord within the civil rights movement, the Board of Education attempted to show unity, declaring that it was unanimous in support of its integration plan and supported its superintendent of schools.[10]

In three heated sessions of the City-Wide Committee, a motion was debated to remove Galamison. Proponents of the measure argued that he often spoke out without approval from the group, putting the organization in embarrassing situations by committing it to actions that it had not agreed to support. Backers of the measure included the NAACP and national CORE, while supporters of Galamison included the Parents' Workshop and the Harlem Parents Committee. Galamison's supporters argued that it was necessary to present a united front, warning that the movement could fall apart. Supporters of the outspoken minister eventually were able to save him by postponing the vote for new officers until June.[11]

However, in a surprise move, the thirteen New York chapters of the NAACP announced their withdrawal from the City-Wide Committee for Integrated Schools, marking the first open break in the New York civil rights movement. Frederick D. Jones, state education chairman of the NAACP, declared the NAACP would still cooperate with the committee; however, it would act independently to integrate the schools of New York. Although Jones did not say why the NAACP chapters were leaving the coalition, it was clear they objected to Galamison's leadership and his decision to call for a second boycott. Some members of the NAACP told reporters that if the integration drive failed, it would be Galamison's fault. Wilkins and others in the NAACP felt that a second boycott was inadvisable and attempted to deflate the prestige of Galamison and the City-Wide Committee. While the NAACP did not rule out supporting a second boycott, it planned to issue its own plan for integration and allow the board time to react to it. To make matters worse, the Urban League denied Galamison's claim that it supported a planned second boycott, claiming that it would independently assess the situation before arriving at a decision.[12]

On February 17, Jones issued a statement explaining why the thirteen branches had pulled out of the City-Wide Committee. He argued that the City-Wide Committee, which was supposed to be a coordinating group of organizations, had become a separate entity. He emphasized the point that the withdrawal by the thirteen branches was not a signal of a split in the New York City civil rights movement. June Shagaloff, representing the National NAACP, reiterated Jones's claim that there was no split in the movement. She declared that "gross distortions of the NAACP's position will give short lived comfort to the status-quo supporters, the hesitant white liberal organizations," and editorial writers. She also claimed that the NAACP chapters were committed to demonstrations and a second boycott.[13] However, despite these statements by NAACP officials, it was clear that the movement had been severely wounded by the departure of the organizations and it was not at all clear that these groups supported continued militant action. The fact that they had left right after the movement's most successful demonstration left doubts in the minds of the militants as to the sincerity of the NAACP's claims that it supported a second boycott.

To save face, Galamison announced that the boycott was still on despite the decision of the NAACP chapters. Personally, he was devastated. He complained that he had learned about the NAACP's withdrawal from the coalition the following day when he read the newspaper: "I was amazed to learn at the local newsstand, in a four-inch type headline, that the NAACP had resigned from the City-Wide Committee. There are a number of ways to withdraw from an effort. This tactic, there could no longer be any doubt about it, was designed to hurt. It did!" Reflecting years later on the episode, Galamison concluded that the national organizations were committing sabotage: "My immediate reaction to the strategy of the NAACP and CORE to sabotage the City-Wide Committee was that it was foul and below-the-belt and despicable. The years have given me time to think, however. And my long-term reaction to the strategy of CORE and the NAACP is that it was foul and below-the-belt and despicable."[14]

Galamison claimed that he had made a mistake by relying on the national civil rights organizations. "People and organizations usually have to depend on the sources from which they get their income. And the financial sources that back these groups limit the effectiveness of the groups. Now, that's the kindest way that I can put it. . . . My personal experience with the NAACP and the Urban League, and CORE, to a degree, is that their mission is to capture movements and contain them. In other words, to get on the ground floor, if they can, but to contain the movement—to see that the movement doesn't really threaten what it set out to correct."[15]

Although Galamison attempted to save face, within days the fragile coalition was coming apart at the seams. Groups within the committee began to announce their independence. CORE and the National Association for Puerto Rican Civil Rights said they would decide whether to support another boycott independent of the coalition.[16]

Without discussion, Galamison had committed all the groups to action. He was giving the board an ultimatum, not leaving room for an alternative. The split between Galamison and the national organizations was also a reminder of the long history of distrust between the Siloam pastor and the national leadership of the NAACP. Those feelings were never addressed before and during the coalition period. The NAACP and the other groups that left the City-Wide Committee lacked confidence in another boycott and in the judgment of Galamison. Many had distrusted the Siloam pastor and had only decided on his leadership as a compromise. They had attempted to limit his role to that of a coordinator, having no power to make any decisions. The national organizations did not want to be led down a path of militant action that would jeopardize their good relationship with city officials and strengthen Galamison and the grassroots organizations.[17] On the other hand, Galamison and his supporters believed that these groups were there only to contain their militancy, especially in the heat of battle. Their only recourse to assure the militant tone of the movement was to proceed as quickly as possible with a second boycott.

To no one's surprise, the head of the City-Wide Committee was bitter and depressed over the breakup of the coalition. How could civil rights groups in the coalition abandon him on what he believed was the eve of victory? The forty-year-old pastor concluded that these organizations were merely mouthpieces for white liberals. He would later assert that the national civil rights organizations had been sent in to control him. They had opposed the first boycott but, realizing that they could not stop it, waited for their opportunity, and took it, right after the successful demonstration on February 3. Incapable of self-criticism, the pastor admitted he had made the decision to have a second boycott but insisted that the national groups' withdrawal from the coalition was a conspiracy plotted from the beginning.[18]

Galamison received good news when sixty ministers, representing ministerial groups from Brooklyn, Queens, and the Bronx, publicly supported the Presbyterian's leadership in the school integration struggle. The ministers called for a blue-ribbon panel of educators from around the country to come up with a plan for integrating the schools.[19]

State Education Commissioner James E. Allen announced he had requested that a special advisory committee on integration assess the problem of school integration in New York and report back to him. He disappointed civil rights groups by his failure to give concrete proposals, and

Galamison said that the time had passed for the appointment of committees and proposals. He would announce the date of a second boycott in a few days.[20]

In a move unlikely to be endorsed by CORE and the Urban League, Galamison announced that the second boycott would take place on March 16 and a third demonstration on April 22, the opening day of the World's Fair in New York City. The April 22 demonstration would not necessarily be a school boycott: "This might be another school boycott or something more appropriate to the opening of the World's Fair." The action, he claimed, was supported by the Parents' Workshop and the Harlem Parents Committee.

The Urban League of Greater New York immediately declared that it could not support the "premature" March 16 demonstration. Frederick W. Richmond, the president of the league, claimed he was "amazed and startled" by Galamison's statement, because the date of the second boycott had not been discussed with the league. In fact, Richmond asserted that Galamison had promised a day earlier not to announce a date for the boycott. Richmond said that the league would work as mediator, attempting to bring together board officials and civil rights groups to work for an integration plan acceptable to both sides. CORE and the National Association for Puerto Rican Civil Rights had similar complaints about the proposed March 16 boycott. Neither group had been consulted about the event, and CORE announced that it would hold a closed-door meeting to discuss a response.[21]

For many, Galamison's actions were strange. Knowing that the coalition was in trouble, why would he risk what was left of the group by making an apparently arbitrary decision? Part of the answer was provided by Galamison at a news conference where he announced the date of the second boycott. Asserting that he had called for the demonstration "in response to the demands of thousands of parents throughout the city for direct and dramatic action to speed the pace of school desegregation," he declared: "there is a deliberate campaign in motion to destroy the City-Wide Committee and to frustrate the legitimate aspirations of the people." He did not reveal the names of the people or organizations attempting to destroy the committee but said people should not assume that because the Parents' Workshop and the Harlem Parents Committee had designed the demonstration there were divisions: "We are exercising autonomy which each group in the Committee enjoys." The City-Wide Committee would present a plan for integration in the hopes that the school board would accept it and avoid a second boycott.[22]

Although he was willing to risk his reputation because he knew parents wanted action, Galamison may have decided he did not have much of a choice; it was either fight or die. His conspiracy theory about how national civil rights organizations wanted to destroy the "People's Movement" convinced the Presbyterian minister that he must carry on the struggle for the people. The feisty pastor also confessed that his ego was at stake: "Every time a supporting organization withdrew I got angrier. Every additional obstacle placed in my path made me more determined to have a second demonstration if I had to go to Board of Education headquarters and sit in alone."[23]

The following day, national CORE called for the creation of a "new and more effective city-wide organization" to coordinate the campaign for school integration. In the meantime, the civil rights organization said it would continue struggling for school integration in New York by using direct nonviolent action, such as sit-ins, boycotts, and marches. Norman Hill, national program director, argued that the call for a boycott was premature. National CORE did not take a position on the March 16 protest; the fourteen local chapters would decide independently whether to support the demonstration. Although, as noted, Galamison saw CORE's move as unfair, there was little he could do.[24]

Despite the national organization's position, two of the most militant chapters in CORE, the Brooklyn and Bronx chapters, announced that they would support the boycott. Isaiah Brunson, chairperson of the Brooklyn branch, opposed the national organization's proposal for a new civil rights coordinating group, declaring that action should be taken against the Board of Education for not integrating the schools.[25]

In spite of these chapters' support, Galamison was left without the endorsement of any national civil rights organization. Depressed and embittered, he saw a clear attempt to scuttle "his movement." The Presbyterian pastor recalled some years later: "Because the representatives of the Harlem Parents Committee, who had met with me most of the night, had to go to work, I announced the second boycott alone."[26]

More devastating news for Galamison came when Bayard Rustin, the symbol of the link between the southern and northern civil rights movements, announced at a press conference that he might not support the second boycott. He gave no reason, simply saying that the news conference was not the time or place to discuss such a matter. Several civil rights groups had called for a march on Albany demanding civil rights. Rustin had joined

forces with those who wanted a new organization to work for school integration.[27] Rustin's withdrawal seemed to hurt the minister the most. Of all
the leaders who had deserted the movement, Galamison saved the harshest
attack for the organizer of the March on Washington. He called him a "tro-
jan horse" and a "press-created Negro" sent by white liberals to control the
movement. Rustin, according to Galamison, "permitted himself to be a tool
with which the national organizations tried to destroy my movement."
Galamison's anger toward Rustin did not subside with time. As late as 1987
the Presbyterian pastor, still fuming over Rustin's decision not to support a
second boycott, asserted that "Bayard sold out more Negroes than all the
African chiefs combined."[28]

Galamison's explanation of why Rustin did not support another boycott
was far too simplistic. Although Rustin never publicly stated why he had
decided to leave the campaign, his letter concerning a March on Albany suggests why he walked away from the New York City school integration movement. Rustin claimed that in New York, the campaigns for housing, jobs,
and schools were separate from each other and that the attempt to put pressure on City Hall was meaningless "without legislation and intervention
from Albany."[29]

In his article "From Protest to Politics: The Future of the Civil Rights
Movement," published in *Commentary* one year after the boycott, Rustin
shed further light on his decision not to support a second boycott. The civil
rights organizer had come to the conclusion that social and economic conditions, not civil rights, were the major problems faced by African Americans. Arguing almost twenty years before William Julius Wilson's thesis that
economic-structural changes cause the growth of an urban underclass, Rustin wrote, "And we are in the midst of a technological revolution which is
altering the fundamental structure of the labor force, destroying unskilled
and semi-skilled jobs—jobs in which Negroes are disproportionately con-
centrated." He contended that a radical transformation must take place in
the social, political, and economic institutions of the country in order to reverse the plight of blacks. Billions of dollars must be spent to improve the
school system, eradicate slums, and eliminate poverty.[30]

Rustin had decided that civil rights militants did not have the answer.
In fact, civil rights militancy, the pacifist declared, sought a no-win policy.
"Sharing with many moderates a recognition of the magnitude of the obsta-
cles to freedom, spokesmen for this tendency survey the American scene

and find no forces prepared to move toward radical solutions. From this they conclude that the only viable strategy is shock; above all, the hypocrisy of white liberals must be exposed." These "moralists" lacked a realistic strategy. "But militancy," Rustin wrote, "is a matter of posture and volume and not of effect." Although not criticizing Galamison directly, Rustin probably came to the conclusion that a call for a second boycott was nothing more than an attempt to frighten people to change. Although Rustin was jovial the day after the February 4 boycott when there seemed to be massive support for the militants, the board's decision not to cave in and Galamison's call for a second boycott without the support of the national and regional civil rights leadership probably helped Rustin reach his conclusion about the future direction of the movement.

Galamison and the militants simply lacked a realistic program. Instead of continued militant action, like boycotts, blacks needed political power. Rustin argued that blacks could gain political power only by working in a coalition with others dedicated to social and economic change. African Americans must be willing to compromise and work with people and groups with "common political objectives." They should be willing to make "smaller concessions to win larger ones." The organizer of the March on Washington declared that such a coalition could work because "economic interests are more fundamental than prejudice." Although Rustin took part in demonstrations on the opening day of the World's Fair, he argued that they were ineffective. The so-called stall-ins, an attempt to tie up traffic, probably reduced attendance that day, but few people took part in the demonstrations.[31]

Rustin had delivered the final blow. No national civil rights group or national civil rights leader supported the upcoming boycott. Galamison and the movement had been deserted, denied the groups and personnel needed to organize supporters and provide financial support. More importantly, it was a signal to the Board of Education; the civil rights movement that had successfully launched the largest demonstration in the nation, embarrassing the school agency, would not be in a position to cause such damage again. Its leader had been isolated and made ineffective.

Faced with a choice of going along with conventional civil rights organizations that had contacts with those in power but little dealings with ordinary people, or siding with grassroots groups with little mainstream political clout, Galamison chose ordinary people. He had always drawn his support and strength from those with few formal political connections. Ordi-

nary people were far more militant than the civil rights organizations.
Parents were not interested in the feuding among civil rights groups; they
wanted action and counted on Galamison's support. For years, without the
support of the national organizations, they had struggled to improve the
education of their children. Galamison felt that if he did not deliver, he
would lose his credibility among the grassroots. The Presbyterian pastor was
willing to sacrifice an opportunity to gain political influence; he would side
with the rank and file who wanted to protest injustice. However, by choosing the ordinary people, Galamison removed himself from the negotiations
with the board and civil rights groups. By isolating himself, it became easier
for his opposition to attack him and paint him as an extremist.[32]

As the boycott date grew near, the opposition to bussing for integration
was growing. In a survey reported in the *New York Times*, eighteen of the
twenty-four councilmen surveyed opposed school transfers that required
forced bussing. Both black councilmen, J. Daniel Diggs of Brooklyn and J.
Raymond Jones of Manhattan, argued that the major goal should be to improve the schools. The fact that black elected officials had indirectly criticized the Presbyterian pastor's actions only helped paint him as an extremist in the eyes of those outside of the movement and among his opposition.[33]

In order to bring pressure on the school agency, white parents opposed
to bussing for integration launched a huge demonstration at the Board of
Education's headquarters. The rally was sponsored by the group Parents and
Taxpayers. The demonstration disclosed that foes of school integration were
willing to appropriate tactics from the civil rights movement. Seventy percent of the crowd of fifteen thousand were women, and practically all the
demonstrators were white. (Because the rally took place during the day,
men were at work.) What developed among the forces opposed to integration was a growing reliance on militant action to coerce the Board of Education not to desegregate. Although the demonstrators claimed that they were
protesting the demise of the neighborhood school, their real fear was that
their children were going to bussed out for integration purposes. Picket
signs read: "Can a bus bring a sick child home?" and "Princeton Plan in the
garbage can." It was the first time many opposed to bussing had taken their
case to the streets.[34]

On March 14, the Urban League announced that it would not support
the boycott, voicing publicly what many had known since the middle of
February. Galamison declared that while he did not have the support of the

conventional civil rights groups, he did have the support of twenty-two organizations, including nine branches of CORE. It was later revealed that the Community Council on Housing, a militant housing group that conducted rent strikes, and Adam Clayton Powell would support the boycott. In fact, Powell would march with Galamison to the Board of Education on March 16.[35] Powell gave the demonstration a needed boost. The popular congressman could attract attention and support for the event, not only from his church, the Abyssinian Baptist Church, which had one of the largest congregations in the city, but from his numerous loyal constituents.

In a surprising turn of events, it was learned that Malcolm X, the fiery Muslim leader, would support the boycott. By November of 1963, Malcolm's political situation had dramatically changed. Elijah Muhammad, the leader of the Nation of Islam, had suspended Malcolm for ninety days because (responding to a news reporter on the assassination of President John Kennedy) he had said that the "chickens had come home to roost." The comment touched off a storm; the media reported that Malcolm was glad that the President had been assassinated. Malcolm said later that he was not justifying the assassination, but only noting that the violence used against black people had now been used on others in the United States. However, Elijah Muhammad and those close to him had seen Malcolm as a growing danger. By 1962, Malcolm was arguing that the organization should take a stronger role in the civil rights struggle. He had moved away from the narrow religious agenda of the Nation of Islam to a broader secular one that included an anti-colonial and anti-imperialist dimension. After the ninety-day suspension was over, Elijah Muhammad extended it indefinitely. It became clear to Malcolm that Muhammad and the inner circle were trying to silence him. Malcolm left the Nation of Islam; he was now in a position to make independent decisions.[36]

Finding himself in a vulnerable situation, Malcolm was looking for allies. Although Galamison would deny closeness with Malcolm, the Muslim leader may have been attracted to Galamison's radicalism, courage, and vision. In an interview with Timothy Lee of the *New York Post*, Malcolm likened himself to "Dr. Martin Luther King, Rep. Adam Clayton Powell, and Rev. Milton Galamison." Some religious leaders realized that religion was not enough to liberate blacks. Malcolm had come to the conclusion that the problem went beyond religion: "I'm a religious leader, yes. But religion is not enough. Today the problems of the Negro go beyond religion. They are so complex that any man who thinks he has a simple solution has to look ignorant."[37]

In spite of Galamison's claim that he did not have an ongoing friendship with Malcolm, Malcolm saw Galamison as a close ally. In a moving telegram to the boycott leader sent on April 3, 1964, Malcolm wrote:

Dear Brother,

saw you on news last night. Pleased to see you are not allowing a wedge to be driven between us. I promise you the same. You have my whole-hearted support in your school project. Just let me know how I can help. We will be at Audubon 166th and B'way Sunday April 5 at 8:p.m. subject civil rights vs. human rights. Would you like to speak, RSVP

Your Brother Malcolm X.[38]

A kinder and gentler Malcolm emerged after he left the Nation of Islam. He attempted to reconcile past differences with civil rights leaders. He did not limit membership in his new organization, the Muslim Mosque Inc. by race, religion or political affiliation. Moreover, he said he would not attack persons engaged in civil rights and asked for forgiveness for the "unkind things that he said in the past." Malcolm was hoping to forge an alliance with civil rights groups. Although the young Muslim leader remained a black nationalist and was not in favor of school integration, he declared that he wanted to end school segregation. This was not double talk. There was a distinction between the two. Desegregation was a major objective among groups trying to solve the school crisis. Malcolm defined segregation as the operation of schools with a black student body by whites. He told a crowd that "I am aligned with everyone who will take some action to end this criminal situation in the schools." He wanted better schools for black children, although he opposed integration as an ultimate goal.[39]

Galamison was cautious. The boycott leader told the press, when asked about the black Muslim's support for the boycott: "I have not talked with Malcolm X. If he adheres to nonviolence he will be welcome to the boycott. We don't want to reject any legitimate support but I want it to be legitimate." Apparently, Galamison wanted to gain broad support for the demonstration. He realized that Malcolm's image as an opponent of the tactics and nonviolent philosophy of the civil rights movement could hinder that support. Galamison never claimed to have a close relationship with Malcolm. He stated in his autobiography that he did not know Malcolm very well. Yet the day Malcolm was assassinated in February 1965 Galamison was supposed to have been a speaker at the thirty-nine-year-old Muslim leader's rally. He said he had not made it because he had preached two sermons that day and was exhausted. So he had decided not to come to the Audubon Ballroom.[40]

Despite Galamison's cautionary remarks about Malcolm's support and attempt to win broader support for the second boycott, moderate leaders and organizations were busy voicing their discontent. The Harlem Parents Committee, the Parents' Workshop, the more militant chapters of CORE, Malcolm X, Adam Clayton Powell, and Jesse Gray, a leading tenants' rights advocate and former head of a committee to put the communist leader Ben Davis on the New York ballot, were the major forces behind the demonstration.[41]

In preparation for the March 16 event, boycott organizers prepared numerous flyers and leaflets to persuade parents to keep their children out of school. One flyer featured a drawing of a southern plantation owner with a whip striking black children. The caption read "Move Negro children off Donovan's Plantation, Boycott March 16." The message of the poster was clear. Donovan was a racist and the boycott's objective was to smash white supremacy.[42]

As the date approached, it became apparent that the boycott organizers had added demands to their list. In addition to a desegregation plan and timetable, they were demanding textbooks that included African-American history and more black principals. What was left of the City-Wide Committee for Integrated Schools issued flyers and leaflets calling on the board to provide a comprehensive city-wide plan and timetable for the desegregation of all public schools, with the desegregation of all elementary schools to be completed by September 1965. It urged the board desegregate all junior high schools on a city-wide basis and racially balance all high schools by September; to assign all pupils to integrated schools and to educate and prepare all New York City parents for participation in an integrated school program; to build new schools only in areas where appropriate and effective desegregation methods, such as rezoning, pairing, and changing the feeder patterns, could be employed. It called on the school agency to stop con-

struction of schools in segregated areas. Other demands included the publication of a racially unbiased textbook that accurately depicted minority
communities; the appointment of a Puerto Rican, agreeable to the Puerto
Rican community, to the Board of Education; and summer schools for students who were a year or more behind in reading grade level.[43]

Two hundred picket lines would be set up near schools. As in the first
boycott, demonstrators from the Bronx and Manhattan would go to City
Hall at noon for a rally and would seek a meeting with members of the City
Council. At one in the afternoon, protesters from Brooklyn and Queens
would be led by Galamison to the Board of Education's headquarters.[44]

Still bitter about the breakup of the coalition, Galamison told the press
two days before the protest that the boycott could not be a failure. Disap-
pointments were due not to indifference but to "sabotage." The national
civil rights organizations had attempted to undermine the movement. Despite Galamison's accusations, it did not matter at that point who was at
fault for the breakup of the coalition. That question would have to be dealt
with later. The important question was whether he could get out the forces
for the demonstration.[45]

## The Second Time Around

The second boycott was far less dramatic than the first. The Board of Education estimated that 267,459 children were absent from school on March
16. (It later confessed that the figures were wrong because it did not report
any absentees among kindergarten children.) Schools in Harlem, Bedford-
Stuyvesant, and other predominantly black and Hispanic communities were
almost empty. Although it was half the size of the first boycott, Galamison
and the grassroots had managed to keep at least 26 percent of the students
home, without the support of the national civil rights groups. Seventy-
seven schools were picketed in Brooklyn, forty-nine in Manhattan, and seventeen each in the Bronx and Queens.[46]

The second boycott was more militant in tone than the first, and
Galamison called it a success. At the rally at 110 Livingston Street, he told a
crowd of 2,500 demonstrators combatively: "If we have to come down here
again, we are going to take this building." Thelma Hamilton declared: "If
they don't give us what we want we'll tie up this whole damn city." However,

this may have been histrionics. Leaders stressed that though the event was nonviolent, violence remained an option in the future, but they may have been exhibiting desperation.[47]

Despite the large number of absentees, the boycott as a method did not coerce the Board of Education into action. Heartened by the fact that the March 16 event had attracted half as many protesters as the first boycott, James Donovan proclaimed: "We are encouraged that the boycott method of expressing a point of view is regarded with markedly diminishing favor." The board president was right. Although the numbers were formidable, especially in the black communities, Galamison needed figures equal to the February 3 protest. A decrease, especially by half, only indicated to the board that Galamison had not gained support and indeed had actually lost favor with New Yorkers. In the Puerto Rican sections of New York, attendance was almost normal. The decision of the National Association for Puerto Rican Civil Rights to withdraw its support for the boycott was devastating. The Puerto Rican community was probably angry at the black leadership for withholding support from a March 2 demonstration sponsored by the National Association for Puerto Rican Civil Rights. Even Galamison, who claimed that Gerberto Gerena Valentin, head of the Puerto Rican organization, was a close ally, showed up late to the rally, demonstrating to the Puerto Rican organizers that their concerns were not one of his top priorities.[48]

To exhibit independence from the City-Wide Committee, put pressure on the board, and win support for their position, the NAACP and CORE organized a "March for Democratic Schools." Rustin, director of the march, called on New Yorkers to join the demonstration targeted at the board, the mayor, and the governor, to force all three to the bargaining table. Norman Hill of National CORE, Gilberto Valentin, Leon Davis (head of Local 1199 of the Drug and Hospital Workers), A. Philip Randolph, and Cleveland Robinson of the New York Human Rights Commission addressed the crowd of 3,000 in Albany. The leaders of the event later met with Governor Rockefeller but claimed that little was gained from the meeting.[49]

Unwilling to participate in the March 16 boycott, the conventional civil rights groups had boxed themselves into a corner. By contending that the period for negotiation was at hand, they had split the movement. They soon found out that the board was not willing to compromise, despite its numerous statements.

In March there was an attempt to forge a new coalition among the civil rights groups. Although the Board of Education asserted that it would take steps to integrate the schools, it became apparent to those who had advocated negotiation that the board would not live up to its promises. Gross announced that the school agency would scale back on its moderate proposal on pairing because white parents objected. The NAACP and other civil rights groups reacted by threatening a boycott. In April, Gross invited civil rights groups to secretly negotiate with him.[50]

The militant groups were distrustful of the board and city officials. Annie Stein accused city officials of failing to show leadership, asking why Mayor Wagner had not sat down with parent groups. An angry Stein accused city officials of going after Galamison because of his World's Fair protest, instead of seriously negotiating.[51]

To recapture the massive support the boycott movement had first enjoyed among whites, EQUAL, an organization of white parents struggling for integration, planned a "freedom day" rally. Ellen Lurie, the group's president, called on Stein to join a group that represented twenty-eight predominantly white neighborhoods in New York City that were struggling for integrated quality education. Proclaiming that the fight to achieve freedom is "everybody's struggle," Lurie contended that those who fight to pressure their neighborhood have forgotten that "freedom is a much more precious objective."[52]

Galamison was reluctant to join with the same civil rights groups that had abandoned the second boycott. He had also come to the conclusion that the board was not serious, contending that negotiating was part of the strategy to stall and hinder civil rights groups. Instead of sitting down with the board, he believed that civil rights groups should be organizing for another demonstration. The militant pastor also opposed secret negotiations because the rank and file were excluded from the meetings; they would see these talks as a way of selling them out. For the most part, Galamison had always operated in the open. No doubt the result of the Downstate settlement was still fresh in his mind.[53]

Despite his fear that the board was stalling, Galamison decided to join the negotiating team of civil rights groups and see what the board's next move would be. Superintendent Gross had pledged that he would bargain in good faith, and the militant civil rights leader was willing to wait to see if the board would produce anything substantial. Calling for boycotts when the superintendent was willing to negotiate might have cost the movement public support. Galamison would have been accused of trying to sabotage fruitful negotiations. Galamison's allies in the movement, including Ellen Lurie of EQUAL, had already expressed their support for the Allen plan and were willing to modify their demand for an immediate plan for integration and timetable.

By April, a new negotiating team had been formed to bargain with the superintendent, and the board was established with representatives from the NAACP, CORE, the Commonwealth of Puerto Rico, the Puerto Rican Civil Rights Committee, EQUAL, the Conference for Quality Integrated Education (an organization of labor, religious and civil groups), the Harlem Parents Committee, and the Parents' Workshop. The groups agreed not to select a leader; public statements by any representative of a member group had to cleared by the other members of the coalition.[54]

On May 12, the State Education Commissioner's Advisory Committee on Human Relations and Community Tensions submitted its report, "Desegregating the Public Schools of New York City." The objective of the report was to "stimulate immediate, direct, decisive action by the Board and Superintendent to desegregate and improve education." The report evaluated past programs and current plans for desegregation; it also proposed further steps. The three-person advisory committee, which included Kenneth Clark, asserted that early attempts by the board to desegregate the schools, including recommendations by the Committee on Integration and the Open Enrollment program, had failed because the board had not implemented the committee's recommendations; only 16,000 students, or 1 percent of the school population, were affected by the voluntary program.

According to the committee, the board's school-building program reinforced "the historic pattern of building on sites within the most segregated areas" because "To date, desegregation has not been a main factor in the programming of construction and physical renovation." Building plans were designed in response to population increases and other factors, not the need for desegregation.[55]

The advisory committee asserted that the Free Choice program, initiated in 1963, would have little impact on the city-wide level because, like Open Enrollment, it was a voluntary program. In its evaluation of the jun-

ior high school feeder pattern changes, the committee noted that the number of segregated junior high schools had increased from twelve (10 percent) in 1958 to twenty-five (19 percent) in 1963. During that same period
the number of predominantly white junior high schools had decreased
from 43 percent to 22 percent. Forty-five percent of black and Puerto Rican
children enrolled in a public school in New York City attended a segregated
institution. The committee claimed that the Princeton Plan would only desegregate one percent of the 25 predominantly black and Puerto Rican
junior high schools by the 1964–1965 school year.[56]

In a blunt critique of the board, the three-member committee declared:

We must conclude that nothing undertaken by the New York City
Board of Education since 1954, and nothing proposed since 1963, has
contributed or will contribute in any meaningful degree to desegregating the public schools of the City. Each past effort, each current
plan, and each projected proposal, is either not aimed at reducing segregation or is developed in too limited a fashion to stimulate even
slight progress toward desegregation.

After noting that high schools had the best chance of desegregating because
only one-third were segregated, it dejectedly contended that the board had
not addressed desegregating these schools.[57]

The advisory committee also predicted that the number of segregated
elementary schools would increase from 22 percent in 1963 to 31 percent
by 1970. Pairing twenty schools a year might bring the percentage to 24
percent in 1970. There were underlying forces hindering desegregation that
were not the fault of the board: "School segregation is a by-product of patterns of segregation in settlement and housing." Migration had led to a
dramatic increase of black and Puerto Rican communities in New York.
Whites were moving to the suburbs decreasing the white population of the
city, and many whites were opting to send their children to private and
parochial schools.

The advisory committee predicted three trends. Minority school population would increase by 50 percent by 1965 and by 70 percent by 1975. The
increases would be differentially distributed. Manhattan would have a greater increase in black and Puerto Rican segregated schools than Queens and
Staten Island. The increase would be due to residential segregation. Noting

that these trends would make it difficult for the board to desegregate the schools, because there was no way to prevent the growth of minority populations, the committee urged the school agency to take some step to prevent "extreme school segregation."

Indirectly criticizing the civil rights groups, the committee argued that putting pressure on the board would not lead to total desegregation. In fact, the remedy of long-distance bussing for elementary schools, favored by civil rights groups, would impose a tremendous hardship on black and Puerto Rican children and parents. Any solution must be mutually accepted by both "whites and minority groups." The committee proposed a large-scale program of construction and development of comprehensive high schools to integrate schools and reduce overcrowding.[58]

To desegregate the lower grades, the committee proposed the establishment of new middle schools to include the fifth through the eighth grades, thus eliminating junior high schools. The first target should be the ones in ghetto areas. Intermediate schools would decrease the dropout rate by exposing seventh and eighth graders to secondary education and giving them the status of "senior members of their school communities." The committee also recommended a new unit extending from pre-kindergarten to the fourth grade. These schools or units would exceed 500 students, although two or more units might be housed in a building. Such small units would help make the children feel they were members of a community. The committee also recommended modernizing facilities and recruiting black and Puerto Rican teachers and administrators.[59]

The report won praise from civil rights groups. Both CORE and the NAACP issued a statement welcoming the report because it replaced the "piecemeal desegregation proposals of the past with overall, basic plans for total reorganization of the schools and academic programs." Although they did not agree on all the points, for example, the assertion that some middle schools could be segregated, it was comprehensive and far-reaching. The two civil rights groups backed the 4–4–4 reorganization plan (four years primary, four years middle schools and four years of comprehensive high schools combining academic and vocational programs). They backed the creation of educational parks to replace the high schools, middle, and primary schools. These parks should be in areas assuring integration. They called on the board to create a rezoning plan for elementary schools and to use the Princeton plan for an unspecified number of elementary schools.[60]

EQUAL, which had established a borough-wide subcommittee to study the Allen plan's recommendations and its potential impact, concluded that the plan should be supported.[61]

Superintendent Gross was not of the same mind. He responded by issuing an alternative proposal, advocating the transfer of thousands of sixth graders in segregated schools to other segregated schools. He also promised to reexamine present and future construction plans to promote integration. The Gross plan recommended the creation of four pairings and three junior high school rezoning schemes, with no further integration measures for the coming year.

Though Roy Wilkins praised the plan, calling it a "giant step forward," the thirteen chapters of the NAACP in New York disagreed. A spokesperson for the groups took exception to the "critical departure from the Allen Plan." Galamison, speaking for Brooklyn CORE, the HPC, and the Parents' Workshop and never giving up his belief in mass protest, contended: "Behind the smokescreen of make believe re-organization, there lies only another little token. And all that a token can accomplish these days is to put another demonstrator through the [subway] turnstile on his way to 110 Livingston Street."[62]

After five grueling sessions in a two-week period, involving the superintendent, six staff members of the board, and the negotiating committee of the various civil rights groups, the board agreed to take steps to desegregate the schools by September 1964 and produce subsequent desegregation plans. The superintendent also agreed not to send thousands of black and Puerto Rican children from segregated elementary to segregated junior high schools. The September 1964 plan would be formulated by the superintendent in consultation with civil rights groups and Dr. Robert Dentler of the Institute of Urban Studies at Columbia University. Dentler and the board would consult on which educational complexes should be the first ones established. Both sides also agreed to "stress the elimination of de facto segregated junior high schools," while discussing ways to promote high school integration. Gross would work with the civil rights groups throughout the summer to create a comprehensive desegregation plan for September 1965, specifically examining the construction budget in order to establish educational parks and complexes. These plans would be in accord with the recommendations of the Allen plan.[63]

As the board announced new integration plans, Parents and Taxpayers (PAT) publicly opposed any effort to desegregate the public schools, attacking zoning changes they claimed would create hardship by increasing the distance children must travel. Children walking great distances would be forced to cross dangerous intersections. Playing the race card in an attempt to attract white parents, PAT claimed that children would spend part of their day in dangerous neighborhoods. According to PAT, the board's plan would increase racial tension by forcing integration. Threatening legal action and demonstrations if the board initiated involuntary integration plans, PAT called for the board to upgrade schools in every neighborhood. It decided to continue using the tactics of the civil rights groups by calling for a city-wide boycott on September 14.[64]

Civil rights groups were aware that a large boycott could destroy any progress that had been made between them and the board. They decided to counter the anti-integration boycott by launching a campaign to urge parents to send their children to school. EQUAL produced 10,000 copies of a flyer under the title "Go to School September 14," while David Livingston, co-chair of the Conference for Quality Integrated Education, issued a press release accusing PAT of racism. Asserting that progress had been made in school integration talks, the Superintendent had agreed to substantially desegregate junior high schools, and he had accepted the Allen plan, Livingston claimed this progress was what the anti-integration forces wished to destroy.[65]

When James Donovan, President of the Board of Education, refused to meet with PAT and the Joint Council for Better Education, another parent organization opposing the board's plans to integrate the schools, the boycott against integration was inevitable. On September, 14, 275,638 pupils stayed home, about 175,000 more than the usual number. The largest number of absences were reported by schools where students had been transferred. The foes of integration did not give up militant grassroots action after September 14. The following day they managed to keep 233,000 children out of school and nine days later, 7,500 parents demonstrated at City Hall. They attempted on several occasions to get the City Council to oppose pairing but failed. Yet despite their inability to get the City Council to act, the parents opposition to integration continued. Besides hundreds of parents attempting to storm a Queens school in order to force two transfer students out, six hundred PAT members held a 48-hour vigil outside of Gracie Mansion beginning on October 9.[66]

Although James Donovan asserted that the board was not going to change its plans and there were no incidents reported in schools where children were transferred, the anti-integration boycott demonstrated to school officials that PAT and its allies were formidable opponents. They had managed to keep a quarter of the children out of the school and asserted they would take further action if the board did not protect the neighborhood-school concept.

Despite the September accord, by October, relations between the civil rights negotiating team and the board had hit rock bottom. In an attempt to pressure the board civil rights groups publicly announced a failure to reach agreement with the school agency. Although the board had agreed to a "cooperative planning" effort to work out integration steps for September 1965 and seriously discuss educational complexes, as well as to consult with Dr. Robert Dentler and the civil rights groups to eliminate segregated junior and senior high schools, after twelve meetings they had reached an impasse.[67]

The civil rights negotiating team issued a memorandum urging the board to suspend plans to build schools in segregated areas and to follow the advisory committee reorganization plan. The board refused to halt construction plans, increasing tension. Contracts for conventional elementary and junior high school plants were still being awarded in a "business-as-usual" way. Although the civil rights groups sent a letter to Gross on September 3, 1964, complaining about the board's construction program, there was no reply. The groups accused the board of jeopardizing any plan for integration "as it further entrenches segregation in our school system." The civil rights groups promised to hold a series of borough-wide meetings to inform and get feedback from the community, but despite their threatening tone, they had lost strength.[68] By negotiating over a long period of time and not preparing for mass action, they had lost public support for their cause, and they remained fragmented. The board was in a winning position. Although a group of thirty-one clergy issued a statement demanding that the Board of Education come up with a city-wide plan for integration, and the group promised to "utilize civil disobedience," they were not part of the City-Wide Committee nor were they in coalition with the more militant faction of the civil rights groups that favored street protest.[69]

Galamison did not attend most of the meetings because he felt they were a waste of time. Joel Chaseman, general manager of the all-news radio station WINS, asserted that a member of his staff had met with Galamison and observed that the Presbyterian pastor was depressed over the school integration struggle. Chaseman claimed that Galamison was " 'determined to cause some sort of school shut-down.' "[70]

Galamison's absence from the meetings was used by James Donovan to level attacks at the Presbyterian pastor. In a letter to Joel Chaseman, the Board of Education president declared:

> So that you can understand the type of individual with whom you are dealing in Mr. Galamison, Dr. Gross informs me that he has had three informal conferences with a selected group of civil rights leaders since the opening of school and that, although invited to each of these meetings, Mr. Galamison has never attended one.
>
> May I add my own personal experience. I carefully sent to Mr. Galamison a confidential advanced copy of our entire "Five-Year Crash Program for Quality Education" (a copy of which I enclose), and to this day I have not had even the courtesy of acknowledgement. I have received enthusiastic replies from virtually every other leader in the community.
>
> I have been irresistibly drawn to the conclusion that Mr. Galamison is not interested in anything constructive and is primarily concerned with continuing to drive around his poor parish in his white Lincoln Continental.[71]

By the late fall of 1964, the fragile civil rights coalition had split, with the more militant wing giving up on negotiation and deciding that direct action was their only alternative. Galamison was the first to walk out of the talks. In a letter to Stanley Lowell, chair of the Human Rights Commission, Galamison urged Lowell to intervene and mediate between the Board of Education and the forces struggling for school integration, now that the talks had been terminated. Galamison pointed out that, despite the board's promises, it had done little to promote integration. The Presbyterian pastor attacked the board's integration plan, referring to pairing as a "piecemeal, tokenism program," and noted that the civil rights groups had operated in good faith. They had met with the board's professional staff twelve times during the summer but to no avail. Striking a note of great concern, Galamison contended: "We can no longer keep faith with the people we represent and continue to meet with those at the Board who make a farce of discussion and negotiation."[72]

But The Siloam pastor was not relying on mediation. Galamison notified

Lowell that the militant groups involved planned to shut down all "600" schools in the city (schools for violent juveniles) if his demands were not met. Demands included the upgrading of 165 black and Puerto Rican teachers to supervisory positions; revising of the construction program to conform with a city-wide plan for desegregation; issuance of, or commitment to the issuance of, a city-wide plan and timetable for school desegregation; an objective evaluation by a study group with no relationship to the board; institution of a curriculum in the 600 schools; the institution of a screening process or admissions procedure for pupils to the 600 schools; and their return to the mainstream of the school system.[73] Galamison had to answer to his constituents. Accordingly, he was unwilling to continue fruitless negotiations while black and Puerto Rican parents were demanding results. Although he had attempted to negotiate, Galamison doubted that this tactic could work because the board was not serious about negotiating. He was convinced that the only way to win integration was through protracted protests that could disrupt normal procedures.

Galamison may have targeted the 600 schools because he did have the support to launch a city-wide protest. He calculated, however, that he could garner enough support from parents with children in these institutions, who—more than other parents—faced hostile school authorities who stigmatized and punished their children. They, like other parents, wanted the best for their children, but most were poor with little recourse. Galamison was hoping that he could draw support by focusing on their plight. He argued that no objective method was used to decide whether a child belongs in these alternative schools. The militant pastor claimed that there were few counseling services for students and many students were simply misplaced. Galamison referred to children who attended the "600" schools as prisoners. Just as important, the Siloam pastor probably counted on manipulating the fear of the public. The notion of countless numbers of children who were seen as juvenile delinquents running the streets of New York might strike fear in city officials as well as the general public, forcing the board to concede.[74]

Soon after Galamison left the negotiating team, Ellen Lurie of EQUAL also walked out of the talks, realizing that nothing was being accomplished. Backing Galamison and the City-Wide Committee's call to arms, Lurie called on community organizations to develop a "broad spectrum of actions suitable for each community which demonstrates such support."[75] Although the activists' aims were noble, attempting to pressure the board into accepting their demands was not practical; the movement was divided and the militants were too ineffectual. More importantly, the left fringe's call for action was coming at a bad time, as people were growing weary of unending protests with little to show for them. Black Power by the mid-1960s was gaining momentum, especially in the urban North, and its goal was not integration but black control of the educational, political, and economic institutions of the black community. Because of the failure of the civil rights movement to dramatically change the social conditions for the ghetto poor and a growing revival of black nationalism, integration to many blacks became undesirable and even counterproductive. Integration was seen as a tool to weaken blacks. What people of African origin needed was power to determine their destiny.

On January 12, 1965, in yet another attempt to bring pressure on the Board of Education, Galamison made it clear that the left was gearing up for action. He pointed his finger at the board's construction budget, asserting that thirty-nine schools were scheduled to be built in exclusively black and Puerto Rican areas with sixteen in white communities. The Siloam pastor declared: "we have no alternative but to shut down the inferior, segregated schools as recommended by the Allen report."[76] The civil rights groups decided on Operation Shutdown, selecting schools that would be forced to close until the demands of the civil rights negotiating team were met. In an attempt to win support for Operation Shutdown, the militants held meetings and printed materials explaining the reason for the action. One flyer noted that since February 1964, black, Hispanic, and white leaders had negotiated with the board: "We have talked and talked and talked and talked. . . . The schools are still segregated." Arguing that the city refused to desegregate and that "Now is the Time for Action!" it called on all supporters to attend a meeting on January 19.[77]

Galamison and the City-Wide Committee for Integrated Schools had been marginalized after the first boycott and were further marginalized by hopeless actions like Operation Shutdown. Knowing that they could no longer cripple the entire system, they selected particular schools, choosing in January Junior High School 49 in Williamsburg. The City-Wide Committee, asserting that it had been paid enough lip service from the board, turned to the grassroots. Although the militant pastor gained support from groups such as EQUAL, the Harlem Parents Committee, and various CORE chapters, he did not have the clout he had in February 1964. EQUAL declared in a tone of righteous indignation that, after eight months of fruitless negotiation and public appeals, "there is no other recourse." However, the big question remained: how many were willing to take to the streets?[78]

The project received some support from high school and college teachers, who established a freedom school in the Chapel of the Intercession at 155th Street and Old Broadway, serving lunch to the children. The staff offered a curriculum that included African history, dramatics, sports, arts and crafts, social studies, mathematics, and foreign languages.[79]

In certain areas the shutdown seemed to be effective. Because of the shutdown campaign at Junior High School 164 and four other schools in the area, the freedom school at the Chapel of the Intercession had so many children that nearby churches were used to house children. Parents and students joined the picket lines from 7:30 to 9:00 A.M. Monday through Friday. Organizers hoped that this form of protest could actually "break the back of the Board of Education."[80]

Despite the optimism of the organizers, they had little chance of winning. Unlike the massive boycott, this one had only limited support. It did not shut down the schools. Although some parents supported the campaign, others had become irritated at the attempted disruption of their children's school day. There was little support for the shutdown in the Puerto Rican community, and it was nonexistent in the white areas of the city.

Galamison and the militants were being accused of using children for their own purposes. The board fought back by gaining court injunctions restraining encouragement of the boycott. As could be expected, the leaders of the national civil rights organizations, with the exception of James Farmer, who announced his support during a rally at City College, did not give their support.[81]

In response to the lack of support by the NAACP, the Harlem Youth Committee organized by the Harlem Parents Committee targeted both the Board of Education and the civil rights organization. The group of 200 youths took to the streets and protested in front of the NAACP headquarters on February 23 to gain support for Operation Shutdown and persuade its legal defense fund to file a federal suit against the board. Despite the demonstration, Wilkins did not respond to their demands.[82]

Even the famed baseball legend Jackie Robinson, who had participated in the demonstrations at the construction site of Downstate Medical Center in the summer of 1963, blasted Galamison for his latest protest effort. By advocating the shutdown of 600 schools, Galamison was using children for his own political goals. According to the baseball player turned columnist, Galamison was using disadvantaged children as "pawns" in the struggle for integration. He acknowledged that Martin Luther King and other civil rights leaders had used children in Birmingham, but New York was different. The Board of Education had acted earnestly to desegregate the school system, while Birmingham had used force to maintain segregation.[83]

Giving his support for the demonstration, James Farmer denied the accusation that children were pawns: "We have rejected the concept that youngsters should not participate in civil rights demonstrations. They are not being forced to do anything against their will. In fact, most of the motivation for the Civil Rights struggle has come from the youth."[84]

Despite the noble effort, the struggle for integration was over. By early March, the 600-schools campaign had ended. The board paid no attention to the demonstrations, simply because the organizers had little support. The board's decision to move away from the issue of integration as a major priority was demonstrated in the inaugural address of the new superintendent, Bernard Donovan, in September 1965. Donovan declared that all of the efforts of the board "will be geared to the provision of a program of excellence for children of the City of New York." Although integration was mentioned as an "important aspect" of this goal, education was the board's "primary function," according to Donovan. High rates of pupil mobility, the dropout rate, manpower retraining programs, and testing programs were Donovan's focus. The superintendent asserted that the mastery of the tools of learning was at the core of his program: "The development of skill mastery on the part of every pupil is not only an essential ingredient of a program of excellence in the schools but is an inescapable necessity for any program which seeks to further integration in this city."[85]

In a unmistakable message to civil rights groups, Donovan maintained that he was willing to work with these groups, but their advice and help must be "specific and constructive. We shall be ready at all times to participate with persons and groups in the City who wish to pursue purposeful and productive programs." The integration programs would move forward, and progress would be made in the intermediate and high school building programs, rezoning, and open enrollment. But it was clear that the protest had no effect on the board.[86]

Unlike the first boycott, the subsequent events led by the militant New York City civil rights movement could not win support from the general public because it had not convinced those who once had supported the crusade that its tactics and, more importantly, its objectives, were still sound. In the end the militants did not have the clout to bring out the numbers they needed to launch an effective demonstration. To be sure, some people who had participated in the ten-year campaign were wary of ongoing campaigns and convinced that the movement could not make a difference. But the withdrawal from the coalition of the conventional civil rights organizations as well as the National Association for Puerto Rican Civil Rights, the lack of support from liberals and labor, and the futile Operation Shutdown campaign zapped the movement of its strength and created the perception that it was in chaos. The public withdrawal of organizations from the coalition and the perception that the school integration movement was divided could only lead to demoralization among partisans of the movement and loss of their support. Thus, by 1965 the vigorous campaign for integration, led by Galamison, had come to an end.

Although the New York City school integration movement had perished, Galamison's activities as a leader for school reform did not cease. By the end of 1966, the Brooklyn pastor would be swept into the movement for community control.

# chapter seven

# THE PEOPLE'S BOARD OF EDUCATION, OCEAN HILL–BROWNSVILLE, AND THE LAST HURRAH

Milton Galamison found himself in a political as well as ideological dilemma by the end of the struggle for school integration. He had led the school integration movement for a decade and in numerous speeches and sermons had spoken on the moral necessity for an integrated society, asserting that it was the best way to destroy all notions of superiority and inferiority in people. Moreover, he had stressed that an integrated society would help create a community where all could be provided equally with the resources for success. Galamison contended that segregation, on the other hand, was immoral because it led to a feeling of inferiority among the victims and the closing of avenues of success. Consistent with his views on racial separation, he had spoken out against black nationalism, at times comparing it to white supremacy ideology. In a sermon in 1961, he contended: "What if, after defeating race supremacy, the victors become race supremacists? What if, after overcoming exploitation, the victors become exploiters? What if, after winning the victory over the Ku Kl[u]x Klanism and the White Citiz[e]ns men?"[1] Black nationalists' plans would only encourage whites to deny access to power and wealth to African Americans. It was clearly a dangerous movement in the eyes of the integrationist.

But by 1965 the black power movement was emerging in black communities across the nation. The civil rights movement had worked for an integrated society but had not rid the nation of urban slums, inadequate health care, segregated schools, and black unemployment, especially among youths. By the mid-1960s, black power advocates criticized the civil rights leaders' attempt to forge an integrated society. Instead these proponents of black nationalism called for community empowerment and control over institutions in the black community as a viable means of improving the circumstances of African Americans. They asserted that the only possible solution to relieve black suffering was not integration but black political and economic empowerment.

The transformation of Brooklyn CORE is a good illustration of the movement toward black power. By the mid-1960s, new members advocating a more nationalist approach joined the Brooklyn organization. Brooklyn CORE targeted low-income blacks for membership. In order to appeal to them, it emphasized black power and moved away from the goal of integration. The nationalists within the civil rights group contended that for blacks to win control of the institutions in their community, they must be in control of their organizations. "The Man" (whites) should not play a vital role in these black organizations because he did not have black interests at heart. Integration, black power advocates contended, was only a scheme to assure white control of the black movement for liberation. White liberals, feeling uneasy and unwelcome, began leaving the Brooklyn organization. David Feingold, a member of Brooklyn CORE complained:

At the end of last year [1966] Brooklyn CORE's loyal membership was not as active as it had been. The liberals had been turned off by black power; many militant black persons had gotten anti-poverty jobs; the black power controversy had alienated others, including black members.

A vacuum was created. Into this vacuum a number of Nationalists moved. CORE welcomed them, seeing new blood, as well as persons who could be used constructively.

According to Feingold, by February the nationalists had dominated Brooklyn CORE and "harassed" white members and black integrationists. In response to Feingold's charges, Brooklyn CORE leaders noted that whites in the organization could "help in private conferences with the black organizers" and could be used as "resource" persons but they should not be organizers. The message coming out of CORE was clear: blacks should run the operation, signifying the direction toward black power.[2]

Galamison had attacked class inequality; he thought that integration was the means of breaking down economic barriers. He maintained that desegregation would assure a fair distribution of resources to the disadvantaged. When the integration movement failed to win substantial gains and community control had gained momentum, he was dismayed. Shuddering at the "prospect of a separate state for blacks," he argued that blacks should not be denied the wealth that they had helped create. Despite his advocacy for integration, by 1966 he and his movement had become marginal in the black community.[3]

Galamison confessed that he was lost when community control had gained momentum. The community control movement had first appeared to him as a black separatist movement struggling for all he had opposed, a separate but equal society. Although Galamison actively opposed the community control movement, Annie Stein, his friend and close collaborator, felt differently. Stein had contended that progressive whites must follow the leadership and sentiment of the black community. As early as 1960, she had suggested to Galamison that it might be necessary for blacks to abandon the integration struggle and pursue black empowerment. Throughout her political career, Stein had argued that blacks must define and lead their own struggle for liberation. It was the job of progressive whites to support the black struggle but not step to the fore and grab leadership. When the black power and community control movement emerged, Stein embraced it.[4]

Despite his distaste for community control, by 1966 Galamison publicly supported the movement. In an article in the left journal *Freedomways*, he asserted that the community-control struggle was an attempt to end colonization. Segregation would continue but blacks would be in positions of power. "If the schools had to be segregated, they would be segregated at every level. Non-resident whites could not reap the economic benefits of working in the black Community while black children suffered the degradation of unwantedness."[5]

At first glance, it seemed that he had joined the nationalist camp. But this was not the case. In an interview soon after the Ocean Hill–Brownsville confrontation (to be discussed below) Galamison admitted that nationalists supported community control but he denied that community control emphasized racial separation. "What emerged was something that black people could live with, and that was a community-controlled program that neither emphasized integration nor segregation, but which addressed itself to local community power." Community control became a means for the community to initiate school reform. A few years later, the Presbyterian pastor again presented a non-nationalistic argument for community control. Community control, he contended, was not necessarily synonymous with black separatism. "It is my conviction that the current stream of Black consciousness is not a rejection of racial unity as a desirable goal nor is it a negation of unity as an ideal. It is not an abandonment of wholesome objectives. The current Black consciousness is one important aspect of the search for a better way. It means community empowerment." The school system had failed to educate children and it now was up to parents to control the educational institutions where their children attended.[6] He simply dissociated the issue of black nationalism from the issue of community control and instead focused on parent empowerment.

Galamison went so far as to argue that community control could actually promote parent and teacher unity. Besides allowing teachers to become more creative by escaping a bureaucracy that shackled them, the Siloam pastor asserted that community control would allow parents and teachers to "work shoulder to shoulder for the welfare of the children and as a result, one would hope to create the kind of atmosphere in which teaching and learning can take place." Integration remained a personal and preferred goal of the pastor. But support of community control assured him that he would not be isolated from the black community.[7]

It should be noted that although Galamison continued to stress black and white unity, he differed with many on the left on the major benefit of community control. The Peace and Freedom Party argued a class and race view by asserting that the school system was designed to assure that white affluent children would take their position in society as skilled workers, professionals, and leaders of society. Black and Hispanic children were miseducated so they could take their place among the unskilled and unemployed. In order to end this practice, the leftist organization declared, parents must take over the schools. The Peace and Freedom Party called for the elimination of the Board of Education, and its replacement by local community boards with the power to hire and fire school personnel, determine the curriculum, and manage all financial matters of the schools. Attempting to build a bridge among the white working-class members of the Board of Education (teachers) and the working class made up of people of color (black and Latino communities), the group contended that teachers must be partners with parents in this revolution. Attempting to claim that both groups were natural allies, and that community control did not mean anti-white or anti-Jewish, it claimed that the enemy of teachers and parents was the board. The Board of Education feared an alliance between the two groups because a united front would force a change in the status quo. However, the union leadership had sided with the board by using fear and advocating racist policies. The Peace and Freedom Party realized that not all teachers would yield to this appeal so it argued that community control assured professionalism.[8]

Unlike the Peace and Freedom Party and other groups who called for a unified working class to battle class exploitation, Galamison did not stress a working-class alliance. The preeminent evil of society for Galamison remained racism. While Galamison and Stein both argued that the educational structure was a colonial system set up to exploit blacks and Latinos, the militant pastor continued to emphasize that a harmonious community where democracy could reign could be brought about not just through working-class unity, but also through community organizing and a spiritual awakening and a commitment to high spiritual principles to set the nation straight. Fair play on the part of those who held power was the solution. "What is on trial is the total democratic process in which the rights and needs of the minority are at the mercy of a willful and insensitive majority. The majority people, like those on the front end of a long line, may feel *that a line is a good thing.* But there are others, like minority people, on the tail end of the line, who may have a different idea." According to Galamison, the end result of the refusal of whites to see the moral imperative of being fair was violence.[9]

## The People's Board of Education

Although by 1966 the school integration movement was extinct, community activism was still teeming in the black and Latino communities. Commu-

nity activists and concerned parents began struggling for community control of schools. They demanded the right to hire teachers, make decisions on
the school's curriculum, control fiscal and capital budgets, and negotiate
union contracts.[10] One of these groups organized by community activists
was the People's Board of Education.

The People's Board of Education had its origins in the school integration struggle in Brownsville, Brooklyn, in the 1960s. Community activists,
including Galamison, Ellen Lurie of EQUAL, Thelma Hamilton, and the
Reverend John Powis attempted to persuade the board to relieve overcrowding of the schools in that community. Powis, who became associate
pastor of Saint Benedict's Roman Catholic Church in Brooklyn in 1963, remembers that children of the community did not receive a full day of instruction because of overcrowding. They demanded that Superintendent
Bernard Donovan transfer children attending overcrowded schools in
Brownsville to underutilized schools in Brooklyn and Queens. In the summer of 1965, Donovan agreed and asked Lurie and others to sign up families in Brownsville who would be willing to send their children to Bay
Ridge, Brooklyn. Powis claimed that they were able to sign up the parents
of 1,700 children.[11]

On the opening day of school in September 1965, Powis recalls accom-
panying a group of children from Brownsville to a school in Bay Ridge.
When the bus reached its destination in the mostly Italian and Catholic community, Powis described it as a "scene out of hell." Neighborhood residents
greeted the children by throwing eggs at them and calling them "niggers."
Powis, although dressed as a priest, was not spared from the egg-throwing
mob. He "received as much egg as anyone else."[12]

As the school year went on, conditions for the children did not improve.
The Brownsville parents of the children who were bussed complained that
their children were put in segregated classes and were treated harshly by
other children and the professional staff. By the end of the first year parents
began withdrawing their children from the schools. The traumatic experience convinced many activists and parents that the only viable solution for
assuring quality education for black and Latino children was community
control. Powis, Ellen Lurie, Thelma Hamilton, and other community leaders met with Donovan and argued that black and Puerto Rican children
were not wanted in predominantly white areas, thus they should be granted the opportunity to operate the schools in their communities. In order to

bring community forces together, work for community control, and improve conditions, Powis, Hamilton, and others helped establish the Brownsville Community Council, Inc.[13]

The group asserted that the black and Latino parents must have a say in the education of their children. It called for stronger PTAs in black and Latino areas, involvement of these communities in the selection of administrators, and control over schools' budgets, curriculums, and zoning. Moreover, the community organization contended that the school staff should be accountable to the taxpayers "with wage increases and promotions based as much on increased achievement of pupils as on seniority."[14]

Community activists from the Brownsville Community Council, the Independent Local School Board 17 (a group that worked for a special decentralized district in Brownsville), EQUAL, PTAs, and other community groups attended Board of Education meetings to express their concern about educational matters. On December 19, 1966, at a public Board of Education hearing on the budget, Lillian Wagner, president of the PTA of J.H.S. 263 in Brownsville, went to the microphone and attempted to inform the board members about the conditions in the junior high school. She was challenged by Alfred A. Giardino, Vice President of the board, who asserted that she had not followed the correct procedures. Speakers were required to request time to speak in advance of the meeting. Wagner had failed to do so. When Wagner insisted on speaking, the crowd of parents and activists from Harlem, East Harlem, the Lower East Side of Manhattan, the Bronx, and Brooklyn rallied around Wagner and began to shout, Giardino called a ten-minute recess to restore order. However, when the meeting resumed Wagner was still at the microphone and insisted on speaking. She had been joined by others who waited their turn to address the meeting. Lloyd K. Garrison, president of the board, took over the meeting and denied Wagner's request to speak, noting she had not followed procedure. When the crowd disrupted the meeting insisting on her right to speak, board members left the hearing room.[15]

In what seemed to be a spontaneous move, the demonstrators decided to create the Ad Hoc Board of Education of the People of the City of New York (AHPB). Powis recalls someone approaching him and asking "would you want to be a member of the People's Board of Education?" Although reluctant to say yes because he had no idea how his diocese felt about the matter, he eventually agreed, believing that the activists' struggle might be brought to the public's attention. Ellen Lurie also contended that the parents at the budget hearing reacted to the board's walkout by appointing "their own People's Board of Education." Galamison, who had not attended the meet- ing, was called by a supporter informing him of events at the board. He immediately rushed to the scene and joined the takeover.[16]

The parents and activists at the board that day elected several members to the AHPB, including Galamison, who served as President; Evelina Antonetty of The United Bronx Parents, who served as Vice President; Powis; Babette Edwards of the East Harlem Union and a member of the I.S. 201 Negotiating Committee, one of the first parent groups to advocate community control; Ellen Lurie of EQUAL; David Spencer, Chair of the I.S. 201 Negotiating Committee; Rev. Robert Nichol of East Harlem Parish; Thelma Hamilton of the Brownsville Community Council; Rosalie Stutz of EQUAL; Dolores Costello, a member of the P.S. 36–125 Committee; William Hall of SNCC, and Vincent Negron, a member of Christians for Social Action.[17]

The list of board members of the AHPB suggests why Galamison was contacted. Many of these people were veterans of the school integration struggle and allies of the Siloam pastor, including Lurie and Hamilton, who had worked closely with him in the school integration campaign. Powis had also worked with Galamison in the struggle to relieve overcrowding in Brownsville. They realized that Galamison's participation in the takeover would bring a great deal of attention to the event because of his notoriety. For Galamison the takeover offered an opportunity to lead another community struggle. He was no longer watching from the sidelines: this new organization put Galamison back into a leadership position, challenging his old nemesis, the Board of Education.[18]

The AHPB members took the seats of the official board members and sent a telegram to the new mayor, John Lindsay, informing him of the takeover and demanding that he meet with them. They also demanded that Lindsay declare a "state of emergency in the administration of public education in New York City," officially remove the present Board of Education members, establish a selection committee consisting of the Chancellor of the University of the State of New York and the president of the PEA, and that persons be appointed to the Board of Education who "would be responsive to parent-community concerns." The Ad Hoc People's Board of Education also asserted that it would meet every day and not give up its seats until its demands were met.[19]

The AHPB began conducting hearings. Parents gave testimony about educational conditions and the lack of adequate resources in the schools their children attended. The AHPB also released a position paper addressing the issues of decentralization, accountability, community participation, and selection of principals. It planned to hold borough-wide hearings, establish its own local school boards, appoint district superintendents, and call community meetings. The AHPB noted it would rely on militant tactics such as boycotting school programs and other special events that did not pertain to the concerns of black and Latino parents.[20] Unquestionably, the objective of the AHPB was to win legitimacy and respect among the parents and children of predominantly black and Latino communities.

After a three-day occupation of the hearing room, Assistant Superintendent Thomas F. Nevins, with the help of the police, entered, approached the dais, and asked the demonstrators to leave. Apparently the board feared that arresting the demonstrators would result in greater support for the protestors. However, Galamison knew the longer he waited, the less competent the board would seem. Having been arrested on several occasions, Galamison was fully aware of the image projected by people willing to go to jail for their cause. During the civil rights struggles, becoming a "jailbird for freedom" helped win sympathy from the general public because it proclaimed the sacrifice people were willing to make for a moral cause. In this case, Galamison attempted to convey the sacrifice he and others were willing to make on the behalf of the children. He responded to Nevins by asserting "We will have to be placed under arrest."

A crowd of about fifty were in the room and cheered the AHPB. Playing to his supporters, Galamison declared "We will not turn our backs on our children. We will continue to hold hearings here today as the People's Board." A police officer first took the Presbyterian pastor by the arm and led him out of the chamber. Soon the others were led out and saw a crowd of supporters who carried signs that read "Free the Real Board of Education." That evening when the board attempted to resume its budget hearings, demonstrators interrupted the meeting.[21]

In order to gain momentum and not lose support, Galamison and the AHPB submitted a press release a few days after their removal from 110 Livingston Street. The group announced that it would enjoin the "Garrison Board of Education" from ratifying the 1967–1968 school budget. AHPB complained that the official board had arbitrarily adjourned a legal public hearing before all who were present could address the issue. It also claimed that the board's proposed budget violated the civil rights of black and Puerto Rican students because it provided them with a less than adequate education.[22]

The AHPB accused the Board of Education of misleading the public by reporting that reading scores had improved. According to the group, the board deliberately concealed the fact that "the number of students retarded more than one year also increased" in Harlem and Washington Heights. The group asserted that in District 6 in Harlem the number of second graders who were one or more years behind grade level had increased from 22 percent in October 1965 to 50 percent by May 1966. It alleged that between October 1965 and May 1966, the average fifth-grade class in District 6 had gone from 14 percent who were behind grade level to 33 percent. The group chided the board for not recognizing that it was responsible for the setback in the black and Latino communities while noting that the scores in the predominantly white, affluent District 26 in Queens were above grade level. The average second-grade score was 3.6 and the average fifth-grade score was 8.0. The AHPB declared: "The very purpose of public education is to reduce the gaps that exist because children . . . have different socio-economic backgrounds, but after five years in a New York City public school it is evident that the disadvantages are compounded by the public schools themselves."[23]

The AHPB announced that its "Bureau of Educational Research" would conduct a proper study of the reading scores because the board had not taken into account several factors, such as the exclusion of children from testing variations in achievement among schools with similar and dissimilar populations. The group argued that because the board's budget had not addressed these problems it should be opposed.[24]

The People's Board declared itself an alternative body to the official board. On January 3, 1967, the AHPB outlined its position on a number of vital issues including decentralization. It argued that parents and community groups should control their children's education and the Board of Education must be held accountable to the parents of children who were educated in the schools. Moreover, parents must have the opportunity to participate in the "day to day operation of the school system at the local and city-wide levels."[25]

The AHPB contended that the board should recruit people from the community and train them as assistant teachers (paraprofessionals) because they had a wealth of knowledge about the children and the community. By calling for the training of community people to work in the schools, the People's Board was avoiding the charge that it was advocating that unqualified people work with children. By training community people, the board would be tapping into an important resource in the community. Despite their education, teachers were portrayed as outsiders, not having knowledge of or ties to the Black and Hispanic communities. Their unfamiliarity with and lack of ties to the communities were often cited by community activists as reasons for student failure. Teachers were unconcerned and would not spend time after school to assist students. On the other hand, the men and women of the community, the parents of the children who attended the public schools in these areas, could add to the pedagogical expertise of teaching. This scheme was a means of involving the community in the schools.

The People's Board of Education, which by January had dropped the Ad Hoc label, also opposed "Garrison's plan for a city-wide task force to find answers to the problems of education in disadvantaged communities." Noting that although the board had conducted numerous earlier studies seeking answers to the problem of the disadvantaged from experts, it had failed to act on their recommendations. The People's Board criticized the use of "outsiders as experts" and called on the board to rely on community people. "A task force, no matter how prestigious and well meaning its participants, would have the effect of interjecting a third party between local communities and the Garrison Board at a time when residents of the ghetto are beginning to force the school system to recognize their right to participate in their children's education."[26]

The militant group argued that at its January meeting real experts, parents and community leaders, would inform the board what action should be taken. It promised that it would continue to listen to the concerns of parents and fight for decentralization.[27]

In order to minimize fighting within the organization, members of the People's Board suggested that no member speak for the group without a full discussion of the entire People's Board. Moreover, in order to make itself visible throughout the black and Latino communities, it established one office in the South Bronx, two in Brooklyn, one in Lower Manhattan, and one in East Harlem. The Student Non-Violent Coordinating Committee (SNCC) provided office space to the People's Board in its Harlem office.[28]

The People's Board of Education helped Galamison stay connected to the grassroots. Like the Parents' Workshop, it gave him the opportunity to speak to community groups and stay in contact with ordinary people. Although Galamison did not invoke a nationalist appeal, his argument for community control, putting education in the hands of parents because the board had failed to educate them, appealed to black nationalists as well as those who called for black and white unity. His fate seemed to be linked to the black and Latino communities of New York.

But in February, the *World Journal Tribune* reported that the head of the People's Board of Education was expected to accept the position of head of the Opportunities Industrialization Centers (OIC). The goal of the program was to train thousands of ghetto teens for jobs. According to the *Tribune*, a source in the city's Human Resources Administration said Galamison was going to make his announcement in three weeks.[29]

Despite Galamison's alliance with community activists who were battling the school system, he was also developing another agenda. While he was waging a battle for community control and attacking the board, the Presbyterian pastor was also becoming a power broker. With years of street protest having failed to provide substantial gains, he came to the conclusion that as an insider he could accomplish a lot more for the community than he could as a protest leader. Moreover, despite his public position about community control, he still held grave doubts about its objectives. In addition, Mayor John Lindsay, a liberal Republican, had developed close ties with the ministerial powers of the city by providing money for anti-poverty programs. Galamison also became one of the beneficiaries of the Lindsay gravy train. Besides the OIC position, he had been serving on the city-wide Council Against Poverty, an agency that made policy and approved anti-poverty programs. He had also become an unofficial adviser to the Mayor.[30]

Probably fearing that he might be labeled a person who capitulated to the power structure as he moved to become a power broker, Galamison attempted to remain loyal to his protest politics. At the same time that he was contemplating becoming head of the New York OIC he continued as president of the People's Board of Education. He was attempting to juggle both roles, power broker and protest leader. With Galamison as its president, the People's Board of Education continued to hold public meetings, demanding community control. Galamison and the People's Board's major targets were the Board of Education and teachers. At a March meeting in front of an estimated crowd of 250, the People's Board proposed that the official board relinquish its authority to the people. Members of the radical group declared that the power of the official board should be invested in local school boards, giving them the right to hire and fire school personnel.[31]

On another occasion Galamison declared that the "Garrison" Board of Education was no longer in control of the school system and had abandoned the children. The professional staff, according to the pastor, was not educating children and could not maintain order in Bronx schools. He noted that if teachers were willing to "abdicate" their authority, then parents and community groups should demand the power to operate the schools. He pointed out that in P.S. 36 in Manhattan, parents had already stepped to the fore by establishing a committee that had been conducting a full educational program for 1,200 children. He called on parents throughout the city to hold sympathy demonstrations.[32]

Galamison and the People's Board of Education argued that teachers were paid a salary for expected performance. "The standard for teachers must be student achievement." Hence, parents in the black and Hispanic communities must have a voice in determining the employment of school personnel. Although Galamison spoke of the possibilities of a teacher-parent alliance, in 1967 it was not a reality. Galamison and other community leaders contended that teachers were more interested in their comfort and improving their livelihood than in the education of black and Latino children.

Galamison's attacks on teachers reflected his view of the transformation of teacher unionism in New York City by the 1960s. By the early 1960s, the TU had folded and the United Federation of Teachers had become the voice of teachers. Unlike the TU, the UFT espoused a more conservative trade unionism. Its major focus was on improving wages and working conditions. Although it urged that additional services and professionals be assigned to "ghetto schools," it maintained the problem in the black and Latino communities was a ghetto environment that produced pathological behavior. The UFT contended that the black urban poor must be provided with special assistance to assimilate and succeed. To many, the UFT was taking racism off the hook and simply blaming the victim. It was attempting to protect white privilege.[33] Although Galamison was careful not to refer to race and attack white teachers, he nevertheless painted a picture of teachers as part of the system that oppressed black children. For instance, on April 10, Galamison and other members of the People's Board of Education joined parents from the Two Bridges Neighborhood on the Lower East Side of

Manhattan in a torchlight vigil at three schools. They were protesting the large number of daily teacher absences. Moreover, the community claimed that school officials in the area refused to have parent-teacher conferences in the evening, making it inconvenient for parents who worked.[34]

Galamison contended that teachers were uncaring, had no interest in the black and Latino communities, and were linked to the system of oppression. They had formed an "unholy alliance" with the Board of Education in order to heap destruction on the city's communities. The fact that the UFT did not support a teacher transfer plan recommended by the commission on integration and did not support the citywide boycotts indicated that it was more interested in its positions than in the welfare of black and Latino children and community empowerment.[35]

Galamison portrayed whites not as innately evil racists but as a group of Americans made sick by a racist society. Racism was ingrained in white Americans and racism was endemic to America. The solution for overcoming racism was not black essentialism but for blacks and whites to struggle for interracial unity, a unity that included community political empowerment for the black and Latino communities.[36]

Galamison held the belief that by restricting the school system, teachers could be made more effective. In order to make teachers more sensitive to the needs of black and Latino children, he called for the immediate implementation of an "intensive compulsory course in urban life and education for every teacher who works in the ghetto." He also proposed mandatory two-week to one-month summer resident workshops for teachers who worked in the black and Latino communities. These teachers would be assigned to the areas where they were employed to perform nonteaching duties (duties he not specify). Galamison assumed that the more familiar teachers were with the world of black and Latino children the more successful they would be in educating them.[37] Black and white unity was possible but there needed to be a transformation of consciousness among whites. They must be enlightened about the conditions of people of color.

Black and white unity was not limited to teachers receiving an education about the ghetto. They should have knowledge of the home conditions of the children they taught and work with people from the community. In order to help accomplish this objective, Galamison urged the assignment of a home-liaison person for every classroom in poor black and Latino areas.

This person should be "indigenous, trained by the board, and offered career improvement prospects."[38]

Evidence that the People's Board worked for interracial unity was its "Evening of International, Interracial, Intercultural but Never Interrupted Entertainment" fund raiser in late May. The event, held at Big Wilt Small's Paradise Club in Harlem, featured dancing and an "international fashion show."[39] Obviously, Galamison and the People's Board attempted to strike a balance between integration and community control.

Similar to the Parents' Workshop, the Peoples' Board informed parents how the system operated, how they could voice their concerns, and how they could best change the direction of education in New York City. On one such occasion it released an "Analysis of the Proposed 1967–1968 Executive Budget as it Pertains to Public Education." It told community groups to write at once requesting time to speak at the public hearing. It also urged groups to contact their council representatives, borough presidents, the Comptroller, and President of the City Council to voice their opinions. In an attempt to encourage activism among parents, the People's Board suggested that they pay a surprise visit to the local schools and see firsthand the current impact of the Board of Education's budget. This act of visiting schools would also empower parents by transforming them from inactive persons, detached from their local schools, to men and women who would monitor every aspect of their children's education.[40]

In its analysis of the proposed expense budget, the People's Board of Education focused on remedial programs and class size. It contended that reading programs failed, because they begin working with children who were at least two years behind grade level, making it difficult to overcome the reading deficiency. Successful intervention took place when the child was a year or less behind grade level. Continuing to take aim at teachers, the People's Board declared that of the 54,235 teachers in the system, only 170 regular and 82 substitutes had been given unsatisfactory ratings in the last five years, which indicated that the board had not found ways of monitoring and dealing with unsatisfactory teachers. The organization implied that the Board of Education and the teachers union were more interested in protecting white teachers' privileges than they were in educating black and Latino children. The People's Board linked teachers to a system of oppression of black children.[41]

In addition, the People's Board asserted that the board wanted to spend only one million dollars in training teachers, clearly not enough to make

teachers sensitive to the needs of black and Latino children. The report also
noted that the board continued to operate the Board of Examiners, an institution that had been accused of hindering the hiring of teachers of color.
Because of its oral examination, Galamison and others asserted that black
applicants with a southern dialect and Latino applicants who spoke with a
Spanish accent found it difficult to pass the teachers examination given by
the Board of Examiners. By continuing this practice, the Board of Education demonstrated little sympathy to the demand for more black and Latino
teachers who could serve as role models for children.[42]

The People's Board proposed that a decentralized budget for each school
or each district be created. This proposition would make it easier for parents to understand how money was spent on a local level. It also called on
the city to allow ghetto parents to be a part of the committee to draw up
plans for decentralization.[43]

Responding to the growing support for community control and seeing
an avenue to gain more money from the state for education, Mayor John
Lindsay set up a panel headed by McGeorge Bundy, President of the Ford
Foundation, to suggest a plan for decentralizing the New York City school
system. The panel called for the creation of a school system that consisted
of thirty to sixty autonomous local governing school boards. Each school
system would be run by a board of six elected and five mayoral appointees.

Galamison, while generally praising the report and asserting that it was
a giant step forward, nevertheless criticized two of the panel's proposals;
if implemented, the present board would remain in existence. He argued
that the people had called for the abolition of the present board and the
creation of a three-member central education commission. Moreover, the
local school board was to be selected by the mayor "after consultation with
parents and community organizations." He suggested that the central education agency submit names to the mayor from a list provided by the community or that three of the five members appointed by the mayor be presented
by the central school agency from the lists drawn up by the community.[44]

## The Ocean Hill–Brownsville Crisis

Although the People's Board had some support among the activists and had
joined with other organizations to form the City-Wide Coalition for Com-

munity Control, it was short lived. Its major problem was that although community activists helped form the board, it had become more of a city-wide protest group and not a community organization with deep roots in any particular community. The People's Board was not in a strong position to negotiate for the establishment of a local school board for any particular community because community negotiating organizations in several neighborhoods, struggling to establish local school boards in their areas, were already in existence.[45]

When both the Lindsay administration and the board demonstrated interest in decentralization and began speaking to community groups, those most active in the People's Board decided to dedicate their energy and work closer with those community groups. When Powis and other community activists established the Brownsville Community Council in February 1967 and began negotiating with Superintendent Bernard Donovan and the Board of Education for community control, they simply stopped working with the People's Board. Consequently, when decentralization became a reality, the People's Board withered away.[46]

Powis, who was now associated with Our Lady of the Presentation Church, had also introduced Mario Fantini of the Ford Foundation to the Brownsville Community Council. Fantini was very much interested in school reform and especially in community control. In early 1967, the foundation decided to provide funds for an experimental district in Ocean Hill to Powis and his small group of activists, who had organized themselves into the Brownsville Ocean-Hill Independent Local School Board. Members of Brooklyn CORE, the Brooklyn Council Against Poverty, and parents, as well as Sandra Feldman from the UFT, worked with the Brownsville Ocean-Hill Independent Local School Board for decentralization. Powis asserts that Feldman was extremely supportive of the group.[47]

In June, the board gave Donovan permission to go ahead and make plans for a decentralization project. The superintendent requested the promised allotment from the Ford Foundation and recognized the Ocean Hill Independent School Board as an official planning group. He assigned his special assistant, Robert Robinson, to work with the community group to help establish an experimental district and to submit to the board a plan outlining its responsibilities and functions. In late June the planning board hired Rhody McCoy as interim unit administrator.[48]

The forty-three year old McCoy, who was acting principal of a "600" school in Manhattan, was born and raised in the Nation's Capital. He had a bachelor's degree from Howard University and a Masters from New York University. McCoy, who had been influenced by the black power movement and Malcolm X in particular, decided to dedicate himself to the advancement of black people. His objective was for blacks to gain control of their destiny. The only way for this to happen was for blacks to be in control of their community institutions.[49]

The Planning board submitted its proposal to the board on July 29. It called for the establishment of a governing board of parents, community, and UFT representatives. Parents from each school in the district would elect a parent representative; teachers from each school would elect teacher representatives; and supervisors would elect a supervisor representative. Moreover, parent representatives would select community representatives from candidates selected by community organizations. Once in place, the governing planning board would select a unit administrator and approve his or her recommendations of principals where vacancies existed. The governing board would also have the power to select a business manager and nominees for community relations liaison among community people. It had the right to determine policy for the guidance of the unit administrator in curriculum and professional personnel. In addition, the proposal called for the governing board to determine the budgetary needs of the district.[50]

Before the Brownsville Planning Council submitted its proposal to the central board for approval, in early July the planning board had set up election procedures, campaigned in Ocean Hill, and registered 2,200 parents. It held an election on August 3, 1967. The planning council asserted that 1,049 parents, or 25 percent of those eligible to vote, did so in the August 3 election. Once the governing board was in place, it elected McCoy as its permanent unit administrator.[51]

Teachers reacted strongly to the developments in Ocean Hill. In a letter signed by seven school chapter leaders and four summer representatives, they claimed that a majority of teachers in the district had not been informed of the project until late June, when they were asked to elect representatives. Teachers did not participate in creating the proposal. They were extremely upset that on June 29 they were told by Powis that McCoy had been picked as the interim unit administrator of the district. The chapter leaders and summer representatives further claimed that when they attempted to clarify certain sections in the proposal that they found "ambiguous," they were accused of trying to destroy its original intent. They also claimed that while community groups made changes in the plan, teachers' suggestions were ignored. A major complaint of the teachers was the selection by McCoy of Herman Ferguson as principal of I.S. 55. Ferguson, a strong proponent of black power, had been indicted for conspiracy to murder Roy Wilkins and Whitney Young. Despite their objections the governing board voted for the nominee.[52]

McCoy contended that the unresolved issues between the community and the teachers were over teacher representation on the board, teacher responsibility to the board, the issue of supervision-tenure-evaluation, voting, and the legality of the decentralization operation. In addition, he admits that the initial proposal was modified, including the selection of the unit administrator. "These two factions [community, parents] together with the teachers, elected a Unit Administrator and a college representative. The name of only one candidate for appointment by the Superintendent of Schools was submitted rather than the requested three names recommended in the original proposal."[53]

Powis argues that the teachers' real opposition was to McCoy as unit administrator. The teachers had backed Jack Bloomfield, principal of J.H.S. 271, who was closely allied with the Ocean Hill Community Council, as well as a group of school officials, local politicians, and community people. According to Powis, the teachers had no idea that the governing board would select anyone but Bloomfield. When the board acted independently of the teachers, according to Powis, they turned against the experiment.[54]

The choice of McCoy for unit administrator by the Ocean Hill–Brownsville governing board and his selection of five principals to fill vacancies in schools in the district led to further conflict, especially with Albert Shanker, UFT President. Shanker, the son of Jewish immigrants, had taken part in sit-ins sponsored by CORE in the late 1950s. In 1964, he became President of the UFT. Both the Council of Supervisors Associations and Shanker filed petitions in the Supreme Court of Kings County (Brooklyn) alleging that the Board of Education was in violation of existing statutory provisions. By choosing McCoy and by his selection of principals who were not on the list of licensed candidates (people who had passed the Board of Examiners' examination for principal), the board was violating civil service procedure. For Shanker and CSA members, the board was undermining a procedure designed to assure that those who worked hard could move up the career ladder. McCoy and community people did not see it that way. They insist-

ed that the test administered by the Board of Examiners for supervisors
was a means of keeping blacks out. McCoy proclaimed that if more blacks
and Latinos were going to be working in the school system as principals,
then they would have to be appointed outside of the list, on which the
names of few blacks could be found.[55] There was little doubt that tensions
were running high in Ocean Hill–Brownsville between the new governing
board and the professional staff.

When the UFT initiated a strike in September of 1967, it listed as one of
its demands the removal of disruptive children from the schools. The strike
infuriated members of the governing board as well as community activists
and parents. They were upset that during the twelve-day strike the teachers
were seeking wage benefits and better working conditions while black and
Latino children were denied an education. They also saw the demand to remove disruptive children as an attack on black and Latino children. Teachers, angry and fearful about events in Ocean Hill–Brownsville, began transferring out of the district. The UFT also forbade union members to join the
Ocean Hill governing board.[56]

By May 1968, the situation in the predominantly black and Latino Brooklyn community reached a crisis. On May 8, thirteen teachers, five assistant
principals, and one principal received a letter signed by McCoy and the chair
of the governing board, Reverend C. Herbert Oliver, informing them that the
board had voted to end their employment "in the schools of this District,"
and "termination of employment is to take effect immediately." The nineteen
teachers and administrators who received the letter were told to report to
"110 Livingston Street, Brooklyn, for reassignment." McCoy and Oliver insisted that the teachers were incompetent and showed disdain for black and
Latino students. McCoy asserted that he wanted the teachers out of the district. Charging them with insubordination, on May 10, McCoy wrote Donovan requesting the immediate suspension of the teachers and the holding of
a hearing. He informed the superintendent that he had suggested to the suspended teachers that they seek transfers out of the district and not return to
their schools. However, once they received the letter they proceeded to their
respective schools, disobeying the unit administrator's directive.[57]

The UFT reacted to the governing board's actions by urging teachers in
the district to walk out until all the teachers were reinstated. By May 24 only
a handful of teachers had reported to work. Out of 63 teachers at P.S. 73,
only 13 reported to school. Only 17 of the 83 teachers showed up at P.S. 144.

One junior high school reported on that day only 55 of a teaching staff of 138 had reported to the school. Not backing down, McCoy notified teachers who walked out that if they did not report to work, he would give them an Unsatisfactory rating. The threat did not work. More than 300 teachers stayed out.[58]

In June, the State Legislature adopted a moderate decentralization bill that expanded the board from nine to thirteen members, the four additional members being appointed by the mayor. It also required that the board submit a plan for decentralization consisting of no fewer than five and no more than thirty local school boards. A selection board, created to propose nominations for the additional members of the Board of Education, recommended several people, including Galamison. In what was clearly a surprise move, the Mayor appointed Galamison. While it may have seemed odd to many that he was willing to join his old nemesis, it should be noted that Galamison and the Parents' Workshop had worked hard to get Galamison on the board. They argued that he would be the people's representative. For some he may have been seen as a tool of Lindsay and not the fiery radical leader of the past, but Galamison insisted that as a member of the board he could be the true representative of the people. He never thought that he was being bought or used by the Mayor.[59]

As a board member, Galamison continued to advocate that local school districts control their expense and capital budgets, be granted the power to hire and fire teachers, determine the curriculum, and decide which contractors should receive contracts to build schools. In August he attacked an opinion poll claiming that parents were opposed to community control. He noted only twenty-five white, twenty-one black, nine Puerto Rican, and two Asian parents were polled, hardly an adequate sample. Although he became a member of the Board of Education, Galamison remained chair of the City-Wide Coalition for Community Control. The City-Wide Coalition for Community Control consisted of Galamison, the Harlem Parents Committee, members of the I.S. 201 complex governing board, the Ocean Hill–Brownsville complex governing board, EQUAL, and other groups. It insisted that community governing boards control total spending (capital and expense budgets), have the right to hire and fire superintendents, principals, assistant principals, and teachers, negotiate union contracts, make construction contracts, and purchase textbooks and supplies. These boards should be chosen by the community through democratic elections. This position was the most radical of all community control proposals. The proponents of this view were demanding that the community have total control over the operation of the schools. To his credit, Galamison was seen by some as a supporter of Ocean Hill–Brownsville. Both McCoy and Oliver maintained that Galamison always remained an ally of the school board.[60]

Community activist Les Campbell noted, however, that community people stopped following Galamison after 1967. Campbell declared that Galamison was not in support of community control and was essentially a "tool of the system." When asked by a reporter to respond to criticism from black power advocates that he was "playing the game," Galamison shot back that the accusation was "garbage."[61] Nevertheless, he was "playing the game." It was evident that he was no longer leading civil rights campaigns and demanding radical changes. Instead he was attempting to win a compromise between the black community and his old adversary, the Board of Education. By May of 1968, Galamison noted that the City-Wide Committee for School Integration had been transformed into the School and Community Organized for Partnership in Education (SCOPE). Galamison noted that the Ford Foundation had given the new organization a one-year grant of $160,000 to help finance its program to enhance communication and cooperation between teachers and parents. Although Galamison refused to admit that he had moved to a more moderate position, accepting money from the Ford Foundation to foster programs to enhance cooperation between teachers and parents was strong evidence that he had moved away from mass action.[62]

As time passed, Galamison would find himself in an exceedingly difficult position as a member of management. By the end of May, both the union and the Ocean Hill governing board agreed that the governing board would bring charges against the teachers it was attempting to transfer and a impartial arbiter should hear the case against them. In late August, special trial examiner Francis E. Rivers, a former judge, found that McCoy and the governing board had failed to provide evidence against the teachers and he recommended that the transfers requested by the district be denied. Despite Rivers's decision, McCoy and the board decided that the teachers should not enter the classrooms.[63]

On September 9, the opening day of school, the UFT called a strike in protest of the Ocean Hill–Brownsville governing board's refusal to reinstate the ten teachers who had been ousted the previous May (three of the original thirteen had transferred out of the district). Shanker declared that governing board members and "militants" were keeping the teachers out of the schools in the district. He insisted that the firing of the teachers was based on "flimsy charges" and that it was illegal. Shanker argued that the Ocean Hill–Brownsville governing board must adhere to "due process and lawful procedures" and teachers must have "other protections before a decentralization plan is implemented." Attempting to couch the dispute in the terms of a labor-management conflict, the union leader argued that collective bargaining agreements must be protected. Although the Board of Education and the union had reached an agreement that ordered the governing board to reinstate the ousted teachers and directed the three hundred teachers who walked out in protest the previous May to return to Ocean Hill and resume their duties, McCoy and Oliver noted that they were not part of any agreement and asserted that the community did not want them back.[64]

When the teachers who had been dismissed from the district returned, McCoy ordered them to report to J.H.S. 271. When they arrived and took seats in the auditorium, they were greeted by about 100 people who verbally attacked them. McCoy arrived and after observing the situation and speaking to community people, he told the teachers to leave because the community was hostile, making it impossible for him to address them. There were reports that one teacher was struck with a flying object and another one was hit on her way out of the auditorium.[65]

Shanker, convinced that the governing board and some community people were not going to allow the teachers to return to the district and that the board had reneged on its agreement, called for a strike. On September 13, the UFT struck for a second time, paralyzing the entire school system.[66]

As a board member, Galamison remained an outspoken supporter of community control and the Ocean Hill–Brownsville governing board. On September 11, he voted against the Memorandum of Understanding between the board and the UFT ordering the governing board to take back the dismissed teachers into the schools. Again in September he cast the only vote against a resolution by the central board suspending the governing board.[67]

In September, he participated in a "Mass Rally for Community Control" at the Manhattan Center. McCoy, as well as Oliver, chair of the governing board at Ocean Hill; Willie Alonso, chair of the Two Bridges governing board; and David Spencer, chair of the I.S. 201 governing board, spoke at the event. In addition, Galamison responded to a request from a group of nonstriking teachers and appeared at Central Commercial High School in Manhattan in an effort to open the school.[68]

In a strong show of support of the Ocean Hill–Brownsville governing board, Galamison asserted that the teachers had never been fired but had merely been transferred out of the district. Parents were attempting to decide who could best educate their children. The decision of who should teach in the black community had been made by the Board of Examiners without consultation with the black community. Moreover, the Presbyterian pastor complained that the UFT's ability to protect incompetent teachers demonstrated that the board and union worked hand in hand against the interests of the black community. Hence, the governing board's decision to remove what it claimed to be incompetent teachers was in the interest of the children and the community.[69]

Galamison claimed that an unholy alliance existed between the Board of Education and the UFT. He noted that 85 percent of ghetto children were performing below grade level. This was the result of the board's refusal to dismiss inept educators. In a clear attempt to defend the governing board's action while not denying that due process had been violated Galamison asserted:

It is very likely that the teachers' behavior about which the Ocean Hill community feels most grieved cannot be proved in a hearing process. Further, it is likely that there is no regulation against the behavior patterns the Governing Board would criticize. There is no law in the school system against ethnocentrism. And there is no law against racial arrogance or prejudice. In the face of the past record on discharging teachers, it is doubtful that the personnel in question would be removed even if charges were preferred. The Governing Board had refused to go through the dubious and historically unsuccessful process of teacher hearings while the community children are being destroyed.[70]

Galamison's assertions were similar to McCoy's views. The unit administrator insisted that he did not first bring charges against the teachers and administrators because he did "not want to play their game." McCoy insisted that the system was designed not to educate black and Latino children but to assure their failure. The Ocean Hill–Brownsville crisis was an ideological conflict. Black nationalists and left-wing groups associated the UFT and the Board of Education with a colonial structure whose mission was to maintain a system of racial exploitation. By controlling the institutions of the black and Latino communities, people of those communities could dismantle the educational colonial structure. Hence, McCoy insisted that the conventional grievance structure, assuring due process, was nothing more than a guarantee that incompetent teachers and those who did not want to educate children of color would remain in the system and he could not "play their game." He had to assure that teachers and administrators were going to provide the best education possible for children. If anyone refused to do so, then that person could not work in his district.[71]

Although the United Federation of Teachers and its head, Al Shanker, had first contended that the Ocean Hill–Brownsville conflict was a labor dispute and had won the support of Bayard Rustin, A. Philip Randolph, and a group of black trade unionists, the UFT president moved away from the labor conflict notion and placed the controversy in a racial context. Shanker had taken a strong position against nationalist struggles and the black power movement because he believed that these movements had been fueled by anti-white black power militants whose goal was the destruction of democracy. In October Shanker said in an interview that throughout the nation, schools were in danger of being taken over by black militants. Attempting to play on the fears of an all-white audience in Houston, the UFT president claimed that New York City teachers were told they would be killed if they stayed in the schools. He implied that if black separatists were allowed to take over New York city schools, Philadelphia, Chicago, Detroit, Los Angeles, and other major cities would follow. In addition, the UFT circulated throughout the city an anonymous and vicious anti-Semitic leaflet it claimed was placed in the mailboxes of teachers at J.H.S. 271. The leaflet called Jews "Middle East Murderers of Colored People" and "Bloodsucking Exploiters" who should not teach African-American history because they would only "brainwash" black children. The leaflet closed with a warning that an enraged black community was preparing to oust all "outsiders" and "missionaries." The circulated leaflet closed with a message from the teachers union, "Is this what you want for your children? The U.F.T. says no!" Shanker's decision to make 500,000 copies of this leaflet and circulate it throughout the city was an attempt to prove to New Yorkers and the nation that the real threat to education came from black nationalists.[72]

In a show of support for McCoy's position, Galamison contended that the governing board's action was a clear message to America that the "black community will no longer work within the rules of a system that has no right to exist."[73] In spite of his public support for the governing board and his denunciation of the present system, he worked hard to assure that the system remain in existence by desperately searching for a middle ground in order to solve the crisis. On September 19 he argued that an "affinity between the teachers union and the Community is needed to safeguard the interest of both groups." To accomplish this objective he proposed that a formula be set up to allow the union, the Board of Education, and the community to assign teachers to schools "in which they are fitted." He also urged the creation of a special panel to recommend due process procedures that would be satisfactory to all concerned parties. In addition, Galamison served on a committee of five board members who were to oversee the implementation of a plan created by State Education Commissioner Allen. The plan called for the reinstatement of the governing board (it had been suspended on September 14 after it refused to reinstate the dismissed teachers) and new discussions among all parties.[74]

As a board member Galamison realized that it was not enough to play the protest leader. As part of management, in a position of authority, he needed some tangible results. He realized that for any plan to succeed it had to be acceptable not only to the governing board but also to Al Shanker and the UFT. To some, his position may have seemed as though he was capitulating to the power structure. To be sure, he found that the role of peacemaker was more difficult than he imagined. The Presbyterian pastor would claim almost twenty years later that he had attempted to get McCoy and Shanker to submit plans for ending the strike. But both failed to submit proposals because, according to Galamison, they were not committed to solving the strike. Although Galamison publicly supported the Ocean Hill–Brownsville governing board, he would later blame its unit administrator along with the UFT for not having any interest in compromising to end the dispute.[75]

Although by September 30 teachers had returned to schools after an agreement was reached between the central board and the UFT, the settlement did not last long. The agreement allowed observation teams consisting of members of the superintendent's staff, an observer selected by the UFT, and one observer selected by the mayor to go into the Ocean Hill–

Brownsville schools with the power to close a school if there was violence or threats of violence. Moreover, the Board of Education assured the union that the dismissed teachers would be allowed to teach in the district.[76]

Notwithstanding the establishment of the observation teams and that most of the 300 hundred teachers who had walked out at the beginning of the crisis had transferred out of the district, Shanker threatened a third strike because McCoy and the governing board were refusing to accept the remaining teachers back into the classrooms. McCoy announced that the eighty-three remaining teachers would have to take a three-day sensitivity development college course. He also noted that he was accountable to the governing board and it had ordered him not to accept the teachers. Oliver had made it clear at a rally held at J.H.S. 271 that the teachers who had been forced back into the district under an agreement between the board and union would be relieved of their assignments. Despite the threat of another teachers strike and although he was risking his job, McCoy insisted that he had to answer to the district and the community. He realized that if had gone against the wishes of the district, not only could it have dismissed him, but he also would have lost credibility in the black community.

For McCoy, therefore, the crisis was a battle for self-determination. McCoy insisted that the issues of due process, union rights, and the union's accusation that board and community members had made anti-Semitic remarks and circulated an anti-Semitic leaflet were a camouflage for the real attempt by the union and central board to destroy community empowerment. McCoy declared that they (the governing board) had to remain "focused," move ahead with their experiment, and not be diverted by anyone; all these accusations were an attempt to get their movement off course. He asserted that the district was making great progress in education; most teachers, unlike in the rest of the schools in the city, were reporting to work and doing a fine job.[77]

Galamison, realizing that union threats could not be ignored, attempted to prevent a third strike. He offered a detailed plan to end the conflict in Ocean Hill. He suggested the Ocean Hill–Brownsville governing board act as an independent school district, autonomous of the board's control. It would be part of an "institution of a scientifically valid experiment in community control." Galamison called for the creation of a graduate school of education in or near Ocean Hill to "upgrade the training and qualifications of teachers" in the district and of an "institute for community leadership development for parents, community agency personnel, organization leaders and future candidates for the district governing board." In order to monitor the experiment, he called for the employment of a research agency to measure its progress for the "guidance of the central Board of Education and the other districts in the city that are either now decentralized or soon will be under a pending plan."[78]

The problem with the plan is that it did not address the current crisis. It said nothing about the Ocean Hill board's refusal to accept the dismissed teachers and the teachers who had walked out as a show of solidarity. Shanker called Galamison's plan "dangerous." The UFT said it was a device by the district to rid itself of the undesired teachers. Responding to Shanker's comments, Galamison asserted that the fellowship was a plum and was voluntary. He declared "[t]he alternative to the plan is to burn down the community. The community is not going to sit still for the conditions that now exist in its schools."[79]

Shanker's reluctance could have been based, in part, on the fact that he did not trust Galamison. In an October 3 letter to chapter leaders and delegates, he accused Galamison of being in collusion with the Ocean Hill–Brownsville governing board.

> Rev. Milton Galamison, who is a member of the special Board of Education committee to assure compliance with the agreement, has actually brought extremists into the school buildings and has publicly stated that UFT teachers should be phased out of the district. Since the Board agreed to return these teachers, such statements by a member of the Board which encourage the future ouster of UFT teachers is an act of bad faith.[80]

Although Galamison was not a neutral party in the dispute, Shanker offered no evidence for his accusations.

The UFT, however, was not the only voice critical of Galamison's plan. Rhody McCoy said that it had "positives and negatives" and that he would not endorse it until the governing board saw it. But he warned that if all sides did not accept it, then it was not "worth the paper it is written on." In an attempt to sell his plan, Galamison invited all sides to a dinner at the Commodore Hotel where members of the Harvard Graduate School of Education were in attendance. Unfortunately, Galamison was unable to sell his suggestions to Shanker. The UFT president eventually denounced the plan, claiming it was an attempt to get rid of the teachers that the community thought were undesirable.[81]

By October 8, one month after the first teacher's walkout, McCoy and seven of the eight principals of Ocean Hill were relieved of their duties and reassigned to central headquarters for violating the board's order to allow the eighty-three teachers back into the district. Donovan contended that he had assured McCoy that he could remain unit administrator if he followed the directives of the board and carried out instructions of the superintendent, but the feisty unit head made it clear that he would not follow the directives of the governing board. Two days earlier Donovan had suspended the governing board for violating the order. On Wednesday, October 9, the Superintendent ordered that J.H.S. 271 be closed for two days because of disturbances caused by outside agitators who threatened the safety of the unwanted teachers assigned to the school.[82]

The United Federation of Teachers initiated a third strike of the city schools on October 14 because the Board of Education had reopened J.H.S. 271 and reinstated the seven suspended principals of the district. Shanker told news reporters that the board should either close J.H.S. 271 or "get the gangsters out of the school so that teachers can teach."[83]

In spite of his efforts to act as a mediator, Galamison publicly remained committed to the Ocean Hill-Brownsville governing board and maintained the support of community people. On October 16, he was elected to the position of Vice President of the Board of Education. John Doar, a Lindsay appointee and a former United States attorney for the Department of Justice, was elected President. The New York Times noted that both Doar and Galamison were officially elected to their positions at a Board meeting. Doar's victory was greeted with "scattered applause" while Galamison received "warm applause." He was greeted with a chant from an estimated crowd of 350 with "He's the One."[84]

However, despite his move to the vice presidency position and his vocal support for community control, he was unable to do much for the governing board except to voice its position. On November 17, after three strikes that lasted forty-four days, a settlement was reached, ending the New York City School crisis. It called for the temporary removal of three principals from Ocean Hill and for the appointment of the Associate State Commissioner, Herbert F. Johnson, as the trustee of the district; it also called for the establishment of a special committee by the state to protect the rights of

teachers and supervisors in the public school system. The seventy-eight
remaining teachers were allowed to return to the district. The agreement also
added ten additional days to the school year and forty-five more minutes to
the school day. Oliver denounced the agreement, declaring that the black and
Puerto Rican communities were not allowed to determine the future of their
children and the agreement probably spelled the end of the Ocean Hill
Community School Board. Powis said it was a capitulation to the UFT.[85]

## Decentralization

In 1969, a decentralization bill was passed. It limited the number of community school districts to 33 with no fewer than 20,000 elementary and
junior high school students in "average daily attendance." All registered vot-
ers in the district were eligible to vote in community school board elections.
Any parents of children attending schools in a community board's jurisdic-
tion were eligible to vote. The bill also outlined qualifications for community board members, nomination procedures, the system for electing board
members, and supervision of board elections. The state also set up a seven-
member interim city board, giving the mayor the power to appoint only two
members, with the others appointed by the five borough presidents. The
title of the chief officer of the new educational system was changed from
school superintendent to chancellor. Employed by the board, the chancellor
had tremendous power including operating all the city high schools, special
programs not operated by the community boards, and city-wide special
education programs.[86]

Galamison argued that by passing this bill, the State Legislature had
assured that community control would not prevail in New York City. He
called it "barbarous." "The bill," Galamison asserted, "has set back the community control effort and the whole school fight, really, about ten years." He
complained that the bill called for borough-wide elections, making it virtually impossible to elect blacks and Puerto Ricans who were independent of
party affiliation. He also argued that the bill was aimed at destroying the
three experimental districts because it required a minimum of 20,000 people in a school district. This meant that the districts which were much
smaller would have to either enlarge or disband. Moreover, Galamison contended that the fact that the bill disbanded the present board was only an

attempt to get rid of him and John Doar, who supported community control. The true beneficiary of this bill, the Presbyterian pastor protested, was the UFT.

Galamison's short term on the board ended after just one year, ending his last battle in the public arena.[87] Galamison claimed years later that he did not continue to struggle for improved education because the integration movement and the community control struggle had run their course, and he and others had come to the conclusion that they could go no further. The Board of Education's bureaucratic structure and the UFT's strength, along with the State Legislature's duplicity, Galamison contended, were too powerful to overcome. In addition, the Siloam pastor asserted, "And what the legislature and unions have done, and whoever else participated in this legislative disgrace, is to embalm a thoroughly unjust system in legislation." Although he said in an interview that no one community can accept embalmed "colonialism," he did not offer to engage in another battle. Years later he noted that Thelma Hamilton suggested that community activists go to 110 Livingston Street and throw rocks at the window. Although Galamison made this comment in jest, it revealed the feeling of hopelessness many had after the long battle to improve education in New York.

By 1968, Galamison concluded that little could be accomplished and the battle had been lost.[88] The struggle for community control may have had more to do with Galamison's fading from the scene of political activism than with a powerful union and a bureaucratic Board of Education. In spite of his public support for community control, Galamison said two decades after the Ocean Hill–Brownsville controversy, "I never was in support of community control. I always supported integration." This was an odd statement from a man who from 1966 until 1969 sided with the Ocean Hill–Brownsville governing board and publicly advocated that local boards be granted immense power. Galamison's public support and private sentiment may seem to suggest that his backing of community control was not genuine but done for political expediency. This is not the case. Galamison saw community control as a means to an end. That end was not black and Latino communities operating neighborhood schools but a harmonious interracial community. Even when he publicly supported community control he never lost sight of his goal of building an interracial society. When the community control movement emerged other community activists, such as Sonny Carson, head of Brooklyn CORE; Les Campbell (Jetu Weusi) and Al

Vann, heads of the pro-black nationalist, Afro-American Teachers Association, and Rhody McCoy had supplanted Galamison's message of a harmonious interracial community with the message of black unity. He was aware that despite his dedication to integration, the winds of change had swept his integrationist approach aside. The black and Latino communities were seeking political and cultural empowerment and integration was not on the agenda of an emerging black nationalist leadership. Jetu Weusi made this clear when he asserted that even when Galamison was supporting community control and the Ocean Hill–Brownsville governing board, he was not seen as an advocate of black power.[89]

Furthermore, Galamison's attempt at being a power broker wretchedly failed. He came up empty handed when negotiating with the school system on behalf of the community. His failure supported the black nationalists' claim that the system was designed to destroy black and Latino children and maintain white supremacy. Galamison's politics were of a different era and he seemed to be out of touch with the growing black power movement. After he was removed from the board, there seemed to be no political space for New York City's foremost integrationist.

# chapter eight

# CONCLUSION

Although he remained active for the rest of his life, Milton Galamison did not renew his involvement with New York City school battles after 1968. He served as a visiting professor of Education and Urban Studies at Harvard School of Education between 1969 and 1970. His time at Harvard helped him concentrate on educational and professional matters. While at the prestigious university, he helped organize the Urban Studies Department. He also taught courses in curriculum redesign and bilingual education.[1]

Instead of continuing grassroots political struggles, he chose to scale back his commitments so that he could focus on outreach programs. Between 1971 and 1976 Siloam housed and cosponsored the Street Academy Program for high school dropouts. It also sponsored and housed a tutorial program for community youths, and in 1985, Siloam proposed the establishment of a community food bank.[2]

By the 1970s, at the same time Galamison's personal and ministerial life was falling apart, his marriage to Gladys had crumbled. It was no secret that the Siloam pastor had been less than faithful in his marriage. People close to him had known about his extramarital activities. He had even been accused of making sexual advances to women in his own congregation. A close ally of Galamison, Elder Charles Wilson, said that the pastor's greatest fault was his "fondness for the ladies." According to Wilson, "Galamison chased the women in the congregation," causing great turmoil in the church and concern over his moral state. However, the congregation seems to have made no effort to oust him. Unfortunately, the Presbyterian pastor's infidelity was more than a mere "fondness for the ladies"—at times it became outright sexual harassment. At least one member said that her close relative left the church because of Galamison's sexual advances.[3] While he battled to eradicate racial inequality, he said little for the fight for gender equality. In fact, his sexual actions and treatment of women reduced him to an adversary of equality for all human beings.

To make matters worse, parishioners accused the Presbyterian pastor of not taking any interest in the affairs of the church. Some felt that years of battle led to Galamison's demoralization. One church member noted that he was different from the Galamison of twenty years before. He lacked a commitment to Siloam. "He was there for services but nothing else."[4] Church members consistently complained about his pastoring. Although he delivered Sunday sermons, they did not have the same fire as before. He seemed to be going through the motions without much conviction. Further, he did not carry out other responsibilities such as delivering spiritual guidance. As one member complained, he was unwilling to perform the most basic responsibilities of a pastor such as visiting the sick and dying of his own congregation. "The one time that you expect your pastor to be there for you is when you are ill or near death." Age and illness had an impact on his pastoring. He did not have the same enthusiasm in his later years that he had possessed in his youth. In the last few years of his life, his eyesight deteriorated, making him unable to drive.

For some, Galamison seemed to have become more alienated from his congregation in his later years. One parishioner argued that he could not tolerate criticism of his leadership. The parishioner noted when Galamison was criticized or suggestions were made to him, he went on the offensive, personally attacking and lining up others to attack the critic. People found him more thin-skinned after 1968.[5]

One frequent criticism of his leadership was over his tight control over the church. Unwilling to share control, the pastor took over the duties of chief administrator, a role reserved for the church's clerk of session. Instead of focusing on pastoring, preaching, lecturing, and giving spiritual guidance, Galamison emphasized control of the church's finances.

In addition Galamison, not noted for his administrative skills, embroiled the church in controversy. Part of the reason for the growing debt was the loss of membership. It was also due, in part, to Galamison's insistence that the church pay apportionment to the Presbytery for a larger membership than it actually possessed, in order to hide declining membership. As membership dropped, Galamison was unwilling to remove names from the church list. Instead Siloam continued to pay for members it did not have, from dues it was not receiving.

Another problem was that the Opportunities Industrialization Corporation school at Siloam was placed in the gymnasium, denying church members and others access to the facility. The gymnasium for decades had served the church and the community by providing young people with a safe, structured opportunity for playing basketball and other sports. By housing an OIC program in Siloam's gym, Galamison lost an important vehicle for building church and community bonds and fighting juvenile delinquency.[6] The Minutes of Session also reveal that the church's property was in constant need of repair. Bricks on the south side wall of the church were cited as a danger zone. A court summons against Galamison was issued for violation of a code in a building in New Rochelle owned by the church. Siloam had a leaking roof and boiler problems. Reverend Sylvester Shannon, the pastor who succeeded Galamison in 1990, confirmed that the roof of the church was in terrible shape when he took over. These and other structural problems were not seriously addressed until after Galamison's death.[7]

Galamison alienated members of the church by failing to utilize the talents and skills of Siloam's membership. Although there were several talented musicians in the congregation who had the ability to conduct a choir, Galamison reserved that duty for himself. He was conductor of the church's chancel choir and bell choir. One member noted that he even sang the solo on Sunday mornings, ignoring the wealth of talent in his congregation. The fact that he was not able to share the spotlight was a sign of both his insecurity and dominance. Galamison controlled so many positions in the church that some parishioners joked that soon the church would not need a custodian.[8]

In the early 1980s, one of the most serious charges rocking the church was the disappearance of church money. The Minutes of Session of Novem-

ber 1983 reveal a heated meeting over this issue. An Elder Steele reported
that a special meeting of the Session on September 1, 1983, had approved a
review of the books and determined that an outside person should conduct
an audit. The audit confirmed Steele's allegation that there was a discrepancy of several thousand dollars. The Session appointed a committee, through
the pastor, to study the audit and to bring back recommendations to the
body. The Special Committee reported to the Session on November 7, as a
result of which the Session subsequently requested the resignation of the
treasurer, Elder Charles B. Wilson. The vote was 12–7 for the resignation,
with two abstentions. Elder Samuel E. Anderson, who was described as "bel-
ligerent," resigned as chairman of the Finance Committee in protest. Wilson
was evasive when questioned by the congregation. Suggestions from the
floor included that there be a complete audit of the books, that the congregation's financial contribution be published monthly, and that there be a
full review each month of income and expenditures. A resolution calling for
a full review of finances to be published each month was carried.[9]

Despite Wilson's resignation, many in the church suspected that he was
the fall guy. They felt that Galamison was really the guilty party. It was
thought that he was either personally stealing or allowing those close to him
to take church money.[10]

Church membership continued to decrease and by the 1980s, Siloam, a
church that had once reported having 2,000 members, now reported fewer
than 500. Part of the decrease could be attributed to the changing demo-
graphics of Bedford-Stuyvesant. More middle-class people were leaving the
area, abandoning it to poor working-class and unemployed blacks. Siloam,
like other churches in Bedford-Stuyvesant, was therefore losing its strong
middle-class base. With few exceptions, these historic black churches were
unable to recover their membership. In addition to this trend, Galamison's
actions further distanced many and they demonstrated it by leaving. Moreover, in the 1980s, when other churches were attempting to develop effective church outreach programs to attract new members, Galamison did
none of this.

Another major reason for the drop in membership during the 1970s is
linked to an inherent problem with Galamison's ministry. Throughout his
career he had stressed a social and political ministry with an emphasis on
direct political action. During the 1950s and 1960s, when he was at his peak
as a protest leader, he was the most prominent pastor in New York City

(next to Adam Clayton Powell), and people flocked to his church. Clearly, many were drawn precisely because of his political activism. As one member said, "They came on Sunday to find out what action Galamison was going to take on Monday morning." Maurice and Winnie Fredricks said that they had joined Siloam because of Galamison's political activity. They wanted to be members of a church where the pastor took part in the day-to-day struggles of ordinary people. The major limitation of this type of growth was that it downplayed spiritual activities. When political activity waned by the 1970s, so too did membership. Many politically active people who were attracted to Galamison's militancy went looking elsewhere for political leadership after Galamison became politically inactive. In 1983, the church lost 150 members simply due to inactivity and nonpayment of dues.[11]

These were tragic events in the life of Milton Galamison. Near the end of his life, instead of being celebrated as a hero and a beloved pastor, he was entangled in church battles and ministering over a divided church, and he was ignored by the civil rights community. New civil rights leaders struggling in the 1970s and 1980s did not consult him. It was almost as if Galamison and the battle he had led for racial equality had been forgotten.

Galamison's personal flaws and church disputes should not cloud his contribution to the struggle for school integration and improving education for children. Galamison and the left forces of the New York school integration movement presented a vision of a society free of racial bigotry. They were not arguing for a "color blind" society but for one where racist barriers that held blacks and Latinos in a low social and economic position would be eradicated, giving all an opportunity for success. As Galamison regularly argued, the United States could not claim to be a democratic and free society when racism curtailed the economic and social opportunities of a large number of its citizens. For the Siloam pastor and his allies, an equitable society was more than a goal; it was essential for the soul of the nation.

As Galamison and the left forces struggling for school integration demonstrated, the South was not the sole terrain of civil rights battles. While the Montgomery Bus Boycott was a crucial event in modern civil rights history, this study suggests that the battle for quality education in New York was also important and should be incorporated in modern civil rights literature. As Galamison argued, de facto segregation crippled the lives of countless black and Latino children and little was being done to reform the school system. Hence, the struggle to improve the schools in the North was (and still is) an

important civil rights issue. The movement for school integration in New
York that evolved in the 1950s and early 1960s is pivotal to understanding
the civil rights movement.

The civil rights leader made many aware of race and class disparity in
New York City. He and others brought the issue of school segregation in
America's most cosmopolitan city to the attention of the nation. To the
astonishment of many New Yorkers and those outside the city, New York,
the melting pot of the United States, was rightfully perceived as a city
plagued by racial and class inequality. At the same time that civil rights campaigns were being waged throughout the South, battles for equality were
fiercely carried on in the North's own backyard.

Just as important, Milton Galamison contributed to the history of grassroots political activism in New York City by organizing demonstrations, sit-
ins, boycotts, and using other tactics whose legacy has continued long after
he left the scene. He helped contribute to and bring to the fore a radical
political culture. People came together across race lines and worked diligently to eliminate racial inequality in the school system. Galamison worked
with ordinary people to build grassroots organizations giving many the
opportunity to become involved in New York City politics. Ordinary people
were able to take a leading role in demanding, mobilizing, and dramatically protesting school agency policies, and negotiating with school board and
city officials. The few steps that the board took are attributable to the efforts
of ordinary people willing to take to the streets to battle institutional
racism. Furthermore, Galamison and the New York school integration
movement's insistence on integrating the teaching and administrative staff
as well as the student body helped lead to the hiring of more black and
Latino teachers and administrators.

In response to grassroots organizing, the Board of Education was forced to
admit shortcomings and adopt several programs, such as Open Enrollment
and Higher Horizons, in an attempt to integrate and improve education for
children of color. Although these programs were limited, reaching only a
small percentage of the student body, they taught a generation of parents and
children that they could make a political impact on the city bureaucracy.

Although Galamison opposed black nationalism, his stress on community activism provided lessons for the community control movement of the
late 1960s. For a decade, the Presbyterian pastor and his allies organized
people in an attempt to empower them in their struggle to win a decent

education for black and Latino children. Community activism was the avenue to winning quality education for children of color. This avenue was adopted by community control advocates. Instead of relying on conventional civil rights leadership and organizations, advocates of community control organized the grassroots to struggle for the right to control schools in black and Latino communities. Like the integration movement, leaders of the community control movement challenged the Board of Education and city and state officials in order to revamp the educational system. Moreover, similar to the movement for integration, community control advocates declared that racism was the vital reason for the educational gap between white children and children of color. Like Galamison, they had come to the conclusion that the school system was protecting white privilege while denying black children a decent education. They contended that only the desire and action of grassroots people could bring about drastic changes in the school system. It should not be surprising that many of Galamison's former allies, who had come to the conclusion that the board was not willing to desegregate the public schools, joined the community-control struggle. If the school board wouldn't improve education through integration, then the only way blacks and Latinos could assure a decent education was to operate themselves the public schools in their communities. Galamison and others were willing to lend their talent and leadership to this struggle. The sabotage of genuine integration pushed the radical integrationists into the community control movement.

This study strongly suggests that race and class were intertwined. Galamison and the school integration movement contended that the disparity in educational levels between affluent white and poor black and Latino children was directly linked to the policy of the Board of Education. Black and Latino children could expect to remain poor because the school system denied them the key to success, a decent education. Thus, the problem of poverty was directly linked to racism.

If a broad coalition for school integration had continued to exist well into the 1970s, not only would it have had the potential to reform the city school system, but also such a coalition could have been the progressive basis for altering the entire political landscape of New York. A coalition of progressives in the white, black, and Latino communities could have fought for adequate housing, health care, and better job opportunities for the working poor, and greater representation of people of color in city government. Instead what emerged after the failure of the school integration movement was greater racial division and the dwindling of a progressive cross-race alliance.

Despite the good intentions of community control advocates, the defeat of more thorough integration allowed voices of division to move to the forefront and exploit racial tension during the 1968 crisis. The use of anti-Semitism on the part of a minority of supporters of community control undoubtedly aggravated tensions between blacks and Jews. Similarly, Al Shanker's attempt to play on the fears of teachers by falsely painting a picture of the whole community control movement as anti-Jewish and out to remove Jewish teachers from their positions further heightened the tension and distrust between the black and Jewish communities. The UFT president's decision to distribute copies of the anonymous anti-Semitic leaflet was a deliberate attempt to create fear and racial division. The battle over community control left a deep wound from which the city has never fully recovered.[12]

Neoconservatives continually point to 1968 and the appearance of the black power and new left movements as the cause of their shift to become more conservative on social and cultural positions. Many of the New York neoconservatives, who are Jewish, point to riots, the attack on Jewish-owned stores in the ghettos, and the 1968 community-control battle as proof that black militants were anti-Semitic and racist. Through such publications as *Commentary* and *The Public Interest*, neoconservatives have assailed black militancy, affirmative action, and black power for support of anti-imperialist struggles in Asia, Africa, and Latin America.[13]

The defeat of progressive causes like school integration, along with the splintering of progressive forces in the 1970s and the 1980s, created a widening vacuum quickly filled by reactionaries and charlatans, with their politics of division and resentment. Mayor Ed Koch's use of the term "poverty pimps," his verbally tarring black leaders as anti-Semitic, and his adamant defense of police officers accused of killing black and Latino citizens were nothing more than the exploitation of race for political expediency. Today, some blacks, like Louis Farrakhan, head of the Nation of Islam, exploit a similar politics of division and resentment for political gain. Using anti-Semitism, sexism, and homophobia Farrakhan has managed to attract large crowds.[14]

Shifts in the global economy, including deindustrialization of northern cities and the loss of jobs, along with the absence of a multiracial progressive movement, have made matters worse. What is needed are forces that can seek to build a movement, that can unify people, instead of dividing them. Milton Galamison pointed in that direction. Throughout his long tenure as head of the school integration movement he never appealed to "racial authenticity" but stressed interracial unity.

Galamison offered a vision of a world where people would gain dignity and a sense of self-worth in a society free of racial discrimination. The fact that he dedicated his life to eradicating injustice makes him important not only for the 1950s and 1960s, but also for today. Segregation of black children in the nation's schools is on the rise due to the concerted effort of a growing conservative electorate, a number of court decisions curtailing school districts' obligations to promote desegregation, and increasing black skepticism of the merit of integration.[15] What is needed is a renewal of spirit on the part of individuals, churches, labor unions, civic and civil rights groups as well as on the part of government officials who struggle for a society where all children have access to a supportive environment and adequate resources for learning, and where people will not feel inferior or superior because of their race, class position, or gender. Galamison's determination and ability to bring together people of diverse backgrounds working to build a multiracial society where all children would share equally in material resources and be given the opportunity to reach their full capabilities is just as desirable and even more necessary as the twenty-first century draws near. Galamison realized a society that denies people equal access to resources and dignity based on race and class position is a society that will never reach its full potential.

# SUPERINTENDENTS DURING THE SCHOOL INTEGRATION STRUGGLE

| Name | Served | Reason for Departure |
| --- | --- | --- |
| William Jansen | 1947–1958 | retired |
| John Theobald | 1958–1962 | resigned after 1957 revelation of construction scandal and his admission that students of a city public vocational high school built a boat for him |
| Calvin Gross | 1963–1965 | resigned because of the lack of support from the top members of the board |
| Bernard Donovan | 1965–1969 | replaced after the new decentralization law came into effect |

## Introduction

1. Interview with Gwendolyn Timmons, 8/29/93.

2. *New York Times*, 3/11/88; *New York Daily News*, 3/11/88.

3. Interview with Gardner C. Taylor, 8/1/88.

4. Miriam Wasserman, *The School Fix, NYC, USA* (New York: Simon and Schuster, 1970), p. 214; Diane Ravitch, *The Great School Wars: A History of New York City Public Schools, 1805–1973* (New York: Basic Books, 1974), pp. 274–279.

5. David Rogers, *110 Livingston Street* (New York: Random House, 1968), pp. 20–29, 101–117; Daniel Hiram Perlstein, "The 1968 New York City School Crisis: Teacher Politics, Racial Politics and the Decline of Liberalism" (Ph.D. dissertation, Stanford University, 1994), pp. 266–297.

6. Charles M. Payne, *I've Got the Light of Freedom: The Organizing Tradition and the Mississippi Freedom Struggle* (Berkeley: University of California Press, 1995), p. 418.

7. John Egerton, *Speak Now Against the Day* (New York: Knopf, 1994); Robin D. G. Kelly, *Hammer and Hoe: Alabama Communists During the Great Depression* (Chapel Hill: University of North Carolina Press, 1990); James Goodman, *Stories of*

*Scottsboro* (New York: Vintage); John Dittmer, *Local People* (Urbana: University of Illinois Press, 1995); Payne, *I've Got the Light of Freedom*; Adam Fairclough, *Race and Democracy: The Civil Rights Struggle in Louisiana, 1915-1972* (Athens: University of Georgia Press, 1995).

## 1. The Shaping of Milton Galamison

1. Roger Lane, *William Dorsey's Philadelphia and Ours* (New York: Oxford University Press, 1991), pp. 355, 360–361.

2. Lane, p. 63.

3. Ibid., p. 63

4. Ibid., pp. 69–71.

5. W. E. B. Du Bois, *The Philadelphia Negro* (Philadelphia: University of Pennsylvania Press, 1996), pp. 115–139.

6. Lane, pp. 171, 197, 210.

7. *The Philadelphia Afro-American*, 4/6/35, 5/18/35; Vincent P. Franklin, *The Education of Black Philadelphia* (Philadelphia: University of Pennsylvania Press, 1979) p. 109.

8. Vincent P. Franklin, *The Education of Black Philadelphia*, p. 105–107.

9. *The Philadelphia Afro-American*, 2/16/35; Franklin, p. 136.

10. *Afro-American*, 6/8/35, Franklin, pp. 141–149.

11. Franklin, pp. 167–171.

12. *The Philadelphia Afro-American*, 7/11/36.

13. William Jones, "Talking It Over," *The Philadelphia Afro-American*, 4/6/35.

14. 1900 U.S. Census (Soundex) Maryland Roll # 41, G452.

15. *Boyd's Philadelphia City Directory* located in the State Historical Society of Pennsylvania.

16. Ibid., p. 684 (see years 1909–1911).

17. City Directories of the United States 1902–1935, Philadelphia (reel 14, 1915–16), (reel 17, 1919–20), (reels 18, 19, 20).

18. 1920 Census Soundex M 1584 224-G 40 Joseph.

19. City Directories of the United States, 1902–1935, Philadelphia (reel 23).

20. Joseph A., salesman, Kathy A. and Oliver W., clerk at the Post Office also resided at 5605 Haverford. Directory (reel 27, 1927–28).

21. Author's interview with William Claxton, Philadelphia, 9/16/94.

22. Author's telephone interview with Gladys Galamison, 8/24/94; Galamison, "Color Me Black," chapter in Galamison's unpublished autobiography, p. 5, box 12, folder 72, Schomburg.

23. Galamison, "Color Me Black," pp. 5–6.

24. Claxton interview; author's interview with Rev. Thomas Logan, Philadelphia, 9/14/94.

25. Gladys Galamison interview.

26. Ibid.

27. Galamison, "Color Me Black," p. 9.

28. Ibid., p. 10.

29. Ibid., pp. 10–11.

30. Galamison, "Color Me Black," p. 12; Fred Powledge, *Free At Last?: The Civil Rights Movement and the People Who Made It* (Boston: Little, Brown, 1991), p. 551.

31. Claxton interview; Gladys Galamison interview.

32. *Afro-American*, 12/8/34.

33. Ibid., 1/19/35.

34. St. Michael's and All Angels' membership list, 1916 (property of Rev. Thomas Logan); Logan interview.

35. Thomas Logan interview.

36. Logan interview; F. L. Cross, ed. *The Oxford Dictionary of the Christian Church* (New York: Oxford University Press: 1983), p. 11; *The Afro-American*, 4/4/40, 4/11/40, 2/20/41.

37. Logan interview; Galamison interview.

38. Author's telephone interview with William Claxton; author's interview with Hermenia Logan, Philadelphia, 9/16/94; author's telephone interview with Lois Hampton, 9/17/94.

39. Thomas Logan interview.

40. Gladys Galamison interview.

41. Saint Augustine's College, Bulletin, 1992–94, pp. 17–20.

42. *Amsterdam News*, 2/16/63. Rev. Logan said he was not aware of the details of the episode, but he was certain that it dealt with food. (Thomas Logan interview).

43. Lincoln University Bulletin, 1991–94, pp. 6–8.

44. Gladys Galamison interview; Sermon, "The Disposition of the Kingdom," 3/9/47, The Milton Galamison Papers (Schomburg), box 50, folder 9.

45. Galamison, "Promises, Promises," pp. 13–14, Galamison Papers (Schomburg), box 12, folder 72.

46. Gladys Galamison interview.

47. Hermenia Logan interview.

48. Gladys Galamison interview; Thomas Logan interview.

49. Gladys Galamison interview; Thomas Logan interview.

50. Gladys Galamison interview.

51. Thomas Logan interview.

## 2. From Witherspoon to Siloam: The Making of a Militant Pastor

1. Telephone interview with Gladys Galamison.

2. Galamison, sermon, "Study in First John Continued" (no date), Galamison Papers, Schomburg Center, box 1, folder 2.

3. Galamison, sermon, "When God Becomes a Christian," 6/29/47, box 1, folder 4.

4. Ibid.

5. Ibid.

6. Galamison, sermon, "The King," 3/30/47, box 1, folder 4.

7. Ibid.

8. Sermon, "The Political Signficance of the Crucifixion," 2/29/48, Galamison Papers, box 1, folder 5 (although it is not clear, this sermon may have been delivered at Siloam).

9. Galamison, Sermon, "God's Will, Man's Won't," 3/14/48, box 1, folder 5.

10. Ibid.

11. Galamison's Sermon, "On Speaking Your Mind," (no date), box 1, folder 5.

12. Gladys Galamison interview.

13. Ibid.

14. Willard B. Gatewood, *Aristocrats of Color* (Bloomington: Indiana University Press, 1990), p. 284.

15. Business Directory, Guide for the Members of Siloam Presbyterian Church (n.d.), Galamison Papers (Schomburg), box 14, folder 93.

16. *Amsterdam News*, 11/6/48.

17. Galamison, "Salvation Themes in the Great Religions," Morning Chapel, "Religion in American Life," 11/16/50, Galamison Papers (Schomburg), box 13, folder 89.

18. Galamison, "The House God Builds," Morning Dumont Chapel, November 10, 1949, Galamison Papers (Schomburg), box 13, folder 89.

19. Galamison, "A Rendezvous with Reality," Radio Chapel, July 20, 1952, Galamison Papers (Schomburg), box 13, folder 90.

20. Galamison, "Temporary Triumphs and Final Failures," Radio Chapel, 8/10/52, Galamison Papers (Schomburg), box 13, folder 90.

21. Galamison, " 'This Day We Sailed On' " Sermon of the Week, *Amsterdam News*, 1/7/50; Galamison, "The Scene in the Sanctuary," Sermon of the Week, *Amsterdam News*, 2/25/50.

22. Protestant Church Directory, p. 148, 1952.

23. Sermon, "The Social Significance of the Crucifixion," 3/31/49, Galamison Papers, box 2, folder 7.

24. Ibid.

25. Ibid.

26. Ibid.

27. Galamison's sermon, "If Wishes Were Horses," delivered 9/26/48, box 2, folder 7.

28. Ibid.

29. Galamison's sermon, "Adding Color to Life," delivered at Siloam on 10/10/48, box 2, folder 6.

30. Sermon, "The Confusion of Tongues," 10/17/48, box 2, folder 6.

31. "Adding Color to Life," 10/10/48, box 2, folder 6.

32. Sermon, "What Are We Anyhow," 3/12/50, box 2, folder 9.

33. Sermon, "How Cheap Is Salvation," 11/5/50, box 2, folder 9.

34. Sermon, "Unexpected Help from Unknown Sources," 11/18/51.

35. Sermon, "Wind Whirling the Dust," 12/10/50, box 2, folder 9.

36. Gary T. Marx, *Protest and Prejudice* (New York: Harper Torchbooks, 1969), p. 99.

37. Interview with Rev. Thomas and Hermenia Logan; interview with William Claxton.

38. Robin D. G. Kelly, *Black Rebels* (New York: The Free Press, 1994), p. 162.

39. Ibid.

40. Claxton interview; Galamison, "Promises, Promises," autobiography, pp. 14–15.

41. Sermon, "Sounds of the Soap Opera," 5/1/77, box 50, folder 9.

42. Sermon, "The Dreamer's Fate," 3/16/47, box 1, folder 4; Sermon, "The Evil of Ease," 6/8/47, box 1, folder 4; Sermon, "What Are We Anyhow?" 3/12/50, box 2, folder 9.

43. Sermon, "What Are We Anyhow?" 3/12/50, box 2, folder 9.

44. Sermon, Galamison, "The Caste of the Unclean," 11/11/56, box 4, folder 18; Perlstein, "The 1968 New York City School Crisis," pp. 285–286; Galamison, "The King," 3/30/47, box 1, folder 1; Galamison, "War in a Closet," 11/7/57, box 4, folder 19.

45. Galamison, "Economic Status of the Negro Worker" (n.d.), Galamison Papers, State Historical Society of Wisconsin, folder 3, reel 1.

46. Galamison, "War in a Closet," 11/17/57, box 4, folder 19.

47. Yvonne McKinney to Galamison, 4/7/58; Galamison to Constance E. Berkley, 2/9/61, Galamison Papers (Wisconsin), folder 6.

48. *Amsterdam News*, 2/7/53.

49. Clarence Taylor, *The Black Churches of Brooklyn* (New York: Columbia University Press, 1994), pp. 117–118.

50. Galamison, on the other hand, not only associated with the group, but also allowed the Bedford Health Congress to use Siloam for a two-day conference. Defending his work with the Health Congress and criticizing his fellow clergy for keeping their distance from the organization, Galamison noted "I don't know whether there are or not [communists in the Bedford Health Congress]. But, in any case, would the fact that Communists were working for the building of a hospital in [t]his area lessen the need for one?" "How Cheap is Salvation?" 1/5/50, Galamison Papers (Wisconsin). *Health Press*, newsletter of the Bedford-Stuyvesant Health Congress (1958). Copies of the newsletters are located at the Brooklyn Historical Society.

51. *Black Churches of Brooklyn*, p. 119.

52. *Amsterdam News*, 1/28/50.

53. Ibid., 1/28/50.

54. Ibid., 1/28/50; 2/5/50.

55. Sermon, "What Are We Anyhow?" 3/12/50, box 2, folder 9.

56. Galamison, "Promises, Promises," p. 4; Galamison to Bruce Rigdon, 12/7/55, Galamison Papers (Wisconsin), folder 1, African Correspondence and Trip, 1955–57, Cameroon, West Africa, Reel 1.

57. Galamison, "Promises, Promises," pp. 4–5.

58. Ibid., p. 5.

59. Ibid., pp. 5–6.

## 3. The NAACP Years

1. NAACP Brooklyn Branch, Ministerial Lists, June 6/16/42; *Brooklyn Branch NAACP News*, 5/46; James R. Europe to Gloster B. Current, 2/2/47, NAACP Branch files, 1940–55, 1942 folder, Manuscript Division of the Library of Congress; Author's interview with Reverend Gardner C. Taylor, 8/1/88; Protestant Council of the City of New York, Protestant Directory of Metropolitan New York (1950, 1952), *The Amsterdam News*, 12/8/56.

2. Memorandum, Roy Wilkins to Pickens, 3/31/41, NAACP Branch Files, Brooklyn, folder, 1942; James Powers to Governor Thomas Dewey, 2/13/48, NAACP Branch Files, Brooklyn, folder, 1948; NAACP Flyer, "Register To Vote November 2nd" (n.d); Information for New or First Voter (n.d); "How the Ministers of the Community Can Help in This Registration Drive," NAACP Branch Files, Brooklyn, folder, 1948; Gloster B. Current to Branches in New York and New Jersey Metropolitan area, June 10, 1949, NAACP Branch Files, Brooklyn, folder, 1949; *Amsterdam News*, 9/24/45, 10/1/55; *Brooklyn NAACP Spotlight*, June, 1949, NAACP Branch Files, Brooklyn, folder, 1949.

3. Wilkins to Pickens, 3/31/41.

4. Special Meeting of the Executive Board, 10/5/45; Protest letter, by Elmore Baber, Samuel Powers, Marjorie Powers, Alex Drogichen, Blanche Drogichen, Doris Price, George Washington, (n.d), NAACP Branch File, Brooklyn Branch folder, June–December 1946, Rosemary Cunningham to the Chairman and members of the Executive Board of the National Association (n.d); Samuel Powers, Elmore Baber, Marjorie Powers, Rosemary Cunningham, Fred Johnstone, Doris Price to Ella Baker, 3/18/46.

5. *Amsterdam News*, 9/18/48.

6. *Amsterdam News*, 1/21/50.

7. *Amsterdam News*, 3/26/49.

8. *Amsterdam News*, 6/2/51.

9. Author's interview with Eleanor Stein, Albany, New York, 10/5/94; Wilkins to W. P. Riley, 5/29/47, NAACP Branch Files, Brooklyn, folder, 1948.

10. Clarence Taylor, *The Black Churches of Brooklyn* (New York: Columbia University Press, 1994), pp. 107–108.

11. *Amsterdam News*, 11/14/45.

12. Clarence Taylor, *The Black Churches of Brooklyn*, p. 110.

13. Transcript of a Speech by Dr. Kenneth B. Clark at the conference, sponsored by the Intergroup Committee on New York's Public Schools, April 24, 1954, Files on Discrimination, Correspondence folder 2, 1954, Special Collections, Milbank Memorial Library, Teachers College, Columbia University; Diane Ravitch, *The Great School Wars* (New York: Basic Books, 1974), p. 251.

14. Transcript, of a speech by Dr. Kenneth Clark.

15. Ibid.

16. Ibid.

17. Ibid.

18. "Progress of the Integration Program," pp. 3–4, Galamison Papers (Schomburg), box 12, folder 11; Ravitch, *The Great School Wars*, pp. 147, 252–253; Preliminary Statement of the Board of Education Resolution and Action, Files of the Mayor (Robert Wagner), box 31, folder 459, New York City Archives; Board of Education Resolution Establishing a Commission on Integration, Files of the Mayor (Robert Wagner), box 31, folder 459; For Commission on Integration see, Annie Stein Papers, folder on Reports on Integration Reports, Public Education Association, New York and Commission on Integration Series, Special Collection, Milbank Memorial Library.

19. Mayor Wagner's Press Release, 2/23/55, Files of the Mayor, (Robert Wagner), box 31, folder 49; Wagner's Press Release, 11/18/55, Files of the Mayor (Robert Wagner), box 5999, folder 682.

20. Brooklyn Branch of the NAACP, "Progress of the Integration Plan, 1959," State Historical Society, Wisconsin; Ravitch, *The Great School Wars*, p. 253.

21. Author's interview with Anne Filardo, Brooklyn, 5/14/95; author's interview with Eleanor Stein, Albany, 10/5/94; author's interview with Evelyn Weiner, Manhattan, 10/21/94.

22. Stein interview; Weiner interview. Although Stein left the Communist Party during the 1960s, she remained a committed socialist. A year before her death, Stein remarked, "I realize that in the transformation of the world from a capitalist to a socialist system, things are likely to get a bit troublesome."(Morton Stavis, "Friends, Family & Freedom Fighters Pay Tribute to Annie Stein." (March 3, 1913–May 13, 1981), p. 11. Pamphlet provided by family and friends of Annie Stein.

23. Stein interview; "Friends, Family & Freedom Fighters Pay Tribute to Annie Stein," p. 11; "Farewell Reception in Honor of Annie Stein, Sponsored by the Coordinating Committee for the Enforcement of the Washington D.C. Anti-Discrimination Laws," Mary Church Terrell Papers, reel 14, container 21; Lin Shapiro, "Eat Anywhere: A History of the Coordinating Committee for the Enforcement of the Anti-Discrimination Laws of 1872 and 1873" (unpublished paper, 1989).

24. Stein interview, 10/5/94.

25. Stein interview; "Farewell Reception in Honor of Annie Stein"; Shapiro, p. 18.

26. "Farewell Reception in Honor of Annie Stein"; the best work examining Annie Stein's role in the Washington D.C. campaign is Lin Shapiro, "Eat Anywhere: A History of the Coordinating Committee for the Enforcement of the Anti-Discrimination Laws of 1872 and 1873" (unpublished paper, 1989); Minutes of the Coordinating Committee for the Enforcement of the Anti-Discrimination Laws of 1872 and 1873 are found in the Mary Church Terrell Papers, Library of Congress.

27. Mark Naison, *Communists in Harlem During the Depression* (Urbana: University of Illinois Press, 1983), pp. 257–258; Robin Kelley, *Hammer and Hoe* (Chapel Hill: University of North Carolina Press, 1990), pp. 92–99; Stein interview.

28. Stein to Terrell, 9/29/53, Mary Church Terrell Papers, reel 12, container 18; Terrell to Stein, 12/5/53 (property of Eleanor Stein); Stein to Charles Silver, 5/19/55, Files on Discrimination, Correspondence, box 1, folder 3, Special Collections, Milbank Memorial Library, Teachers College, Columbia University; Stein interview. Stein quickly became active and in 1954 was nominated for the Executive Committee, Brooklyn Branch, NAACP. List of nominees for office, NAACP Branch Files, Brooklyn, folder, November–December, 1954.

29. Galamison interview; Anonymous letter to the Brooklyn Branch, NAACP (n.d.), NAACP Branch Department, General Department File, Brooklyn, New York, folder, Branch dispute, 1956–57.

30. Galamison interview; Transcript of Milton Galamison Oral History Interview, Moorland-Spingarn Research Center, Howard University.

31. Galamison to Jansen 5/27/54, Galamison Papers (Wisconsin), folder 31.

32. Conroy to Galamison, 6/3/54, Files on Discrimination, Correspondence folder 2, 1954, Special Collections, Milbank Library, Teachers College, Columbia University.

33. Galamison to Conroy, 6/9/54, Files on Discrimination, Correspondence folder 2, 1954, Special Collections; Brooklyn Branch, NAACP Education Committee, "Summary of Proposals made to Assistant Superintendent Francis A. Turner Central Zoning Unit on Site Selection of New Schools," 4/1/58, in Galamison Papers (Wisconsin), folder 18.

34. Galamison's Statement Before the Subcommission on Zoning of the Commission on Integration, 6/13/56, NAACP Administration Files, General Office File Desegregation New York Schools, folder, Brooklyn, 1956–63; Parents' Workshop, Fact Sheet #3, January 1961, Galamison Papers (Wisconsin), folder 26.

35. Galamison interview; Transcript of Milton Galamison Oral History Interview, Moorland-Spingarn Research Center, Howard University; Galamison, "Promises, Promises," p. 6.

36. NAACP, Brooklyn Branch, Annual Report, Education Committee, 11/29/56, Galamison Papers, box 11, Folder 98; Terrell to Stein 4/2/54 (property of Eleanor Stein).

37. Galamison interview; *New York Age*, 6/24/38, 9/3/38.

38. *Amsterdam News*, 11/23/40, 11/28/42, 1/9/43; *New York Age*, 6/29/40.

39. Author's interview with Mildred Flacks, Santa Barbara, California, 5/23/87; Transcript of M. Gechlik's interview with Mildred Flacks, 1/14/86 (property of Mildred Flacks); *Amsterdam News*, 10/23/43, 2/2/46; Steela Fischer to Rose Shapiro, 1/28/56, Committee on Integration Series, box 261, folder 12, Special Collections, Milbank Memorial Library, Teachers College; Clarence Taylor, *Black Churches of Brooklyn*, p. 108; Author's interview with Anne Filardo, Brooklyn, New York, 5/14/95; Schools Council of Bedford-Stuyvesant and Williamsburg, *Better Schools Today, Better Citizens Tomorrow*, Annual Yearbook, 1946 (property of Mildred Flacks).

40. *Better Schools Today*, Ibid.

41. Stein interview.

42. Memorandum, Stein to Irving Goldaber, 1/16/60, Galamison Papers (Wisconsin), folder 2.

43. Ibid.; Clair Cumberbatch to John Theobald, 9/10/58, Galamison Papers (Wisconsin), folder 13, Education, May 1958–Feb. 1959, reel 1.

44. Robert Korstad and Nelson Lichtenstein use the phrase *alternative social world* in reference to Food, Tobacco, Agricultural, and Allied Workers in Winston-Salem because it linked black workers of various neighborhoods and backgrounds for struggle. Robert Korstad and Nelson Lichtenstein, "Opportunities Found and Lost: Labor, Radicals, and the Early Civil Rights Movement," *Journal of American History* 75 (December 1988), p. 791; Minutes of Conference with Cecile Ruth Sands and the Brooklyn NAACP, 6/9/58, Galamison Papers (Schomburg), box 11, folder 98.

45. Minutes of Conference with Cecile Ruth Sands and the Brooklyn NAACP, Galamison Papers (Schomburg), box 11, folder 98.

46. NAACP, Brooklyn Branch, Annual Report, Education Committee, 11/29/56, Galamison Papers (Schomburg), box 11, folder 98.

47. Ibid.

48. Ibid.

49. Galamison to Jensen, 11/1/56, NAACP, General Office Files, New York Schools, folder, Brooklyn, 1956–65; Galamison, "Promises, Promises," Milton Galamison's unpublished autobiography (n.d.), pp. 5–8, p. 255; Galamison to Wagner, 10/16/56, Robert Wagner Files, 5999, box 687.

50. Ibid.

51. Charles Silver to Galamison, 7/12/56, NAACP Administration Files, 1956–65, General Office File, Desegregation, New York, folder, Brooklyn, 1956–63.

52. Press Release, Galamison's Open Letter to the Superintendent of Schools, Dr. William Jansen, 11/1/56, NAACP Administration General Office Files, Desegregation, New York Schools, folder, Brooklyn, 1956–65.

53. Jansen to Galamison, 11/14/56, NAACP Administration Files, General Office files, Desegregation New York Schools, folder, Brooklyn, 1956–63.

54. Memorandum, John Morsell to Roy Wilkins, 11/14/56; John Morsell to Rev. Grant Shockley, 11/15/56, NAACP Administration Files, Desegregation, New York Schools, folder, Brooklyn, 1956–63.

55. Minutes of the Meeting of New York NAACP Branch Presidents and Chairmen of Education Committees, 11/21/56, NAACP Administration Files, 1956–65, Desegregation New York Schools, folder, Brooklyn, 1956–57.

56. Galamison interview. Galamison claimed that he had never publicly called for the resignation of Jansen. An *Amsterdam News* reporter came to his office and saw a letter written by the minister to Jansen calling for his resignation but he had not intended to send it without the permission of the organization. However, the reporter wrote the story in the *Amsterdam News* and other newspapers picked it up. "Promises, Promises," pp. 9–11.

57. Galamison, "Promises, Promises," pp. 10–11; Transcript of Milton Galamison Oral History Interview, Moorland-Spingarn Research Center, Howard University.

58. *Daily Worker*, 11/11/56.

59. Wilkins to Galamison, 7/15/57, NAACP Administration Files, 1956–65, De-segregation New York Schools, folder, Brooklyn, 1956–57.

60. Galamison to Wilkins, 7/18/57, NAACP Administration Files, Desegregation New York Schools, folder, Brooklyn, 1956–57.

61. Ibid.

62. Brooklyn NAACP's Annual Report, 11/29/56.

63. Ibid.

64. Interview with Galamison; Galamison, Promises, Promises," p. 11; Transcript of Milton Galamison Oral History Interview, Moorland-Spingarn Research Center, Howard University.

65. *Amsterdam News*, 12/13/56.

66. Ruth Lewis to Rev. Grant Shockley, 12/15/56; Ruth Lewis' Affidavit, 12/15/56; Wilkins to Shockley, 1/22/57; Thompson to Wilkins, 2/7/57; Memorandum, Gloster Current to Robert L. Carter, 2/27/57 NAACP Branch Department, General Department File, Brooklyn, New York, Branch Dispute, 1956–57.

67. *Daily Worker*, 2/7/57.

68. Ibid.

69. Report to the Commission on Integration, Board of Education, City of New York by the Sub-Commission on Teachers' Assignments and Personnel, 12/7/56; other sub-commissions were Guidance, Physical Plant, Zoning, and Education and Curriculum; *New York Times*, 2/25/57.

70. *New York Times*, 2/25/57.

71. *New York Post*, 2/29/57.

72. *Amsterdam News*, 3/1/57.

73. Memorandum #2, Brooklyn Branch of the NAACP to Charles Silver, 4/3/57, NAACP Administration File, 1956–65, General Office File Desegregation New York Schools, folder, Brooklyn, 1956–63.

74. *New York Times*, 3/8/57; *New York Daily News*, 3/8/57.

75. *New York Times*, 4/11/57.

76. Edward Lewis to Mayor Wagner, 7/27/57, Wagner Files; *New York Post*, 7/29/57.

77. *New York Times*, 9/20/57.

78. William Jansen, "Report on Integration," 9/19/57, Special Collections, Milbank Memorial Library, Teachers College, Columbia University; newspaper clippings, folder on School Segregation, Schomburg; "Progress of the Integration Program."

79. Statement Presented to Mayor Robert F. Wagner by Delegation of Parents, Read by Ella Baker, 9/19/57, Wagner Files, box 600, folder 691.

80. *New York Times*, 11/17/57.

81. *New York Times*, 11/18/57.

82. Galamison to Morris Warschaver, 1/7/57, Galamison Papers (Wisconsin); Testimony Before the Board of Education, 1/17/57, Special Collections, Milbank Library, Teachers College, Columbia University.

83. Ibid.

84. Galamison Testimony on the 1958 Capital Budget, 11/20/57, Library in the School of Industrial Relations, Cornell University.

85. Ibid.

86. Ravitch, *School Wars*, p. 297.

87. *New York Recorder*, 9/20/58.

88. Galamison's Testimony at the Proposed Capital Budget Hearing of the City Planning Commission 10/17/58, Galamison Papers (Wisconsin), box 11, folder 98.

89. Ibid.

90. "Discriminatory Practices in the Public Schools of Brooklyn New York," Brooklyn NAACP Education Committee, 1/9/57, folder 31.

91. Ibid.

92. Galamison, "Progress of the Integration Program, 4/59," pp. 1–3, folder 19.

93. Ibid., pp. 3–7.

94. Ibid., pp. 9–10.

95. Ibid., p. 11.

96. Ibid., pp. 12–13.

97. Ibid., pp. 13–18.

98. Ibid., pp. 18–23.

99. Ibid., p. 23.

100. Galamison to Executive Board Members of the Brooklyn NAACP, 5/28/58, Galamison Papers (Wisconsin), folder 18; interview with Gwendolyn Timmons.

101. Galamison to Revs. Sandy Ray, Archie Hargraves, Gardner Taylor, Henry Hucles, Benjamin Lowery, Henri Deas, 4/22/59, Galamison Papers (Wisconsin), folder 22, NAACP, Willie Reid Case, 1956, 1959–60.

102. Flyer, Protest Rally, Tues May 19th; Galamison to Pastors, May 11, 1959, folder 22.

103. Roswell B. Perkins to Galamison, 5/14/59; Perkins to William Rand, Galamison Papers (Wisconsin), 5/20/59, folder 19.

104. Report of Campaign Director for Brooklyn NAACP, 5/29/59; NAACP Files, Brooklyn New York, folder, 1959.

105. Galamison to John F. Murphy Jr., 6/24/59, Galamison Papers (Wisconsin), folder 19.

106. NAACP, Annual Report, 1959, Galamison Papers (Wisconsin); Night of Stars, Tentative Financial Report, May 23, 1957, NAACP Branch File .

107. Galamison to Silver, 11/5/58, Galamison Papers (Wisconsin), folder 18.

108. Memorandum, Galamison to Silver and Taylor, 11/5/58, Galamison Papers (Wisconsin), folder 18.

109. Frank Horne to Galamison, 6/17/59; Galamison to Theobald, 6/23/59; Galamison to Frank Horne, 6/23/59, Galamison Papers (Wisconsin), folder 2; Flyer, "Mass Meeting Friday June 26th," Galamison Papers (Wisconsin), folder 19; Ravitch, pp. 258–259; Roy Wilkins also applauded Theobold for his decision, Wilkins to Theobold, 6/25/59, NAACP, 1956–65 General Office Files, Desegregation New York Schools, folder, Brooklyn, 1956–65.

110. Galamison to William Blask, 6/24/59; Galamison letter to Churches, Galamison Papers (Wisconsin), folder 19, reel 1; *New York Recorder*, 6/20/59.

111. Gordon Gravenor letter, 7/14/59, Galamison Papers (Wisconsin), folder 19.

112. Press Release from the Commission on Intergroup Relations, 8/15/59, Galamison Papers (Wisconsin), folder 2.

113. Report from Mrs. Stein on school transfer, 9/14/59, Galamison Papers (Wisconsin), folder 2; *New York Recorder*, 9/26/59.

114. Notes on the Conference with Assistant Superintendent Pitt on Glendale Schools, 10/19/59, Galamison Papers (Wisconsin), folder 2.

115. Transcript of Milton Galamison Oral History Interview, Moorland-Spingarn Research Center, Howard University.

116. Gloster B. Current to Eunace Woodson, 4/17/59, Galamison Papers (Wisconsin), Wisconsin State Historical Society, folder 19.

117. NAACP Campaign Proposals—1959; In June of 1959, the group reported that it had 2,834 members, Membership Drive Report, June 5, 1959, Galamison Papers (Wisconsin), folder 19.

118. Current to Galamison, 4/8/59; Report to the Board of Brooklyn Branch of the NAACP, submitted by Eunace B. Woodson, 4/19/59; Carita V. Roane to Current, 10/26/59, NAACP Branch File, folder, Brooklyn New York, 1959.

119. Roane to Current, 10/26/59.

120. Gloster Current to Galamison, 8/23/57; Galamison to Current, 9/16/57, NAACP Branch File folder, July–December, 1957.

121. Galamison to James Curtis, Galamison Papers (Wisconsin), folder 7.

## 4. The Parents' Workshop for Equality in New York City Schools

1. Galamison to Rose Russell, 11/25/59, Galamison Papers, (Wisconsin), folder 33.

2. Russell to Galamison, 11/30/59, Galamison Papers (Wisconsin), folder 33; Leona Abrams to Galamison, 4/18/60, ibid.

3. Abrams to Galamison, 10/14/60; Galamison to Abrams, 10/21/60, Galamison Papers (Wisconsin), folder 33.

4. Transcript of Milton Galamison Oral History Interview, Moorland-Spingarn Research Center, Howard University.

5. Ibid.; Interview with Galamison, 10/27/87.

6. Statement of Proposal to Create a City-Wide Committee for Equality in Education; Galamison to James Curtis, 3/8/60, Galamison Papers (Wisconsin), folder 7, Committee For Equality in Schools-Citywide, 1960, reel 1.

7. Thelma Hamilton's testimony, "Friends, Family & Freedom Fighters Pay Tribute to Annie Stein" (March 3, 1913–May 13, 1981), pp. 7–8.

8. Parents' Workshop for Equality in New York City Schools Constitution, 1960, Galamison Papers (Wisconsin), folder 26.

9. Ibid.

10. Ibid.

11. Ibid.

12. Ibid.

13. Stein interview; Galamison to to Kenneth Clark, 3/21/60; Agenda, Rally for Equality (n.d.); flyer, Rally for Equality in New York City Schools on 4/21, Galamison Papers (Wisconsin), folder 7.

14. Stein interview.

15. Thelma Hamilton's Testimony, "Friends, Family & Freedom Fighters Pay Tribute to Annie Stein"; News from the Parents' Workshop for Equality in New York City Schools (n.d.), Stein Papers; Esther Linder to Thelma Hamilton, 12/30/62; Clara Krell to Parents' Workshop, 1/7/63, Galamison Papers (Wisconsin), folder 27.

16. Press Release, Open Letter to Mayor Wagner, March 1, 1960, Galamison Papers (Schomburg), box 11, folder 99.

17. Ibid.

18. Galamison to Parents' Association Presidents, 4/16/60, Teachers Union Collection Cornell Labor Archives, Cornell University, School of Industrial Relations, Ithaca, New York.

19. Galamison to Parents' Association Presidents, 4/16/60, Cornell University School of Industrial and Labor Relations; Flyer, "Rally for Equality in New York City Schools," 4/21, Galamison Papers (Wisconsin), folder 26.

20. Interview with Gwendolyn Timmons.

21. Galamison speech, 12/27/61, Galamison Papers (Wisconsin), folder 26.

22. Flyer, Rally for Equality in N.Y. Schools, April 21, Galamison Papers (Wisconsin), folder 26.

23. Press Release, "200 Parents Met with Theobald," Galamison Papers (Wisconsin), folder 26.

24. Introductory Remarks from a conference with Dr. John Theobald, April 25, 1960, Galamison Papers (Wisconsin), folder 26, Parents for Equality in New York City Schools, Bulletins and Data, 1960 . . . 1963.

25. Ibid; Press Release Parents' Workshop, April 25, 1960, Galamison Papers (Wisconsin), folder 26.

26. Parents' Workshop, "Bill of Particulars on Zoning," 4/25/60, Galamison Papers (Wisconsin), folder 26.

27. Ibid.

28. Parents' Workshop, Press Release, 6/8/60, Galamison Papers (Wisconsin), folder 26.

29. Galamison to Theobald, 6/10/60, Galamison Papers (Wisconsin), folder 27.

30. Theobald to Galamison, 6/14/60, Galamison Papers (Wisconsin), folder 27.

31. Dorothy Lane to Area Captains, 8/25/60, Galamison Papers (Wisconsin), folder 27.

32. Galamison to Rev. Samuel R. Johnson Jr, 8/29/60, Galamison Papers (Wisconsin), folder 27.

33. Urban League of Greater New York, "Progress Report on Open Enrollment," Galamison Papers (Wisconsin), folder 26, 4/61; Ravitch, *The Great School Wars*, p. 262.

34. Galamison, draft of an article on integration, 12/27/61, Galamison Papers (Wisconsin), folder 26; Milton Galamison, "An Analysis of the Board of Education Open Enrollment Policy, published by the Parents' Workshop" (n.d.), Galamison Papers (Schomburg), box 11, folder 98.

35. Galamison, draft of a paper on integration, 12/27/61, Galamison Papers (Wisconsin), folder 26.

36. Galamison, "Analysis of the Board of Education Open Enrollment Policy."

37. In one fact sheet it claimed that due to pressure from the Parents' Workshop and the success of the "pilot" Open Enrollment project in September, the board announced the extension of Open Enrollment to all elementary schools that were segregated (90 percent or more black and Puerto Rican). The fact sheet provided details about the receiving schools' reading scores, so parents could make intelligent decisions. After listing schools, their locations, reading grade levels, and the racial make-up of the student body, it gave an explanation for why a child should transfer. "In an integrated school your child will receive the benefits of a democratic education that will enable him to live, play and work with children of all backgrounds. Your child will develop a better appreciation of himself as a human being—born free and equal in dignity and rights with other children. Your child will be exposed to higher educational standards, and be better prepared for future opportunities for specialized training for college. When all children have the opportunity to know children of other backgrounds as equals, they lose any feelings they may have of inferiority or superiority." Galamison, Parents' Workshop, Fact Sheet # 3, Open Enrollment in Queens County, January 1961, Galamison Papers (Wisconsin), folder 26.

38. Parents' Workshop, Junior High School Open Enrollment, Galamison Papers (Wisconsin).

39. "News from the Parents' Workshop for Equality in New York City Schools," 2/61, Galamison Papers (Wisconsin), folder 26.

40. "News from the Parents' Workshop," 10/61, Galamison Papers (Wisconsin), folder 26.

41. Newsletter from the Parents' Workshop, 12/61, Parents' Workshop folder, Annie Stein Papers, Public Education Association, New York.

42. "News From the Parents' Workshop for Equality in New York City Schools," 5/61.

43. Ibid.

44. Ibid.

45. "News from the Parents' Workshop for Equality in New York City Schools," 10/61, Galamison Papers (Wisconsin).

46. "News from the Parent's Workshop," 12/61.

47. "News from the Parents' Workshop for Equality in New York City Schools," 2/61.

48. Ibid.

49. Ibid.

50. "News from the Parents' Workshop for Equality in New York City Schools," 3/61, Parents' Workshop folder, Stein Papers.

51. Ibid.

52. Ibid.

53. The Urban League of Greater New York, "Progress Report on Open Enrollment," Spring, 1961.

54. Ibid.

55. Theobald to Galamison, 3/21/61.

56. "News from the Parents' Workshop for Equality in New York City Schools," April 1961, Stein Papers.

57. Ibid.

58. Silver to Galamison, 4/26/61, Galamison Papers (Wisconsin), folder 27.

59. Galamison to Silver, 5/2/61, Galamison Papers (Wisconsin), folder 27; "News from the Parents' Workshop for Equality in New York City Schools," 5/61.

60. "News from the Parents' Workshop for Equality in New York City Schools," 5/61, Stein Papers, Parents' Workshop folder.

61. Both parties did agree that a new formula would have to be used. Galamison would talk to Theobald's committee with a goal to finding a viable solution. The board agreed to expand Open Enrollment to junior high schools that had been left out. On the elementary school level, consideration was given to reopening applications in the spring. Ibid.

62. "The Open Enrollment Program in the Elementary Schools Progress Report," September 1960 to September 1961, Galamison Papers (Wisconsin).

63. Ibid.

64. "News from the Parents' Workshop for Equality in New York City Schools," 10/61, Galamison Papers (Wisconsin), folder 26.

65. Galamison to Donovan, 9/27/61, Special Collections, Milbank Memorial Library, Teachers College, Columbia University.

66. Donovan to Galamison, 9/29/61, Galamison Papers (Wisconsin).

67. *New York Teacher*, 9/30/61. Copies of *New York Teacher* are located at the Tamiment Library, New York University. "News From the Parents' Workshop for Equality in New York City Schools," 10/61.

68. Ravitch, *The Great School Wars*, p. 260; "News from the Parents' Workshop," 12/61, Stein Papers, Parents' Workshop folder.

69. Ravitch, *The Great School Wars*, p. 263.

70. "News from the Parents' Workshop," 2/62, Galamison Papers (Wisconsin).

71. Ravitch, *The Great School Wars*, pp. 263–264.

72. "News From the Parents' Workshop," 11/62, Stein Papers.

73. Ibid.

74. Francis Fox Piven and Richard Cloward, *Poor People's Movement*, pp. 3–4.

1. Board of Education Press Release, May 10–11, 1961, United Parents' Association, Series 10, box 5, folder 56, Special Collections, Milbank Memorial Library, Teachers College, Columbia University; *New York Times*, 2/1/64, 2/3/64.

2. Between 1960 and 1966, the schools with 90 percent or more blacks and Latinos and junior high schools with more than 85 percent black and Latino students, went from 118 to 201, David Rogers, *110 Livingston Street*, p. 15.

3. Ibid., pp. 16–19.

4. "News from the Parents' Workshop," 1/63, Stein Papers, Parents' Workshop folder.

5. Clarence Taylor, *Black Churches*, pp. 152–155.

6. Ibid., pp. 155–163; Galamison interview.

7. Raymond L. Hall, *Black Separatism in the United States* (Hanover, New Hampshire: University Press of New England, pp. 87–90); Ernest Allen, Jr., "Satokata Takahashi and the Flowering of Black Nationalism," *Black Scholar* 24, 1 (Winter 1994): 23–24.

8. James H. Cone, *Martin and Malcolm: A Dream or a Nightmare?* (Maryknoll, New York: Orbis Books, 1992), pp. 95–100.

9. Galamison, "Five Minute State, Court of Reason," Parents' Workshop, March 27, 1963, in Stein Papers.

10. Ibid.; Galamison, "Period of the Pendulum," pp. 5–7.

11. Galamison, "Period of the Pendulum," pp. 7–8; Bruce Perry, *Malcolm* (Barrytown, New York: Station Hill, 1991, pp. 207–212.

12. Ravitch, *The Great School Wars*, p. 268.

13. "A Statement of Proposal to Create a City-Wide Committee for Equality in Education," Galamison Papers (Wisconsin); David Rogers, *110 Livingston Street*, p. 104; Harlem Parents Committee—Issues and Answers in Seabrook, "Parent Advocacy," pp. 65–66, 73–78. At a closed-door meeting in the summer of 1963, several NAACP branches, June Shagaloff of the national office, Galamison, and Oliver Leeds of Brooklyn CORE had agreed to leave if Superintendent Gross did not offer an integration plan and timetable. But in spite of Gross's failure to offer such a plan, Thelma Johnson complained that the national office representative and the metropolitan chair "did not give the signal to leave." She accused the NAACP of being irresponsible when it came to leadership. Johnson, a member of the New York chapter of the civil rights group, submitted her resignation, claiming that she found it "impossible to serve in an organization whose paid leadership refuses to keep a commitment to principle." She later helped form the Harlem Parents Committee with Isaiah Robinson. Thelma Johnson to Rev. Richard Hildebrand, 8/19/63, Galamison Papers (Wisconsin) folder 3.

14. Author's interview with Oliver and Marjorie Leeds, Brooklyn, August 11, 1988; Elliot Rudwick and August Meier, *CORE: A Study of the Civil Rights Movement 1942–1968* (New York: Oxford University Press, 1973), pp. 199–200.

15. Galamison, "The Process of Isolation," p. 1; Luther Whitfield Seabrook, "Parent Advocacy for Educational Reform: A Case Study of the Harlem Parents Committee" Education Dissertation, University of Massachusetts, 1978, p. 79.

16. Galamison, "The Process of Isolation," in "Promises, Promises," pp. 2–4, Galamison Papers (Schomburg), box 12, folder 71.

17. The group was broken into two bodies. The assembly consisted of representatives of the local civil rights groups, CORE, NAACP, Parents' Workshop, Harlem Parents, Puerto Rican Civil Rights, and the Urban League. The second body was the executive board, which consisted of the national leaders of the civil rights groups and Galamison. According to Galamison, a lot of bickering took place between CORE and the NAACP. CORE demanded representation equal to the NAACP, although it had fewer locals in the committee. "The Process of Isolation," pp. 7–9.

18. "News from the Parents' Workshop," 6/63, Stein Papers.

19. Ibid.

20. Ibid., 7/63.

21. Ibid.

22. Milton Galamison interview.

23. Daniel Perlstein, "The Case Against Community: Bayard Rustin and the 1968 New York School Crisis," Educational Foundations. Years later Galamison claimed that Rustin had been sent by well-meaning "white liberals" (whom he did not identify) to help with the demonstration. He charged that Rustin was a "press created Negro leader." He accused Rustin of allowing himself to be used as a tool by the national civil rights organizations to destroy "my movement." Galamison offered no evidence for this assertion. Galamison would make these claims after the national civil rights groups and Rustin abandoned the second boycott. Galamison, "The Process of Isolation," in "Promises, Promises," pp. 2–4, 5, 10.

24. New York Times, 9/2/63.

25. Ibid.

26. Ibid.

27. "Statement by Stanley Lowell," 8/27/63, United Parents Association Papers, series 10, box 81, folder 59; City Commission On Human Rights, Memorandum To: All City Agencies and to all Interested Civil Rights Groups, Agreement Reached By Representatives of the Board of Education and the City-Wide Committee for Integrated Schools at Meeting at City Commission on Human Rights of New York, September 5, 1963, UPA series 10, box 82, folder 60; "News from the Parents' Workshop," 12/63, Stein Papers; News Release, City-Wide Committee for School Integration, 9/6/63, Galamison Papers (Wisconsin), folder 3.

28. New York Times, 9/6/63.

29. "News From the Parents' Workshop," 12/63, Stein Papers.

30. UFT, "Statement on School Integration," 7/15/63, UPA Papers, series 10, box 81, folder 59; United Federation of Teachers' Statement on School Integration, 12/16/63, Norma Becker Papers, Madison.

31. Ibid.

32. Ibid.

33. Flyer, New York Teachers For Quality Integrated Education" 12/29/63, Norma Becker Papers; Flyer "Is the Boycott Necessary?" Norma Becker Papers.

34. *Amsterdam News*, 12/21/63.

35. *Amsterdam News*, 1/4/64; Luther Whitfield Seabrook, "Parent Advocacy for Educational Reform," pp. 83–84.

36. "School Integration," Norma Becker Papers. The Urban League announced that it would not take part in the boycott because it was not a protest organization.

37. Statement of the National Association for the Advancement of Colored People 13 New York City Branches Before the Board of Education City of New York, 1/6/64, Prepared by Frederick Jones, New York Branch Representative and State Education Chairman, and June Shagaloff, Special Assistant for Education, National NAACP, UPA series 10, box 82, folder 61.

38. "Statement by Roy Wilkins," 1/7/64, UPA series 10, box 82, folder 61; memorandum, Gloster Current to Laplois Ashford, 12/13/63, NAACP Administration 1956–65, General Office File Desegregation, New York Schools, folder, Brooklyn, 1956–63.

39. Minutes of an Exploratory Conference of Persons Interested in National School Boycott, February 3, 1964, Stein Papers, Parents' Workshop folder, Feb. 3, March 16.

40. Ibid.; Alan B. Anderson and George W. Pickering, *Confronting the Color Line* (Athens: University of Georgia, 1986), pp. 118–121.

41. Minutes of an exploratory conference of persons interested in a national school boycott.

42. Ibid.; News Release, Temporary Freedom Day Committee, 1/14/64, Galamison Papers (Wisconsin), folder 29, Parents' Workshop for Equality in New York City Schools, Boycott, 1964.

43. Statement by New York CORE Chapters on School Integration, 1/16/64, Norma Becker Papers.

44. *Amsterdam News*, 1/18/64.

45. Press Release, Bayard Rustin Papers, reel 12.

46. Transcript, WCBS "Newsmakers," 1/19/64, Galamison Papers (Schomburg), box 13, folder 92.

47. Ibid.

48. Ibid.

49. Ibid.

50. Press Release, Monday, 1/20/64, Galamison Papers (Wisconsin).

51. Parents' Workshop Flyer announcing a meeting at Siloam on January 9, [1964?], Galamison Papers (Wisconsin), folder 29; *Amsterdam News*, 1/25/64.

52. Edward P. Gottlieb letter, 12/17/63; Flyer by the New York Teachers for Quality Integrated Education on the Cocktail Party, 12/29/63, Norma Becker Papers, State Historical Society of Wisconsin.

53. *Amsterdam News*, 1/25/64.

54. City-wide Committee for Integrated Schools flyer, 2/3/64; Galamison Papers (Wisconsin); *Amsterdam News*, 1/25/64; *New York Times*, 2/3/64.

55. Doug McAdam, *Freedom Summer* (New York: Oxford University Press, 1988), pp. 83–86; John Dittmer, *Local People*, pp. 257–261; Charles Payne, *I've Got the Light of Freedom*, pp. 301–316. "Freedom School Battle," Charles Currier Papers, Wisconsin Historical Society, Madison.

56. City-Wide List of Freedom Schools, Bayard Rustin Papers, reel 12.

57. Board of Education, "Plan for Better Education through Integration," 1/29/64, Record Group iv, Educational Administration Records, box 6, Special Collections, Milbank Memorial Library, Teachers College.

58. Ibid.

59. News Release, City-Wide Committee for School Integration, 1/29/64, Galamison Papers (Wisconsin), folder 29; *New York Times*, 1/31/64.

60. City-Wide Committee on Integrated Schools, Press Release, January 30, 1964, Galamison Papers (Wisconsin), folder 29.

61. *Amsterdam News*, 2/1/64; Associated Press writer, Junius Griffen, Galamison Papers (Wisconsin), folder 29.

62. Interview with Leon Modeste, Syracuse, 12/4/93; interview with Gwendolyn Timmons; Ministerial form for February 3 boycott, Bayard Rustin Papers, reel 13.

63. *New York Times*, 2/1/64.

64. Ibid., 2/2/64.

65. Ibid.

66. Western Union Telegram from Civil Rights Groups to Mayor Wagner, February 2, 1964, Wagner Files, box 6002, folder 708.

67. *New York Times*, 2/3/64.

68. *New York Times*, 2/2/64.

69. Flyer, Parents' Action Committee for Equality (n.d.), Stein Papers, Boycott folder.

70. Flyer, Astoria-Long Island Community NAACP, Stein Papers, Boycott folder, 2/2/64, 3/16/64.

71. Manual for School Boycott, Monday, 2/3/64, Bayard Rustin Papers, reel 3.

72. City-Wide Committee for Integrated Schools, "Questions & Answers," Stein Papers, Boycott folder, 2/3/64, 3/16/64.

73. Ibid.

74. "Instructions to Picket Captains," Stein Papers, Boycott folder, 2/3/64, 3/16/64.

75. Galamison letter, 1/29/64, Galamison Papers (Wisconsin) 29; *New York Times*, 2/3/64.

76. Galamison, "The Hooky Party, p. 1," in "Promises, Promises." Galaminson Papers, box 12, folder 71;

77. *New York Times*, 2/4/64.

78. Ibid., 2/3/4.

79. Galamison, "The Hooky Party," p. 2; Interview with Galamison; *New York Times*, 2/4/64.

80. Interview, Anne Filardo; Interview with Arnold Goldwag (Goldwag was a member and Public Relations Director of Brooklyn CORE from 1962 to 1967), Brook-

lyn, 7/27/88; Interview with Oliver and Marjorie Leeds (Oliver Leeds was president of Brooklyn CORE in the early 1960s), Brooklyn, August 1988; *Amsterdam News*, 2/8/64.

81. *Amsterdam News*, 2/8/64.

82. *New York Times*, 2/4/64.

83. *Amsterdam News*, 2/8/64.

84. Interview with Elana Levy, 8/20/93.

85. *New York Times*, 2/4/64.

86. *Amsterdam News*, 2/8/64.

87. *New York Times*, 2/5/64.

88. Ibid.

89. Ibid.

90. Ibid.

91. Ibid.

### 6. The Second School Boycott: The End of the Movement

1. *New York Times*, 2/4/64.

2. *New York Times*, 2/6/64.

3. David Rogers, *110 Livingston Street*, pp. 149–154, 192–201; *United Teacher*, 12/16/63; *New York Times*, 2/8/64.

4. Galamison, "The Process of Isolation," pp. 9–10.

5. *New York Times*, 2/10/64.

6. Galamison interview; Galamison, "The Hooky Party," pp. 16–17; *New York Times*, 2/11/64, 2/14/64; David Rogers, *110 Livingston Street*, p. 114.

7. Western Union Telegram from Frederick Jones to Mayor Wagner, 2/6/64, Wagner Files, box 6002, folder 707.

8. Galamison interview.

9. Galamison, "Isolation," pp. 9–10; Modeste interview.

10. *New York Times*, 2/11/64.

11. *New York Times*, 2/12/64.

12. Statement by Frederick Jones, 2/14/64, UPA series 10, box 82, folder 62; Galamison, "The Process of Isolation," pp. 10–12; Galamison, "The Hooky Party," p. 16; David Rogers notes that the 13 chapters of the NAACP met and voted 11–2 to withdraw from the coalition, *110 Livingston Street*, p. 108; *New York Times*, 2/14/64.

13. Statement by Frederick Jones, Education Chairman, New York State Conference of the NAACP Branches, 2/17/64; Statement of June Shagaloff, Special Assistant for Education, National NAACP, 2/17/64, UPA series 10, box 82, folder 62.

14. Galamison, "Isolation," pp. 12–13.

15. Fred Powledge, *Free at Last?: The Civil Rights Movement and the People Who Made It*. (Boston: Little, Brown, 1991), pp. 551–554.

16. *New York Times*, 2/15/64.

17. Interview with Milton Galamison; Rogers, *100 Livingston Street*, p. 113.

18. Interview with Galamison; Galamison, "Isolation," pp. 5- 6, 10; Galamison, "The Hooky Party," p. 16.

19. *Amsterdam News*, 2/22/64.

20. *New York Times*, 2/25/64.

21. Galamison, "The Process of Isolation," p. 12; *New York Times*, 2/27/64.

22. *New York Times*, 2/27/64; Galamison, "The Process of Isolation," pp. 4–5. The charge that those in power were out to destroy the City-Wide Committee was a protracted theme of Galamison's (Galamison interview). In an interview with Melvin Urofsky, Galamison alleged that "those who withdrew didn't just withdraw quietly, they withdrew with big public announcements and news headlines; it was a really vicious sellout kind of activity, there's no question about it. This was unquestionably due to a concerted effort in the power structure to remove all support from the struggle, even though the struggle had failed to achieve its goal." Melvin I. Urofsky, ed., p. 301, *Why Teachers Strike* (Garden City: Anchor Books, 1970).

23. Galamison, "The Hooky Party," pp. 16–17.

24. *New York Times*, 2/28/64; Galamison, "The Process of Isolation," pp. 12–13.

25. Ibid.

26. Galamison, "The Process of Isolation," p. 17.

27. *New York Times*, 3/3/64.

28. March on Albany Mobilization Meeting letter, February 8, 1964, Bayard Rustin Papers, reel 3; Manual, March on Albany, Tuesday, March 10, 1964, Bayard Rustin Papers, reel 3; Galamison, "The Process of Isolation," pp. 4–5; Author's interview with Galamison.

29. Bayard Rustin Letter on the March on Albany, 2/28/64, Bayard Rustin Papers, reel 13.

30. Bayard Rustin, "From Protest to Politics: The Future of the Civil Rights Movement," *Commentary* 39, 2 (February 1965): 25–27.

31. Ibid., pp. 27–30; Jervis Anderson, *Bayard Rustin: Troubles I've Seen* (New York: HarperCollins, 1997), pp. 268–272.

32. Galamison, "The Hooky Party," pp. 14–15; Taylor, *Black Churches of Brooklyn*, pp. 139–163; *New York Times*, 2/28/64.

33. *New York Times*, 3/12/64.

34. *New York Times*, 3/13/64.

35. Galamison, "The Hooky Party," pp. 18–19; *New York Times*, 3/16/64.

36. Bruce Perry, *Malcolm*, pp. 239–250; William Sales, Jr., *From Civil Rights to Black Liberation: Malcolm X and the Organization of Afro-American Unity* (Boston: South End Press, 1994), pp. 69–70; Galamison, "The Hooky Party," p. 19.

37. Steve Clark, ed., *February 1965, The Final Speeches of Malcolm X* (New York: Pathfinder, 1992), p. 182.

38. Western Union Telegram, Malcolm X to Galamison, Galamison Papers (Wisconsin).

39. James Shabazz to Galamison, Galamison Papers (Wisconsin), folder 3.

40. Galamison, "Period of the Pendulum," pp. 1–9.

41. Gerald Horne, *Black Liberation/Red Scare: Ben Davis and the Communist Party* (Newark: University of Delaware Press, 1994), p. 59.

42. Flyer on the Second Boycott, March 16, 1961, Galamison Papers (Wisconsin); Galamison, "The Hooky Party," pp. 18–19.

43. Flyer, " 'Fizzle Number 2'; Information Leaflet on March 16th School Boycott," Stein Papers, Boycott folder, 2/3 and 3/16/64.

44. *New York Times*, 3/15/64.

45. Ibid.

46. Galamison, "The Hooky Party," p. 21; *New York Times*, 3/17/64.

47. *New York Times*, 3/17/64.

48. Galamison argued that Valentin's decision not to support the boycott stemmed from his having been red-baited by the largest Spanish-speaking newspaper in New York, *El Diario*, Galamison, "The Process of Isolation," pp. 13–15; Melvin Urofsky, *Why Teachers Strike*, p. 301; *New York Times*, 3/2/64.

49. Bayard Rustin letter concerning the NAACP/CORE "March for Democratic Schools," Stein Papers; *New York Times*, 3/11/64.

50. Rogers, *110 Livingston Street*, p. 117.

51. Annie Stein, Letter to Editor, 4/15/64, Stein Papers, Fruitless Negotiations folder.

52. Ellen Lurie to Annie Stein, 4/27/64, Stein Papers, Fruitless Negotiations folder.

53. His view that negotiating was a waste of time was made obvious to all just by the lack of negotiating sessions he attended. The City-Wide Committee was usually represented by Thelma Johnson of Harlem Parents Committee, Rogers, *110 Livingston Street*, pp. 116–119.

54. Ibid., p. 117.

55. "Desegregating the Public Schools of New York City: A Report prepared for the Board of Education of the City of New York by The State Education Commissioner's Advisory Committee on Human Relations and Community Tensions," 5/12/64, Stein Papers, Fruitless Negotiations folder. A summary of the report is also found in Educational Administration Records of the Board of Education, box 9, Special Collections, Milbank Memorial Library.

56. Ibid.

57. Ibid.

58. It argued that the comprehensive high schools should accommodate the ninth grade. The sites of the schools should be predominantly white areas or "well selected sites" to encourage school integration. These schools would offer academic, vocational, and commercial courses. It also suggested that high schools should be open to students on a city-wide basis. All these methods would help desegregate high schools, Ibid.

59. Ibid.

60. The NAACP and CORE Statement of New York Board of Education and Su-

perintendent of Schools on Commissioner Allen's Report, May 28, 1964, Stein Papers, Fruitless Negotiations folder.

61. EQUAL Newsletter, July 1964, Stein Papers, Fruitless Negotiations folder.

62. EQUAL Newsletter, July 1964, Stein Papers; Rogers, *110 Livingston Street*, pp. 116–117.

63. Statement by the NAACP, CORE, Harlem Parents Committee, City-Wide Committee for Integrated Schools, the Urban League, the Commonwealth of Puerto Rico, EQUAL, and the Conference for Quality Integrated Education, Stein Papers, Fruitless Negotiations folder. The negotiating team consisted of Thelma Hamilton from the Parents' Workshop, Ellen Lurie of EQUAL, Rosa Estades of the Commonwealth of Puerto Rico, Dorothy Jones of the Civil Rights Commission, Fred Jones and June Shagaloff of the NAACP, Norman Hill of CORE, Carl Fields of CORE, and two reps from the Conference, EQUAL Newsletter, July 1964, Stein Papers, Fruitless Negotiations folder.

64. Report of Reactions to the Interim Report and Recommendation for Plans for the Future of Parents and Taxpayers Coordinating Council, Stein Papers, PAT boycott folder.

65. EQUAL Newsletter # 2: Preparation for the Opening Day of School, 7/28/64, Stein Papers, PAT Boycott folder; Conference for Quality Integrated Education, Press Release (n.d.), Stein Papers, PAT Boycott folder.

66. *New York Times*, 9/15/64; Barry Gottehrer, *New York City in Crisis* (New York: David McKay, 1965), p. 150.

67. Report to the Community by Civil rights and other Groups on the Current Status of their Discussions with the Board of Education Concerning School Integration, October 13, 1964, Stein Papers, Fruitless Negotiations folder. Dentler was a sociologist who did the research for the Allen Report, Rogers, *110 Livingston Street*, pp. 34, 416–422.

68. Report to the Community by Civil Rights and Their Groups.

69. Letter from Clergy Committed for Better Schools, Stein Papers, Fruitless Negotiations folder.

70. Joel Chaseman to Julius C. C. Edelstein, 11/9/64, Wagner Files, box 6002, folder 707.

71. James Donovan to Joel Chaseman, 11/10/64, Wagner Files, box 6002, folder 707.

72. Galamison to Stanley Lowell, Galamison Papers (Wisconsin).

73. Ibid.; Galamison, "The Hooky Party," pp. 25–26.

74. Galamison, "The Hooky Party," p. 26. Rhody McCoy has noted that Galamison was nervous about turning students of the 600 schools out on the streets. McCoy reassured the Siloam pastor that violence would not erupt during the demonstration, Author's interview with Rhody McCoy.

75. EQUAL, Press Release, November 23, 1964, Stein Papers, Fruitless Negotiations folder.

76. Press Release, January 12, 1965, Stein Papers, Fruitless Negotiations folder.

77. Flyer, "Why 'Operation Shutdown' at Junior High School 49?" Stein Papers, Fruitless Negotiations folder.

78. Jewel Cruvin of New York CORE and Ruth Singer of the Harlem Parents Committee, Letter, 1/21/65; Statement on EQUAL's Position Concerning the Allen Report and the School Shutdown, 1/28/65, Stein Papers, Fruitless Negotiations folder.

79. Flyer, "Let Freedom Ring," Stein Papers, Fruitless Negotiations folder.

80. Joseph Peterson and Calvin Cba, Letter to Parents, 2/12/65.

81. "Views," Harlem Parents Committee, February 1965, Stein Papers, Boycott/ 1965 folder.

82. "Views."

83. Jackie Robinson, "There Must Be a Better Way," *Amsterdam News*, 1/30/65.

84. "Views," Harlem Parents Committee, February, 1965.

85. Bernard Donovan's Inaugural Speech, September, 5, 1965, Published by the board of Education; Stein Papers, Boycott/ 1965 folder.

86. Ibid.

## 7. The People's Board of Education, Ocean Hill–Brownsville, and the Last Hurrah

1. Sermon, "The Enemy's Gods,"7/16/61, Galamison Papers (Schomburg), box 4, folder 23; Sermon, "The New Patriotism," 2/21/60, Galamison Papers (Schomburg), box 4, folder 21.

2. William Van De Berg, *New Day in Babylon* (Chicago: The University of Chicago Press, 1992), pp. 11–28, 112–124; Memorandum, David Feingold to Valerie Jorrin, 2/6/67, The Feingold Papers; Memo to Valerie Jorrin, supervisor, CORE Unit, (n.d), David Feingold Papers, Wisconsin State Historical Society; Taylor, *Black Churches of Brooklyn*, pp.159–160.

3. Galamison, "Period of the Pendulum," pp. 14–15, Galamison Papers (Schomburg), box 12, folder 71.

4. Galamison, "Period of the Pendulum," p.13; Interview with Eleanor Stein; A Response by Annie Stein to Barley L. McSwine's "The Need for Community Control of Education," *Black Scholar* (March 1975): 43–47.

5. Milton Galamison, "Educational Values and Community Power," *Freedomways* (Fourth Quarter, 1968): 313.

6. Melvin Urofsky, *Why Teachers Strike* (Garden City: Anchor Books, 1970), p. 304; Galamison, "Period of the Pendulum," pp. 12–16.

7. Urofsky, p. 313; Milton Galamison interview.

8. School Affairs Committee of the West Side Peace and Freedom Party's "Position Paper on Community Control of Schools," Stein Papers, Decentralization folder. Likewise, the Communist Party of New York State argued that the present board, "hand picked by the large corporations, has proven the need for the people—

Negro, Puerto Rican, and white—to gain democratic control of the school system."
Statement of the Communist Party of New York State on the proposed Decentralization and Community Control of the New York City Public Schools, 2/13/68 (author's personal copy).

9. Galamison, "The Ocean Hill–Brownsville Dispute," *Christianity and Crisis*, 10/14/68, p. 241; Galamison, "Educational Values and Community Power," pp. 316–318.

10. On February 12, parents from the Joan of Arc Junior High School, and from Public Schools 179, 163, 84, and 75, elected a negotiating committee. The group would later join the City-Wide Coalition for Community Control of Public Schools, West Side Committee for Decentralization, Flyer "Report Back Meeting," Annie Stein Papers, Decentralization folder.

11. Interview with Rev. John Powis, 3/9/96.

12. Ibid.

13. Powis interview.

14. Brownsville Community Council, Inc., Bernard Donovan Files, box 18; Interview with Rev. John Powers.

15. Jack Bloomfield, "The Untold Story of Ocean Hill," reprinted from the *New York Daily Column* and the *New York Knickerbocker*, 1969; Preston R. Wilcox, " 'Trouble Makers' at the Board of Education: Fact or Fantasy" (n.d.), Stein Papers, People's Board of Education Folder; Harlem Parents Committee, "Chronology: The People's Board of Education, New York City," in UPA series 10, box 81, folder 50. The papers of the HPC are found in the UPA papers; see also Luther Whitfield Seabrook, "Parent Advocacy For Educational Reform: A Case Study of the Harlem Parents Committee," Ed.D Dissertation, University of Massachusetts, 1978, pp. 243–245.

16. Powis interview; "Chronology: The People's Board of Education"; *New York Times*, 12/22/66; Seabrook, p. 243.

17. Powis interview; Chronology The People's Board of Education; Seabrook, p. 243; *New York Times*, 12/22/66; David Rogers, *110 Livingston Street*, pp. 364–369; Ellen Lurie, "How to Change the Schools: A Parents' Action Handbook on How to Fight the System (New York: Random House, 1970), p. 6.

18. Powis interview; Preston Wilcox, " 'Troublemakers' at the Board of Education," p. 3.

19. Seabrook, pp. 243–245.

20. Preston R. Wilcox, Trouble Makers at the Board of Education; Powis interview.

21. *New York Times*, 12/22/66.

22. People's Board of Education Press Release, 12/26/66, Stein Papers, People's Board of Education Folder.

23. Ibid.

24. Ibid.

25. People's Board of Education Position Paper, January 3, 1967, Stein's Papers.

26. People's Board of Education, Press Release, 1/3/67, Stein Papers.

27. Ibid.

28. "Suggested Agenda for the People's Board of Education Executive Session," 1/18/67, Galamison Papers, Box 14, Folder 100.

29. *World Journal Tribune*, 2/8/67.

30. *World Journal Tribune*, 2/8/67.

31. *New York Times*, 3/1/67.

32. People's Board of Education, Press Release, 3/17/67, Stein Papers, People's Board of Education folder

33. Daniel Hiram Perlstein, "The 1968 New York City School Crisis: Teacher Politics, Racial Politics and the Decline of Liberalism" (Ph.D Dissertation, Stanford University, 1994), pp. 46–47

34. People's Board of Education, Press Release, 4/4/67, Stein Papers, People's Board of Education Folder.

35. Galamison, "The Ocean Hill–Brownsville Dispute," *Christianity and Crisis*, October 14, 1968, p. 240; Galamison, "Educational Values and Community Control," p. 315; Milton Galamison interview.

36. Galamison, "Educational Values and Community Power," pp. 311–313.

37. Memorandum, Galamison to Kenneth Clark, Galamison Papers, Box 14, Folder 100.

38. Ibid.

39. People's Board of Education, Flyer, "Evening of International, Interracial, Intercultural but Never Interrupted Entertainment," 5/24/67, Stein Papers, People's Board of Education Folder.

40. People's Board of Education "Analysis of the Proposed 1967–1968 Executive Budget as it Pertains to Public Education," Stein Papers, People's Board of Education Folder.

41. Ibid.

42. Ibid.

43. Ibid.

44. Galamison to McGeorge Bundy, 11/15/67, Stein Papers, Decentralization Debate, 11/15/67.

45. Preston R. Wilcox, "The Controversy over I.S. 201," *Urban Review*, July 1966.

46. Powis interview; Naomi Levine, *Ocean Hill–Brownsville: A Case History of Schools in Crisis* (New York: Popular Library, 1969) p. 32.

47. Naomi Levine, *Ocean Hill-Brownsville: A Case Study of Schools in Crisis* (New York: Popular Library, 1969), pp. 30–32; Powis interview; Jack Bloomfield, "The Untold Story of Ocean Hill"; Rhody McCoy, "The Year of the Dragon," a paper submitted to the Harvard University Graduate School of Education Office for Metropolitan Educational Collaboration's Conference on Educational Sub-Systems, January 24–26, 1968, Ravitch Papers, box 1, chapter 29.

48. Donovan to Mario Fantini, 6/19/67, Donovan File, box 14, folder 2; Donovan to Powis, 6/29/67, Donovan Files, box 14, folder 2, Special Collections, Milbank Memorial Library, Teachers College; Niaomi Levine *Ocean Hill–Brownsville*, pp. 33–34.

49. Rhody McCoy interview; Jonathan Kaufman, *Broken Alliance: The Turbulent Times Between Blacks and Jews in America* (New York: Touchstone, published by Simon and Schuster, 1995), pp. 129–135.

50. "A Plan for An Experimental School District: Ocean Hill–Brownsville" Ravitch Papers, box 1, folder 6, Special Collections Milbank Memorial Library, Teachers College. A copy of the plan is also found in the Donovan Files; McCoy, "Year of the Dragon," p. 8.

51. McCoy interview. Although the governing board did not produce any evidence that more than 1,000 parents voted, the Niemeyer Report did not find any evidence of fraud. Naomi Levine, "Ocean Hill–Brownsville: A Case Study of Schools in Crisis," pp. 37–38; Ocean Hill–Brownsville School District Fact Sheet, September 1968; Rhody McCoy, "The Year of the Dragon," p. 8; Ravitch Papers, box 1, folder 6.

52. Statement by the Teachers of Ocean Hill–Brownsville Experimental District, Bernard Donovan Files, box 14, folder 21; Levine, "Ocean Hill–Brownsville," pp. 33–34.

53. McCoy, "Year of the Dragon," p. 9.

54. Powis interview; Ocean Hill–Brownsville School District Fact Sheet, September 1968 (copy of Anne Filardo).

55. Petition by Al Shanker Against the Board of Education, Supreme Court of the State of New York, October 2, 1967, Subject Files of Bernard F. Donovan, box 14, folder 2; Order to Show Cause Against the Board of Education filed by the Council of Supervisors Associations in the Supreme Court of the State of New York, Order to Show Cause Against the Board of Education, filed by Al Shanker, October 3, 1967; Subject Files of Bernard Donovan, box 14, folder 2; McCoy interview.

56. McCoy, "The Year of the Dragon," p. 10; Levine, "Ocean Hill–Brownsville," p. 51. Two other experimental districts had been established with the assistance of Ford Foundation money, one in Two Bridges in lower Manhattan, and the other in the I.S. 201 complex in Harlem.

57. Letter of dismissal from the district, Donovan Files, box 18, folder G; McCoy interview; Oliver interview; McCoy to Donovan, 5/10/68, Donovan Files, box 14, folder 4; Fact Sheet: To the People of Our Community, Donovan Files, box 18, folder G.

58. Report on Teacher and Pupil Attendance, 5/24/67, Donovan Files, box 17, folder 14; McCoy's letter, June 19, 1967, Donovan Files, box 14, folder 4.

59. Francis Plimpton to Mayor Lindsay, 7/3/68, Mayoral Papers (John Lindsay), box 6619, folder 212; Lindsay to Galamison, 7/12/68, Mayoral Papers (John Lindsay), box 6619, folder 212; The Public Schools of New York City Staff Bulletin, September 24, 1968, vol. vii, no. 1, pp. 1, 4–5; Levine, "Ocean Hill–Brownsville," pp. 57–58; Annie Stein, "Strategies for Failure," *Harvard Educational Review* 41, 2 (May 1971): 174; Charles R. Morris, *The Cost of Good Intentions* (New York: McGraw-Hill, 1980), pp. 111–112; Gladys Galamison interview.

60. Annie Stein, "Strategies for Failure," p. 175; Press Release, 8/68, Stein Papers, Decentralization Folder; Announcement of a Press Conference by the City-wide Coa-

lition for Community Control, 8/23/68, Stein Papers, Decentralization folder; McCoy interview; Oliver interview; City-wide Coalition for Community Control of Public Schools, Position Paper (n.d.), Stein Papers, Decentralization Debate Folder. In December 1968, Galamison, along with Rhody McCoy and 17 others, were paid tribute by community groups as leaders of Community Control. Flyer, "Tribute to Leaders of Community Control," Stein Papers, Decentralization Debate folder.

61. Daniel Hiram Perlstein, "The 1968 New York City School Crisis: Teacher Politics, Racial Politics and the Decline of Liberalism" (Ph.D. dissertation, Stanford University, 1994), p. 280; *New York Times*, 5/22/68.

62. *New York Times*, 5/22/68.

63. Agreement between CSA, UFT, and the Ocean Hill–Brownsville Governing Board, 5/31/68, Donovan Files, box 18, folder E; Report and Recommendation of Francis E. Rivers, Esq., Special Trial Examiner, August 26, 1968, Bernard Donovan Files, box 18, folder L.

64. Shanker to membership, 9/5/68, Shanker's Letter to Parents informing them of the crisis in Ocean Hill, 9/6/68, UFT Collection, box 1, folder 8; *New York Times*, 9/10/68; Agreement among the Governing Council of Ocean Hill–Brownsville, the United Federation of Teachers, and the Council of Supervisory Associations, 5/31/68 (copy of author).

65. Arlene Ranchnasky's letter on events at J.H.S. 271 on September 11, 1968, UFT Collection, Box 1, Folder 8; Levine, pp. 75–77; *New York Times*, 9/12/68.

66. *New York Times*, 9/14/68.

67. *New York Times*, 9/12/68; Memorandum of Understanding Between the UFT and the Board of Education; *New York Times*, 9/16/68.

68. Flyer, "Mass Rally For Community Control, Wednesday, September 25, 1968," Stein Papers, Decentralization Folder; *New York Times*, 9/18/68.

69. Milton Galamison, "The Ocean Hill–Brownsville Dispute," *Christianity and Crisis*, 10/14/68, p. 240.

70. Ibid.

71. McCoy interview.

72. "An Appeal to the Community from Black Trade Unionists," Sponsored by the A. Philip Randolph Institute, Bayard Rustin Papers, reel 6; *New York Times*, 10/21/68. The author received a copy of the anonymous leaflet from Irving Jacobson, retired New York City schoolteacher, a copy of the leaflet is also found in the Bayard Rustin Papers, reel 6, and in Jonathan Kaufman, *Broken Alliance* (New York: Touchstone Books, 1995), pp. 153–154.

73. Galamison, "The Ocean Hill–Brownsville Dispute," p. 241.

74. *New York Times*, 9/20/68, 9/21/68.

75. Milton Galamison interview.

76. *New York Times*, 9/30/68.

77. *New York Times*, 10/2/58, 10/5/68. The UFT had made thousands of copies of an anti-Semitic leaflet that it claimed was written by "black militants" in Ocean Hill, UFT Collection, box 2; McCoy interview.

78. Milton Galamison interview; *New York Times*, 10/4/68.

79. Ibid.

80. Albert Shanker to Chapter Chairmen and Delegates, 10/3/68, personal copy of the author.

81. Ibid.; McCoy interview; *New York Times*, 10/5/68.

82. Statement by Bernard Donovan, 10/8/68, Statement by Donovan, 10/11/68, Donovan Files, box 14, folder 4; *New York Times*, 10/7/68, 10/9/68.

83. *New York Times*, 10/12/68, 10/14/68, 10/15/68.

84. *The Public Schools of New York City Staff Bulletin* 7, 2 (October 28, 1968): 1, 11; *New York Times*, 10/21/68.

85. *New York Times*, 11/18/68; Oliver interview; Powis interview.

86. A Summary of the 1969 School Decentralization Law for New York City, prepared as a public service by the Office of Education Affairs, Stein Papers, Decentralization Debate, Post 1968 folder.

87. Ibid.; Melvin Urofsky, *Why Teachers Strike*, p. 311; Milton Galamison interview; Lindsay to Galamison, 5/14/69, Mayoral Papers (John Lindsay), box 6619, folder 212.

88. Urofsky, *Why Teachers Strike*, p. 314; Milton Galamison interview.

89. Milton Galamison interview; Perlstein, "The 1968 New York City School Crisis," p. 280.

## 8. Conclusion

1. "Homecoming Celebration for Milton A. Galamison, Sr., January 25, 1923–March 9, 1988" (author's copy).

2. Ibid.; "Suggested Operations Budget for PEA Patch Food Bank-Ninety Days," property of Siloam Presbyterian Church.

3. Author's interview with Galamison; author's interview with Arnold Goldwag, Brooklyn, 8/27/88; author's interview with Evelyn Weiner; author's interview with member #1 of Siloam Presbyterian Church (this person does not want to be identified); author's interview with Rev. Sylvester Shannon, Brooklyn, 5/10/96; author's interview with Charles Wilson, Brooklyn, 6/11/96.

4. Church member # 1 interview.

5. Shannon interview; church member # 1 interview.

6. Shannon interview; Siloam Presbyterian Church's Minutes of Session, 6/4/84; church member # 2 interview, 5/11/96.

7. Minutes of Session, 6/5/78, 3/2/81, 6/4/84; Shannon interview.

8. Shannon interview; church member # 1 interview.

9. Minutes of Session, 11/7/83.

10. Wilson denies that he knows anything about missing money. Interview with Charles Wilson, Brooklyn, 6/11/96.

11. Interview with Maurice and Winifred Fredricks, Brooklyn, 5/9/90; "That All

May Know!" A Summary of Annual Reports for 1996 Session Members, Siloam Presbyterian Church; Shannon interview.

12. Jonathan Kaufman, *Broken Alliance*, pp. 159, 231.

13. John Ehrman, *The Rise of Neoconservatism: Intellectuals and Foreign Affairs 1945–1994* (New Haven: Yale University Press, 1994), pp. 33–57; Kaufman, pp. 213–215.

14. In 1985, Farrakhan attracted a crowd of 25,000 to Madison Square Garden. The leader of the Nation of Islam attacked Jews claiming he, like Jesus, is hated by them because he "exposed their wicked hypocrisy." He expounded that the Jews use their "stranglehold over the government" to smear him and they have no respect for the truth.

15. Peter Applebome, "A Wave of Suits Seeks a Reversal of School Busing," *New York Times*, 9/26; James Kunen, "The End of Integration," *Time*, 4/29/96, pp. 39–45.

Index compiled by Fred Leise
NOTE: The abbreviation MAG used in this index refers to Milton Arthur Galamison. Information on Milton A. Galamison is divided into the following subjects: activism, organizational activities, personal life, relationships, religious life, sermons, and views and opinions.